Sobek's Adventure Vacations

The Fourth Edition

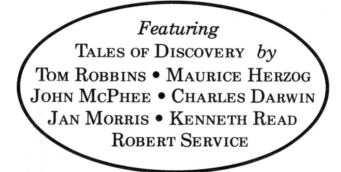

Featuring
TALES OF DISCOVERY *by*
TOM ROBBINS • MAURICE HERZOG
JOHN McPHEE • CHARLES DARWIN
JAN MORRIS • KENNETH READ
ROBERT SERVICE

Edited by Christian Kallen for
SOBEK'S INTERNATIONAL EXPLORERS SOCIETY

Produced by
RICHARD BANGS, JOHN YOST, GEORGE WENDT

RUNNING PRESS • PHILADELPHIA, PENNSYLVANIA

ISBN 0-89471-428-7 (Paper)
ISBN 0-89471-429-5 (Library Binding)

Producers: Richard Bangs, John Yost, George Wendt

Editor: Christian Kallen

Photo Editor: Bart Henderson

Production by Erin Broglio, Laura Taylor

Cover design by Toby Schmidt

Typesetting by Columbia Phototype

Printed and bound in Hong Kong by Progressive Printing Agency

All places and sights described in this book are real and actual. Any resemblance to places imaginary or fictitious is purely coincidental.

This book can be ordered by mail from the publisher. Please include $1.00 for postage and handling. **But try your bookstore first!** Running Press Book Publishers, 125 South 22nd Street, Philadelphia, Pennsylvania 19103.

CONTENTS

HOW TO USE THIS BOOK

This directory to the outstanding travel adventure experiences of the earth makes it easy to live your wildest wilderness fantasies, on the polar ice-caps or in the Amazon jungles. *Sobek's Adventure Vacations* lists trips of every type in every part of the world, twelve months a year. To make it easier for you to match your vacation to the right adventure, we have used seven major geographical sections (Africa, Asia, Europe, North America, Oceania, South America, The Poles) each of which is regionally divided, and convenient activity symbols allowing the reader to quickly determine the important features of any trip. Each trip is further identified with the name of the outfitter selected to operate this trip. Only top quality, experienced outfitters specializing in the area where a trip is being run appear in *Sobek's Adventure Vacations*.

TRIP ACTIVITY SYMBOLS

A **HIKE** or **TREK** is a journey on foot into areas not normally reached by road. Only day gear is carried. A trek is a longer trip, while hikes last just one day.

MOUNTAINEERING includes technical or extended high-country climbing, in either summer or winter. Outfitters generally provide technical gear where necessary (ropes, hardware, etc.). Ski mountaineering trips are indicated by the use of both symbols.

A **NATURAL HISTORY** trip focuses on the ecology, bird, or animal life of a given region. Guides are well-versed in biology, botany and/or geology.

RIDING trips use horses, camels or llamas to carry passengers and their gear into remote areas. In some cases the animals are used for packing gear, not riding.

BACKPACKING trips are extended camping trips where the client is expected to carry all his or her personal gear as well as a share of the communal gear.

SKIING includes both downhill (alpine) and cross-country (nordic) styles of skiing. Style and degree of skill needed are described in the write-ups in greater detail.

EDUCATION trips feature expert guidance and instruction from the trip guides or special teachers on the staff. Often a certificate of completion is issued.

The **CANOEING** symbol includes kayaking as well — small, individual watercraft for one or two persons, usually implying a base camp from which day trips are made. In some cases native craft are used — dugout canoes in the Amazon, *shikharas* in Kashmir.

SAILING trips are cruises on wind-powered craft on lakes, open sea or in sheltered areas such as coves or sounds. The sailboats may serve as home base for the trips or be used only for day trips. Participation in the sailing is a feature of some of these trips.

DIVING includes both scuba diving with underwater breathing apparatus and skin-diving, using only snorkle and mask. Outfitters generally provide underwater equipment, including scuba gear or snorkle, mask, fins, weight belts and air compressors where appropriate.

CULTURE trip places great emphasis on encounters with life-styles different from the Western norm, such as Sherpa villages in Nepal, Quechua Indians in Peru, Papuans in New Guinea, etc. In some cases the culture is encountered through archeological records, ruins, etc.

The **FLYING** symbol is used where flying is a major means of transportation, as in bush fling seaplane trips, or helicopter flights. It is not included where a flight is but a means of reaching the trip proper, as a fly-in to a river trip or trek.

PHOTOGRAPHY trips focus on the skills and techniques needed to make the most out of the photographic opportunities of a trip.

The **FISHING** symbol is used when fishing is a primary part of the trip. Local fishing guides are usually included.

OVERLANDING is travel by van, four-wheel drive vehicle, or other motorized transportation to scenic or cultural highlights of an area. Usually camping is included though sometimes hotel or inn accommodations are used. In some cases other means of transportation may be used along the way — e.g., ferries, brief canoe trips or day hikes.

DOGSLEDDING is a time-honored means of carrying gear over snow and ice in the Arctic and sub-arctic regions of North America. Generally participants can take part in leading, harnessing and maintaining the sled dog teams.

BICYCLING trips use bikes as the primary means of long-distance touring. In such cases, while a minimum amount of gear is carried in panniers, a supply wagon will follow or precede the bikers with heavier camping supplies.

HOT-AIR BALLOONING is the use of nylon balloons to take trips of an hour or more over scenic countryside, relying on the currents of wind for movement.

RAFTING is always river travel with camping equipment and personal gear being carried on inflatable rafts by oars or paddle. In a few cases, it may be a "float trip," but usually implies whitewater.

CRUISE trips use larger motor-powered ships to travel up river, over seas or along coasts for comfortable yet close views of remote areas. Accommodations are in well-appointed cabins, and most meals are taken on board.

CLASS DEFINITIONS

Every description in this book includes a grading for its level of difficulty. Based on the whitewater rating of Class I to Class V, with Class V being the most difficult, the scale is an added guideline to choosing your adventure. Since different people have different tolerances for altitude, duration, remoteness and the like, this scale cannot be exact. It is intended for use in making general distinctions between the offerings in the following pages.

Class I – *EASY:* These trips emphasize the scenic or cultural value of a particular region, using hotel accommodations and travel by comfortable van or bus. Short hikes and gentle river floats may be involved. These are trips suitable for all ages and inclinations.

Class II – *MODERATE:* Mild outdoor programs which immerse the participant a bit more fully in the world of adventure. Camping is often involved, and longer day hikes and/or river trips with whitewater are usually included. However, the degree of exertion is optional, making these trips suitable for all ages as well.

Class III – *AVERAGE:* Camping is the normal means of overnighting on a Class III trip; hikes and river trips may be longer and more difficult. However, some hotel or lodge nights are often included for convenience. Generally, treks of shorter duration (up to 10 days) and/or lower altitudes (below 3000m) are considered of this class. Good health is the only physical requirement, though a minimum age of 12 years is usually requested.

Class IV – *DIFFICULT:* Trips of longer duration, farther from population centers, involving physically demanding activity – such as trekking above 3000 meters or rafting a Class IV-V river – are considered Class IV trips. Previous outdoor experience (camping, hiking, etc.) is often helpful, and a physician's certificate of health is generally required. Age limits vary with individual trips, operators and participants, but most Class IV trips have an 18 years age minimum.

Class V – *STRENUOUS:* When previous technical experience and skills are required, the trips are classed as strenuous, to make their restrictions clear. Generally these trips are of an exploratory nature, in sparsely populated areas, and they may demand previous whitewater, rock climbing or similar skills. Treks of long duration (a month or more) which reach an altitude of over 5500 meters are included in this category.

ON TRIP PRICING

An important consideration in choosing a trip from *Sobek's Adventure Vacations* is its price. The land cost of an adventure trip—the cost of a trip excluding all air transportation, except where specified—can vary dramatically. Certain types of travel, or particular areas of the world, dictate high costs regardless of the level of service supplied. The arctic regions are expensive, as are certain countries such as China and North Yemen. Cruise ships and hotel trips have high accommodation costs built in, reflecting the more comfortable features of these programs. These considerations can be the dominating factors in trip pricing, but they are not the only ones.

The single most important determinant of cost is still value: You get what you pay for. Features such as guide-to-client ratio, inclusion of hotels and in-city meals, domestic air transport or charter services, park and museum fees, the quality and amount of equipment used, and the use of non-local guide services can all explain the price-tag of one trip relative to another. International river trips tend to be more expensive than treks, for a variety of reasons. Inflatable rafts carry three or four passengers and a guide, dictating high per-person guide costs (and more guides per trip). The equipment itself is expensive, requires periodic repair and replacement, and is heavy and difficult to transport from trip-to-trip. Providing quality cuisine in remote river corridors, far from the local *tienda* or vineyard, necessitates heavier loads and more careful planning. The contrast with a trekking group of 15-20 people, led by a native guide, which buys much of its food along the way and carries little specialized equipment, explains why there are two ends to the price spectrum.

With this edition of *Sobek's Adventure Vacations*, Sobek's International Explorers Society uses **Trip Value Coding**, making it easy to compare trip costs, and facilitating the selection of trips within certain price ranges. Each write-up herein is followed by a listing of the months of operation for that trip, and a one-word code indicative of trip costs, based on a per-day price range.

> **Moderate** trips cost under $75/day per person.
> **Medium** trips are between $75 and $125/day.
> **Premium** trips cost more than $125/day.

Sobek's Adventure Vacations is designed to provide the widest possible selection of programs available in all areas— location, activity, and cost. Some trips are included that sacrifice comfort for cost, and include few extra services; yet these are the very programs sought by some adventurous souls. The level of service and of trip value for the many excellent operators in this book is explained in detailed trip literature, available for each trip upon request from Sobek's International Explorers Society. The choice is yours.

Detailed information, including current dates and prices, equipment lists, health and travel advice, day-by-day itineraries, suggested reading and much more, is available for every trip. General information on reservations, deposits, and other topics is located toward the back of the book.

OMO NATIVE   Stan Boor

ON THE RUFIGI   Judy Gordon

RADIO EDEN: AN AFRICAN ODYSSEY

by Tom Robbins

*T*he Selous is the largest uninhabited game reserve in the world. Located in central Tanzania, a couple of hundred miles south of Mount Kilimanjaro, the Selous is no national park where tourists sprawl on rattan sofas, sipping gin and listening to the BBC as from the air-conditioned safety of posh lodges they spy shamelessly on mating lions. In the Selous, one doesn't catch a safari bus to the corner of Giraffe and Warthog. To see the Selous, one hikes and one paddles. And when an aggravated hippopotamus is charging one's rubber raft, one paddles very hard, indeed.

When I announced to family and friends that I was going hiking and river rafting through a vast patch of African cabbage, they didn't ask why. They must have realized that after three years bent over an idling and backfiring novel, skinning my knuckles on every bolt and wrench in the literary toolbox, I needed to blow a little carbon out of my own exhaust. Perhaps they also sensed that after my recent dealings with editors, agents, lawyers, producers, and reviewers, I might be primed for the company of crocodiles.

EAST

SELOUS RAFTING

THE LARGEST UNINHABITED game reserve in the world is drained by the Rufiji, a riverine avenue to the wild hinterlands of East Africa. Tanzania's superb Selous Game Reserve presents a wildlife extravaganza, celebrated in legend and literature; the Rufiji is our silent route through the center of the Selous. We paddle past hippos, crocodiles, elephants and birds, and hike away from the river to track antelope, buffalo, zebra, lion and more of the African menagerie. Several nights in comfortable game lodges combine with the excitement of whitewater in Stiegler's Gorge and the otherworldly landscapes of the Lake Tagalala palm swamps, to reveal a new face of traditional African game-viewing. The Selous Rafting safari can be combined with the Mount Kilimanjaro trek or safaris to the northern Tanzania game parks, for a complete view of African wildlife unmatched in modern times.

ITINERARY: Days 1-2: En route to Dar-es-Salaam. Day 3: Dar. Day 4-6: To Selous game lodges. Days 7-14: On river. Days 15-16: Game camps. Day 17: Return.

✈ 🦢   Class III   **Premium**
December, January
Sobek Expeditions   AF13

THE OMO RIVER

THE AFRICAN QUEEN is repeatedly ranked as the world's finest river experience for one good reason – the Omo River is truly amazing. A remnant of Stanley's Dark Continent, it is wild, beautiful, beyond man's imprint. Scores of cataracts, 1200-meter forested gorges, savannah, hills, forest, thousands of hippos, crocodiles, antelope, warthogs, baboons, fish, birds and many other blessings of nature abound on the river's banks. Bodi, Mursi and Bacha tribespeople eke out a timeless existence on the lower shores of the river, to touch this wildness with a human element. Our half-trip options make this ultimate African journey more accessible. The first half accents whitewater and side hikes, gorges and action. It is shorter, cooler and greener. The second half is wildlife and primitive people, with warmer days and slower water. Both portions include a little of everything that the Omo offers, but with different balances. And all our Omo trips include time in Addis Ababa to see the proud highlands of ancient Abyssinia.

ITINERARY: Days 1-3: Addis Ababa. Days 4-15: River first half. Day 16: Bus to Addis or join trip from Addis; continue river. Days 17-29: River second half. Days 30-31: Game Park and flight to Addis. Day 32: Return.

✈ 🦢 🏺   Class IV   **Medium**
September, October
Sobek Expeditions   AF9

I WAS INOCULATED AGAINST most tropical diseases (there's no [yawn] serum to ward off "sleeping sickness"), and . . . the very fact that the Selous is unoccupied by humans or farm animals means disease is rarely contracted there. In the Selous, the tsetse is all pester and no siesta. Ah, but I'd overlooked one thing. The Selous itself is a tropical disease: feverish, lethargic, exotic, achy, sweaty, hallucinogenic, and, as I've learned since coming home, recurrent.

Just when I think that I am over it, that rush-hour traffic, income tax forms, and two viewings of Amadeus have worked their civilizing cures, I suffer yet another attack of Selous. It comes on with a humid vapor, with a vibration of membrane, with howls and hoofbeats that nobody else in the room can hear, and although I might be in the midst of something truly important such as choosing which brand of burglar alarm to install in my newly violated door, it never fails to distract me with memories of a sweeter, if less comfortable, place; a place where even time is honest, and primitive equalities prevail. . . .

RWANDA GORILLA   Michael Nichols

RWANDA/ZAIRE

THE HIRSUTE HOMINIDS of the Central African volcanoes are restricted in habitat to a small area of two countries, Rwanda and Zaire. The pressures of land-clearing by a rapidly expanding population have cornered the gentle gorillas into small areas set aside by the governments of two countries, national parks that are refuges for the few remaining families of the largest primates. For the amateur or professional naturalist wishing to observe the gorillas, Kahuzi-Benga and Virunga national parks must be explored. Yet until recently the logistics of a Rwanda-Zaire journey were immensely complicated, and seldom attempted. No longer. Through special arrangements we can not only offer the ultimate gorilla-tracking experience, but also include visits to the traditional homeland of the pygmies, encountering the most skilled hunters and trackers in the world today. Two weeks of the wildest sights Africa can offer are topped off with the plains game of Akagera park to feast the eye and mind.

ITINERARY: Days 1-2: To Kigali. Day 3: Lake Kivu. Day 4: Bukavu. Day 5: Kahuza-Beiga. Day 6: Goma. Days 7-8: Virunga Park. Days 9-11: Mount Hoyo. Day 12: Butembo. Day 13: Goma. Days 14-16: Akagera. Day 17: Return.

	Class III	**Premium**
Year-round		
Safaricentre	AF53	

CRADLE OF MANKIND

THERE IS MORE TO KENYA than the heavily-touristed game parks. Escape from the crowds of zebra-striped vans clustered around every moving object with a journey into the western and northern reaches of Kenya. Here both people and wildlife have been more resistant to the impacts of development, isolated by terrain and temperament. We don't neglect the big game, but move beyond it to the tea plantations of Lake Victoria, the slopes of Mt. Elgon, and the banks of Lake Turkana, the "Jade Sea." Traversing the rugged and hostile western shore of the lake, we enter the desert homeland of the nomadic Turkana pastoralists, to view firsthand their extraordinary existence in what appears to be a lifeless environment. National parks both well-known and scarcely visited highlight the journey, and a week's relaxation on the quiet island of Lamu provides a fitting end to an exploration of the other Kenya.

ITINERARY: Days 1-2: To Nairobi. Days 3-4: Masai Mara. Day 5: Lake Victoria. Days 6-7: Mt. Elgon. Days 8-9: Lake Turkana. Day 10: Eldoret. Day 11: Nairobi. Day 12: Amboseli. Day 13: Tsavo. Day 14: Mombasa. Days 15-16: Lamu. Day 17: Mombasa. Day 18: Nairobi and home.

	Class III	**Medium**
Year-round.		
Safaricentre	AF54	

BOTSWANA LIONS   Karen Peterson

KENYA WILDLIFE CIRCUIT

KENYA IS SYNONYMOUS with big game, and what better way to see the lions, the elephants, giraffes and gazelles than to rove by 'Rover through its well-maintained game parks? A journey to the national parks of Kenya is a journey into the past of African exploration, a chance to witness the wealth of plains game that makes the Great Rift Valley, the Aberdares Mountains and Mt. Kenya touchstones for the wildlife lover. This package tour features comfortable hotel and lodge accommodations throughout, shopping sprees in Kenya's capital, sunrise at Victoria Falls and the luxury of golf, squash, tennis, and swimming or fishing within view of Mt. Kenya itself. And of course there's plenty of the big game that has made East Africa the mecca for wildlife photographers ever since Adam bought his first Brownie. Cost includes airfare from New York or other gateway city.

ITINERARY: Day 1: Depart U.S. Day 2: En route. Day 3: Nairobi. Days 4-5: Aberdare Mountains. Days 6-7: Amboseli National Park. Days 8-9: Tsavo National Park. Days 10-11: Harare. Day 12: Return or join *AF45*.

🛶 🚙 　　Class I 　　**Medium**
Year-round
Sobek Expeditions 　　AF48

MOUNTAIN GORILLAS OF RWANDA

THE MIGHTY MASTERS OF AFRICA'S montane rain forests, the mountain gorillas, are magnificent beasts, kings of their domain, whose existence is nevertheless threatened by the encroaching presence of man. The great apes live secluded, high on the forested slopes of the Ruwenzori mountains and Virunga volcanoes, in the border regions of Rwanda, Uganda and Zaire. We maximize our contact with family groups and individuals of the untamed but tolerant creatures by concentrating our visit on one area of Rwanda, and following the lead of rangers and trackers. The result is an incomparable experience of intimate wildlife observation of one of the earth's rarest animals, and one of man's most reclusive relatives. We add a trip to Akagera National Park and its antelope, oribi, hippos, birds and lions for a complete wildlife adventure.

ITINERARY: Days 1-3: Fly to Kigali. Days 4-7: Virunga volcanoes, Ruhengeri. Days 8-11: Akagera. Day 12: Return home.

🛶 🚙 　　Class III 　　**Medium**
December, January
Sobek Expeditions 　　AF16

OUR FIRST DAY IN THE BUSH finds us up at dawn. Having only seen dawn from the other side of the clock, I never imagined daybreak might actually be pleasant. The tsetselike sting of 5:00 A.M. is softened by the sight of an elephant family, Mom, Dad, Bud, and Sis, carelessly mashing a million dewdrops as they Vachel Lindsay down a green valley to a water hole.

We watch the elephants from the veranda of the Stiegler's Gorge Safari Camp, the last outpost of humanity we'll enjoy before we venture into the Selous. We had slept at the camp, or tried to sleep, for an all-night newsboy choir of hyenas periodically sang us awake. Late the previous afternoon, the train had deposited us at a village called Fuga, the end of the line, where we — eighteen of us, including the guides — were met by a trio of Land Rovers and driven for a couple of battering hours down an Armageddon of a road, a moonscape of a lane to Stiegler's Gorge. By the time our gear was stowed in our respective huts, it was dark and a rusty gong had summoned us to a dinner of green beans and steak.

Dave, a veteran guide, had hoisted a morsel of steak aloft in the lanternshine. "Impala," he had said, studying his fork. "At first I thought it might be sable. Africa is an adventure in meat."

MOUNT KILIMANJARO

IN KEEPING WITH SOBEK tradition, our ascent of The White Mountain follows the less-traveled trails to the top. The vistas of Kilimanjaro, its extraordinary forests, moorlands and snow-fields, are too good for the well-worn tourist route; the highest solitary peak in the world deserves better. The Machame Trail winds up through high-altitude rain forest to alpine climes, past the glaciers of the southern face and the Great Breach Wall to the summit. It's a special route to the top – not the easiest way, but a private one. The climb can be combined with a float down the Rufiji River (see *Selous Rafting*) or an extension to the famous parklands of northern Tanzania – Serengeti, Ngorongoro and Lake Manyara.

ITINERARY: Day 1: Arusha, Tanzania. Day 2: En route. Days 3-9: On the mountain. Day 10: Kibo Hotel. Days 11-12: To Arusha and return.

⋔ Class IV **Premium**
December, January
Sobek Expeditions AF14

SERENGETI AND GORILLA SAFARI

SUNLIT PLAINS AND MIST-BOUND forests in Rwanda and Tanzania are home to the grandest wildlife parade on earth. The abundance of the Serengeti plains animals contrasts with the rare and reclusive mountain gorilla of Rwanda to give the African aficionado a complete spectrum of fauna photo opportunities. From the black chests of the gorillas to the carmine colorings of the bee-eater bird, every shade is there. Delicate pink on flamingo flight-feathers, the subtle tans of a gazelle, menacing crocodile green, and the camouflage hues of the cheetah challenge your Kodachrome to capture every nuance of color. The dazzling display ranges

ON KILIMANJARO   Jim Slade

from Lake Manyara to the volcanoes of Rwanda, across the Serengeti plains and around Lake Victoria. Predators and prey provide an unforgettable living panorama. Color it exciting!

ITINERARY: Days 1-2: To Arusha. Day 3: Arusha. Day 4: Lake Manyara. Days 5-6: Ngorongoro. Days 7-10: Serengeti. Days 11-13: Lake Victoria. Day 14. Kigali. Days 15-18: Parc des Volcans. Day 19: Kigali. Day 20: Return U.S.

⛵ 🚙 Class III **Medium**
June-January
Overseas Adventure Travel AF55

THE SAVANNA GRASS IS GREEN but dry, and it crunches underfoot. J'nanga, our native game guide, steps noiselessly on the bare patches between clumps of grass, but we cement-footed Americans sound as if we're breakdancing in a silo of Rice Krispies. Our gauche sneakers scuff at fresh cheetah tracks, at shiny licorice drops of wildebeest dung, at impala skulls as bleached as a surfer's eyebrows, short wildflowers, and a mega-Manhattan of ants.

Scattered about the plain are trees that resemble huge stone jars; trees that resemble delicatessens festooned with salami and pepperoni; trees that appear to be growing upside down; trees that look like Fifties haircuts, their foliage barbered into Sha Na Na flattops; and, most prevalent, leafless trees bristling with thorns so long and sharp they could pierce the heart of a bureaucrat.

ELEPHANT SUNSET   Karen Petersen

THE NEXT MORNING the real fun begins. Bleary-eyed from the insomnolent effects of hyena serenade, we put our rafts in the water and paddle into the Selous. For the next two weeks, we'll see no other humans, just animals, birds, fang-snapping reptiles — and, of course, the gods of the river.

Sobek employees are quite familiar with river gods. Anybody who does much river rafting gets to recognize the invisible deities who rule each particular river, sometimes each particular rapid in a river. The very name Sobek is borrowed from the crocodile god of the Nile. It was chosen as both a charm and a homage.

Rivers are the true highways of life. They transport the ancient tears of disappeared races, they propel the foams that will impregnate the millennium. In flood or in sullen repose, the river's power cannot be overestimated, and only men modernized to the point of moronity will be surprised when rivers eventually take their revenge on those who dam and defile them. River gods, some muddy, others transparent, ride those highways, singing the world's inexhaustible song.

In terms of white water, the Rufiji, the river that drains the Selous, is a pussycat. Once free of the confines of Stiegler's Gorge, it hums a barely audible refrain. Ah, but though the gods of the Rufiji are fairly silent gods, we are soon to learn that their mouths are open wide.

TANZANIAN TRAVELS

A NON-STOP BARRAGE of superior wildlife viewing areas makes northern Tanzania justly famous in the world of adventure. There is simply no rival for the sheer number, variety and accessibility of wildlife to be found anywhere in the world—from the plains of Serengeti to the floor of Ngorongoro Crater, the excitement doesn't quit. Traveling in comfortable safari vehicles, we survey the world's largest permanent population of big game at Ngorongoro, mingle with the Masai in their homeland, learn about the origins of humankind at Olduvai Gorge, and traverse a number of different ecological zones along the way. Whether we are cruising the soda-crust shores of Lake Natron, dropping down into Ngorongoro Crater, surveying the giraffe, zebra or ostrich at Serengeti, or the elephants and lions at Manyara, the list of Tanzania's wonders goes on and on. But the song remains the same: "Look over there!"

ITINERARY: Days 1-2: En route. Day 3: Arusha. Days 4-5: Rift Valley. Day 6: Lake Natron. Day 7: Salai Plains. Days 8-9: Serengeti. Day 10: Nubanka. Day 11: Seronera. Days 12-13: Olduvai. Day 14: Ngorongoro. Days 15-16: Lake Manyara. Day 17: Arusha. Day 18: Return.

🚙 ⛵   Class III   **Medium**
Year-round
Overseas Adventure Travel   AF36

WONDER OF AFRICA

THE COMPLEAT EAST AFRICA awaits you on the greatest African experience yet devised— five weeks from the snows of Kilimanjaro to the coast of Kenya. The adventure begins in Arusha, Tanzania, from where we go to the extinct volcanic crater of Ngorongoro, whose wildlife is hemmed in by crater walls. Huge herds of zebra cast a psychedelic spell as they gallop across the dusty plains, a blur of stripes and flying hooves. We follow the Masai escarpment to the Rift Valley and pause to visit the nomadic Masai—tall and stately, bedecked with beads and jewelry, who provide memorable company at every crook in the trail. Lake Natron, in the heart of the Rift Valley, is awash with masses of pink flamingos and occasional bloats of hippos. Then on to the Serengeti for some of the finest game-viewing anywhere. Millions of wildebeest and zebra migrate through these grasslands, while nearby prowl lion, cheetah, leopard, hyena and other predators. Next is Olduvai Gorge, Dr. Leakey's discovery site of early man; then Kilimanjaro, which we climb over a six-day hike. Crossing into Kenya, we come to Tsavo, Kenya's largest national park. Its rugged countryside hosts a host of animals, seen from the swaying back of a camel, to bring us ever closer to the heart of Africa. Finally we fly to Lamu, an ancient Arab island town with white-washed walls, veiled women and a colorful port. The billowing curved sails and creaking of the wooden deck transport us back into another time as we board a *dhow* for a sail back down the coast to taste the full flavor of Kenya. An optional week on Zanzibar or Mt. Kenya can be added, and for those with less time, each component of this trip can be taken separately or in various combinations.

ITINERARY: Days 1-2: To Nairobi. Day 3: Arusha. Days 4-16: Safari. Day 17: To Kibo. Days 18-23: Kilimanjaro trek. Days 24-25: Nairobi. Days 26-36: Tsavo camel trek. Day 31: To Lamu. Days 32-37: Dhow sail. Day 38: To Nairobi. Day 39: Return.

⛵ 🚙 🚶   Class III   **Moderate**
September-March
Australian Himalayan Expeditions   AF52

MASAI MAIDEN   Richard Bangs

VICTORIA FALLS   Bart Henderson

UNEXPLORED MADAGASCAR

An ethnic journey in a land that is off the beaten track may be the truest kind of adventure, for discovery becomes a personal matter as well as a test for your camera and pen. Madagascar, the large island off Africa's Indian Ocean coast, is such a destination. We drive through central and southern Madagascar, visiting the native towns, living among the villagers for several days at a time, and hiking into the remote wooded countryside where the most isolated of the islanders live, for a journey of recurring revelations. The variety of peoples encountered includes Antanosy, Antandroy, Mahafaly, Mikea, Uezo and Zafimaniry tribes, some of whom are as yet unused to the company of tourists. The route includes stops in the city of Antananarivo and a visit to the Berenty Lémur Reserve, with an optional extension to the Mitsio Islands off the northwest coast. If people and foreign cultures fascinate you, immerse yourself in the vibrant villages of the mysterious Malagasy Republic, on the isle of spices, Madagascar.

ITINERARY: Days 1-2: En route. Day 3: Nairobi. Day 4: Antananarivo. Days 5-6: Berenty Lemur Reserve. Day 7: Ampanihy. Days 8-9: Tulear. Day 13: Antsirabe. Days 14-15: Antoetra. Day 16: Antananarivo. Day 17: Return.

🚙 🦆 🛶   Class III   **Medium**
May, June, October
Forum Travel   AF40

SOUTH CENTRAL

ZAMBEZI WILDLIFE SAFARI

The classic African adventure follows trails blazed by Livingstone and Stanley, by Richard Burton and Theodore Roosevelt, on "big game safaris" in the heartlands of Africa. Picture yourself amidst herds of elephant, zebra or giraffe; track a pride of lions circling its prey; relax as the sun kindles a flare of colors on the horizon, while a flock of flamingoes erupts into a geyser of pink against the sunset sky. This is the Technicolor Africa of your dreams, comfortably

WE HAVEN'T COME TO THE Selous to wine and dine, nor to sight-see and shop. We've come to seek an audience with the river gods, to show ourselves to them and accept their banishment or their boons. We've come to test ourselves against water dragons with ears like wads of hairy bubble gum, and the gaping yawn of a million cases of "sleeping sickness" rolled into one. We've come to the Selous to outrace the hippos.

Did I say that we are exhausted at the conclusion of our morning and afternoon paddles? True, we're tired, but we're also exhilarated. We're so elated our bones are practically singing in their weary sockets. and, narrow escapes or not, it is with eagerness that we wrap ourselves against the homicidal sun and go out on the river again.

Because of the naughty habits of the crocodiles, we're forced to bathe onshore, showering with buckets of muddy water drawn cautiously from the stream. Now, Chicago Eddie might whine that he'd rather be soaking in a tub in some fancy hotel, but nobody believes him. The Rufiji pantheon, lurid of feather, strong of tooth, has wired an ancient tingle in Eddie's cells, and, like the other seventeen of us, he broadcasts secret signals of ecstasy — Radio Eden — as he penetrates ever deeper into the Selous.

packaged to maximize wildlife and minimize hardship. Featured highlights include a luxury chalet overlooking Lake Kariba, personable game guides driving through clutches of buffalo and rhino, a treehouse overlooking a watering hole, and the spectacle of the pride of Africa, Victoria Falls. One-day whitewater rafting trips on the Zambezi River below the falls or wildlife floats above the falls are also included. It's the classic African adventure, complete with airfare from New York and other U.S. gateway cities.

ITINERARY: Day 1: Depart U.S. Day 2: En route to Harare. Days 3-4: Bumi Hills. Days 5-7: Hwange Park. Day 8: Victoria Falls. Day 9: Zambezi River trip (*AF2* or *AF32*). Day 10: Victoria Falls. Day 11: To Harare and return or join *AF46* or *AF1*.

⌐ 🚙   Class I   **Medium**
Year-round
Sobek Expeditions   AF45

THE ZAMBEZI   Michael Nichols

THE ZAMBEZI RIVER

FROM THE SPRAY OF VICTORIA FALLS, one of the seven wonders of the world and the greatest sight Africa has to offer, the roaring waters of the Zambezi enter a canyon crammed with adventure. The local name for the Falls, Musi-O-Tunya (Smoke That Thunders), shows appropriate awe for the two-kilometer wide curtain of falling water where we begin a week-long navigation of the river that carved the Great Zambezi Gorges. David Livingstone discovered the Falls in 1855 on an exploratory canoe expedition down the Zambezi; he wisely decided to detour around the gorges, and left unrun Africa's wildest river corridor – until 1981, when Sobek negotiated the first descent with an ABC television crew. The rapids were Bio-Bio big, the scenery stunning, the wildlife wondrous. Now, the epic expedition is available to wild river connoisseurs – the full 100-kilometer course, from the base of the booming Falls themselves to the headwaters of Lake Kariba. This is incontestably one of the world's finest whitewater and wildlife adventures!

ITINERARY: Day 1: Livingstone, Zambia. Days 2-6: On the Zambezi. Day 7: Arrive Lake Kariba, return Livingstone.

⌐ ⌐   Class IV   **Premium**
August-December
Sobek Expeditions   AF1

UPPER ZAMBEZI

FLOAT THE MAGIC of Africa's grandeur in one easy stroke: a day-long raft trip down the upper reaches of the Zambezi River to the brink of Victoria Falls. The river winds through easy whitewater among the islands of the Zambezi, rolling over the course David Livingstone paddled when he discovered the great river and Musi-O-Tunya over a century ago. We drift through an African menagerie where crocs and hippos ply the banks, where kudu and other plains animals come to the shore, where an elephant may sound his call—creatures in a living diorama of game-viewing from a new perspective. A sumptuous picnic lunch on a riverine island heralds the day for hikers who want to wander this wilderness island on their own, to see what its mid-river secrecy contains. When we continue downstream, we can explore the Musi-O-Tunya Game Park on the Zambia side before the trip ends, if departures are from the Intercontinental Hotel in Livingstone; Zimbabwe departures are from the Victoria Falls Hotel. Both trips conclude with "the Smoke that Thunders"—the vertiginous Victoria Falls. A relaxing, safe and informative look at the wild wonderland of the Zambezi.

ITINERARY: One-day floats begin and end at Victoria Falls, Zimbabwe.

⌐ ⌐   Class I   **Medium**
Year-round
Sobek Expeditions   AF32

ZAMBEZI ONE-DAYS

ANY VISITOR TO VICTORIA FALLS can now experience the world's most exciting day-long whitewater run, bar none. From the Boiling Pot at the base of the Falls, accessible by a short trail, expert river guides row through 10 major rapids couched in the setting of a spectacular, twisting, narrow basalt gorge. Between thrills we stop at limestone caverns, hike to a fairy-tale waterfall, dally at a pleasant swimming hole and feast on a sumptuous lunch. If your travel plans include Victoria Falls, they should also include the Zambezi River.

ITINERARY: One-day trips begin and end at Victoria Falls, Zimbabwe.

✈	Class III	Medium
August-December		
Sobek Expeditions	AF2	

NAMIBIA OVERLAND

TOWERING SAND DUNES, vast plateaus of aridity, flocks of flamingoes pink against the cerulean sun, and a paradoxical heritage makes Namibia unique in all Africa. We explore all the known attractions of this vivid and constantly changing landscape, from its world-record dunes to its German colonial character, as well as paying our dues in the game parks of this southwestern African nation. Towns like Swakopmund, Luderitz, and the capital of Windhoek boast a anachronistic German heritage, while ornately dressed Hetero women, wizened tribesmen and descendants of the Bushmen bespeak a different background. We travel by minibus or four-wheel drive to several game-viewing areas, including the famous Etosha Pan, spend two full days in the celebrated Namib Desert, and visit the stark Grand Canyon-like terrain of Fish River. A close look at a country often overlooked, but never equalled.

ITINERARY: Day 1: Johannesburg to Kuruman. Day 2: Kalahari. Day 3: Hardap Dam. Day 4: Windhoek. Days 5-8: Etosha Pan. Day 9: Damaraland. Days 10-11: Swakopmund. Days 12-13: Namib Desert. Days 14-16: Fish River Canyon. Days 17: Augrabies Park. Day 18: Kimberly. Day 19: Johannesburg. Day 20: Return.

🚜 🛶 🛖	Class II	Moderate
Year-round		
Afroventures	AF35	

BOTSWANA

BOTSWANA SAFARI

THE REAL AFRICA is more incredible than any dime novel or summer cinema entertainment. It's a land where huge rivers turn desolation into a wildlife heaven, where a mile-wide waterfall plummets hundreds of feet into narrow gorges, where flocks of flamingoes flood the skies. Our Botswana Safari is an ideal way to strike out into the heart of Africa, with extended stays at the Moremi Wildlife Reserve in the Okavango Delta, in the elephant country of Chobe National Park, and at Victoria Falls where we bask in the cool spray and test the turbulent whitewater of the Zambezi River. Botswana is a country the size of France, with almost a quarter of its area devoted to wildlife conservation, some of it administered by the native Botswana tribes. First hand encounters with crocodiles, hippo, buffalo and lions make this camping safari one for the young – and strong – of heart.

JOHNNY WEISMULLER, the consummate movie Tarzan, was the tallest hero of my boyhood, and more often during my life than is socially acceptable I've been moved to imitate his famous yell. To some, the Tarzan yodel is corny, campy, childish, and vulgar. To me, it's more stirring than the bravest battle cry, more glorious than the loftiest operatic aria, more profound than the most golden outpouring of oratory. The Tarzan yell is the Rexultant cry of man the innocent, man the free. It warbles back and forth across the boundary between human and beast, expressing in its extremes and convolutions all the unrestrained and holy joy of ultimate aliveness.

In the past, unfortunately, I've usually bounced my Tarzan yells off the insensitive ears of cocktail-lounge commandos. Here, at last, in the glades of the Selous, it is released in its proper context. It gives me that old Weismuller Saturday-matinee primal chill as it comes quavering out of my throat to mix in the Selous twilight with the smoker's coughs of a distant pride of lions, the spooky erotic murmurs of a treeful of waking bats, and that ceaseless pulsebeat of body Africana, the echoing hoot of the emerald-throated wood dove.

ITINERARY: Day 1: Johannesburg to Botswana. Days 2-4: Maun, Okavango Delta. Days 5-6: Moremi Wildlife Reserve. Days 7-10: Chobe National Park. Day 11: Victoria Falls. Day 12: Zambezi River run. Day 13: En route. Day 14: Ben Lavin Nature Reserve. Day 15: Johannesburg.

🚙 🛶 ✈ Class III   **Medium**
Year-round
Afroventures   AF30

PARKS OF BOTSWANA

THE INLAND DELTA of the Okavango hosts bird and animal life beyond imagining, as the waters of the great river come to their quiescence in the desert, creating a zoological wonderland. Land Rovers, bush planes and dugout canoes take us through the finest game parks of southern Africa on a grand circle route from Victoria Falls. Wildebeest, antelope, lion, hyena, rhino, elephant and many more animals crowd the views of this region, and the unique inland marshes and isolated isles of the Okavango are sure to make a birder crow with joy. The four-wheel drive vans take us through Chobe's fields in the company of expert game guides; we canoe through the riverine passages surrounding Xaxaba Island along papyrus shores; then we fly over the remotest reaches of Savuti Channel to a tented camp in the heart of the Okavango's wildlife region. A free day at Victoria Falls follows, and a visit to the Ewanrigg Botanical Gardens, a treasure trove of colorful aloes and ancient cycads. Cost includes airfare in Africa.

ITINERARY: Day 1: Victoria Falls to Chobe National Park, Botswana. Day 2: Chobe. Day 3: Savuti camp. Days 4-5: Khwai River camp. Day 6: Kubu camp. Day 7: Maun. Day 8: Victoria Falls. Day 9: To Harare and return.

🛶 🚙 ✈ Class III   **Premium**
Year-round
Sobek Expeditions   AF46

OKAVANGO FLY-IN SAFARI

THE DELTA OF THE OKAVANGO is one of the world's most unusual features— the inland terminus of a great river, and a haven for wildlife like no other. Chobe National Park, on the northeast corner of this immense swamp, harbors huge herds of elephant and antelope, as well as rare puku, red lechwe, cheetah and other animal life typically found in Africa's abundant savannahland. But in the delta itself, water-oriented wildlife is in striking contrast to that found at Chobe: antelope like the lechwe and sassaby; egrets, storks and herons; and the white-marked fish eagle more common along African rivers. We reach the heart of the Okavango by charter plane, giving us an overview of this natural wonder. With visits to Kavango, Chobe and Maun, and travels to Victoria Falls and the metropolis of Johannesburg, this is an overview of southern Africa in more ways than one. Accommodation is a mixture of hotels, lodges, chalets and camping, with four nights spent under canvas in the game reserves themselves. And while in southern Africa, may we suggest taking a whitewater or wildlife float down the Zambezi River at Victoria Falls?

8-DAY ITINERARY: Day 1: Victoria Falls. Days 2-4: Chobe. Day 5: Maun. Days 6-7: Moremi. Day 8: Maun and return. *Reverse itinerary every alternate departure.*

15-DAY ITINERARY: Day 0: Arrive Johannesburg. Day 1: To Palapye, Botswana. Day 2: Maun. Days 3-4: Okavango Delta. Days 5-6: Moremi. Days 7-10: Chobe. Days 11-12: Victoria Falls. Days 13-14: En route. Day 15: Johannesburg and return. *Reverse itinerary on alternate dates.*

🚙 🛶 ✈ Class II   **Medium**
March-November
Afroventures   AF41

HERERO TRIBES WOMEN   Karen Peterson

ITINERARY: Day 1: En route. Day 2: Cairo. Days 5-6: Luxor. Days 7-11: Nile sail. Day 12-14: Aswan. Day 15: Cairo. Day 16: Return.

▲ 火 ☕   Class II   **Moderate**
Year-round
Overseas Adventure Travel   AF23

NORTH

NILE SAIL TREK

SAILING THE NILE RIVER by felucca is a timeless experience, one repeated by Egyptians for scores of centuries, reaching back to the days of the Pharoahs. We cruise for five days through history, from modern Aswan to the ruins of No-Amon (Thebes), the ancient Egyptian capital and one of the most remarkable archaeological sites in the world. Along our way pyramids pierce the sky, the Sphinx rears her mute head, and the *felaheen* farm as they have from the beginnings of time, following the cyclic patterns. Our meals are traditional—and tasty—Egyptian cuisine; our nights are spent beneath the primordial constellations; and our dreams may be filled with the chambers of Karnak, the temples of Kom Ombo, the mausoleum of the Aga Khan.

HOGGAR CAMEL SAFARI

DISCOVER THE LUNAR LANDSCAPES of Algeria's famed Tassili du Hoggar at the casual pace of our *meharis*, or camels. We share the lives of Tuareg nomads, meandering along camel paths from the mountain passes across searing Saharan sands to welcome oases. Out of Tamanrasset we ride to plateaus of the north, where we are surrounded by the phantasmagoric colors and shapes of the desert rocks, vistas of mountain peaks and the abrupt topography of the Hoggar. A wonderland ride on the ships of the desert.

ITINERARY: Day 1: Fly Paris/Algiers. Day 2: Fly Algiers/Tamanrasset. Days 3-9: On the camels. Day 10: Tamanrasset. Day 11: Fly to Paris.

🐪 🐫   Class III   **Medium**
February-March, July-August
Visages du Monde   AF20

OUR LAST DAY IN THE SELOUS is structured much like the others: up at dawn for a game walk into the bush, breakfast, break camp, two hours on the river, lunch, rest, two more hours playing Dodg'em car with the hippos, set up camp, another game walk before dark, dinner, bed. At the end of such a day, one requires no tsetse injection to speed one's slumber. On this final eve, however, many of us lie conscious, listening, holding on to every note of the ninety-piece orchestra of the African night. It is as if we dread the morning and our return to what we call civilization.

I'll bet that Bob, in the adjacent tent, is recalling the impalas we had seen that dusk, crossing a narrow ridge single file, so that we could count them the way a child at a crossing will count boxcars: there were exactly sixty-five silhouetted against the setting sun. . . .

Certainly M'sengala, with his goofy, infectious laugh, is in my thoughts. I'm remembering how shocked he'd looked when Curt had slipped the Sony Walkman headset over his leathery ears and turned up Huey Lewis and the News, and how quickly he'd begun to grin and then to dance, as if he could not stop himself from dancing. M'sengala got down! The Selous, itself, gets down. Down to basics, to the curious if natural rhythms of life.

And death. For if there's abundant life in the Selous, there's abundant death as well. . . . Yes, there are ongoing dramas of death in the Selous, but except for the small amount imported by poachers, there's no unnecessary violence, no greed, no cruelty. Nor is there politics, religion, trendiness, ambition, hype, or sales pitch. Perhaps its the very purity of the Selous that makes us cling to it, reluctant to let it go.

For two weeks, we have traveled in the realm of the eternal. There is no escape from the prison of the past, no interest in the uncertainties of the future. There is no other place. The Selous is here. There is no other time. The Selous is now.

And as we lie in our tents on the grassy plain of eternity it must occur to each and every one of us that the Selous is the way the world was meant to be — and everything else is a mistake.

▲

THE HIGH ATLAS

THE MAGICAL CITY OF MARRAKECH needs no backdrop of snow-capped mountains, but it has one. The Atlas Range sprawls across the southern horizon, tempting us out of the labyrinthine streets and old souks into the Moroccan backcountry. We base our two-week trek in the Berber village of Arroumd, whose mud-and-wood houses are surrounded by the terraced terrain and towering peaks of this ancient frontier. Then after the hidden secrets of the hills we trek, accompanied by pack mules and native guides, toward North Africa's highest summit. Ascent of this peak, Toubkal (4165m), is optional, but from its summit the Atlas stretch to east and west, the Sahara spreads southward, and the blue Mediterranean limns the northern sky. Berber hospitality, with its constant spring of sweet mint tea and the spinning, weaving, cooking and dancing of these traditional mountain people, lets us link our high enthusiasms with the color and vitality of the human element.

ITINERARY: Day 1: Arrive Marrakech. Day 2: Marrakech. Days 3-13: To the High Atlas; trekking. Days 14-15: Marrakech. Day 16: Return.

			Class IV	**Moderate**
April-October
Exodus   AF43

TRANS-AFRICA
GRAND SAFARI

THE MAGIC OF THE WILDS is captured in the shimmering of sun-baked plains, the tranquility of hidden streams, the chaos of raging waterfalls and the tentative lift of an impala's head. For over three weeks we safari through Namibia, Botswana, Zimbabwe and South Africa on a grand adventure of animal life, native traditions and colonial influence. The arid tracts of the Kalahari Desert surround the lush anomaly of Okavango. The unique Namib Desert, bound on one side by Atlantic surf, is elsewhere surrounded by German farmers. Contrasts and controversy are played out over time against the constant face of a compelling continent, where words like "spectacular" are as commonplace as they are true. This camping safari by four-wheel drive van may vary its route due to road and weather conditions.

ITINERARY: Day 1: Kuruman. Day 2: Augrabies Falls. Days 3-4: Fish River Canyon. Days 5-6: Namib Desert. Days 7-8: Swakopmund. Day 9: Windhoek. Day 10: Kalahari Desert. Day 11: Lake Ngami. Days 12-13: Maun, Okavango Swamp. Days 14-15: Moremi National Park. Days 16-17: Savuti (Southern Chobe). Days 18-19: Serondela (Northern Chobe). Day 20: Victoria Falls. Day 21: Zambezi River Whitewater Run. Day 22: En route. Day 23: Ben Lavin Nature Reserve. Day 24: Johannesburg.

			Class III	**Moderate**
Year-round
Afroventures   AF28

TRANS-AFRICA

THE ESSENCE OF AFRICA is distilled on a trans-continental truck expedition, a modern motorized homage to the great safaris of the past. We travel through landscapes little-altered by the march of progress, peopled by tribes whose way of life has remained unchanged for thousands of years. This rugged trip requires the ability to cope with the delays and hardships made inevitable by primitive conditions, harsh weather and long distances. Yet our journey is a celebration of extraordinary scenery, people and wildlife. In northern Africa, Arab, Berber and Moor rub shoulders in the crowded bazaars; across the High Atlas Berbers give way to Tuareg nomads as we enter the fringes of the immense Sahara, a varied landscape of 100-meter high dunes, ancient volcanic ranges and gravel plateaus. South of the Sahara the black tribes take over, first Hausa and Fulani in the Sahel, then numerous small groups, each with distinct beliefs and traditions as we enter the Cameroons. Continuing through the rain forest of Zaire we emerge into the vast plains of East Africa, with its fantastic diversity of large tribal groupings. This is still an explorer's continent, much as it was in the 19th century. If you want it to yield you some of its secrets, join us on one or all of the legs of a Trans-Africa safari between London, Kano (Nigeria), Nairobi (Kenya) and Johannesburg (South Africa) or the reverse. Segments last from 4 to 19 weeks, and each one is a special adventure unto itself.

ITINERARY: Day 1: Begin London, Nairobi or Johannesburg. *Note:* Complete trip lasts 21 weeks; Nairobi to London portion lasts 15 weeks. Various segments of the trip may be booked separately upon arrangement. Alternate departures follow reserve route.

			Class III	**Moderate**
Year-round
Exodus   AF50

WAT ARUN, THAILAND   Michael Ingram

ASIA

DHAULAGIRI VIEW   Liz Hymans

THE ASCENT OF ANNAPURNA

by Maurice Herzog

*A*ll the nine members of the Expedition will have more than one reason for cherishing this record. Together we knew toil, joy and pain. My fervent wish is that the nine of us who were united in face of death should remain fraternally united through life.

In overstepping our limitations, in touching the extreme boundaries of man's world, we have come to know something of its true splendor. In my worst moments of anguish, I seemed to discover the deep significance of existence of which till then I had been unaware. I saw that it was better to be true than to be strong. The marks of the ordeal are apparent on my body. I was saved and I had won my freedom. This freedom, which I shall never lose, has given me the assurance and serenity of a man who has fulfilled himself. It has given me the rare joy of loving that which I used to despise. A new and splendid life has opened out before me.

In this narrative we do more than record our adventures, we bear witness: events that seem to make no sense may sometimes have a deep significance of their own....

NEPAL

GATEWAY TO NEPAL

FROM THE STREETS OF KATHMANDU to the skies over Everest, with a taste of trekking for the intrepid: an introductory package to Nepal that features the mountain trails that have made the mountain kingdom famous. From departure to return, this complete travel experience investigates the heartlands and hinterlands of Nepal, including the bustling side-streets and market places of Kathmandu, the icy flanks of Mt. Everest as seen from the air, the fabulous lowland wildlife of Chitwan National Park (including tiger, leopard, bear and the very elephant that carries you through the jungle), and finally the remote tracks of pilgrims and trekkers into the Annapurna massif. The trek route begins in Pokhara, in the center of the country, and slices toward Chandrikot and Nanada, with excellent views all along the impressive Annapurnas. In the style of classic mountain expeditions, porters bear the burden of overnight gear and supplies, leaving you with eyes wide and hands free to appreciate the wonders of Nepal. It's just three days on the trail, but three days you'll neither regret nor forget. Travelers who choose not to make the optional Annapurna trek spend extra time in Pokhara and Kathmandu to visit the cultural sights of Nepal.

ITININERARY: Day 1: Depart gateway city. Day 2: En route. Day 3: Kathmandu. Day 4: Everest fly-over. Day 5: To Pokhara; begin trek. Day 6: On trek. Day 7: End trek. Day 8: Drive to Chitwan. Day 9: Chitwan. Day 10: Kathmandu. Day 11: Return or join *AS80*.

🍴 🐘 🥾   Class II   **Moderate**
August-May
Sobek Expeditions   AS78

MOUNT EVEREST VIEW

THE INTRODUCTION TO NEPAL provided by our *Gateway to Nepal* adventure trip is incomplete without a trailside view of Everest, the Goddess Mountain. A short trek out of Lukla, the famous high-altitude trekkers' airstrip, is all that is needed for clear and compelling views of the great mountain. Weather permitting (since inclement conditions can prevent flying into or out of Lukla, causing delays in anyone's Everest plans), this eight-day option has all the elements of a top Himalayan trek. Thyangboche's monastery, where Buddhism is still practiced in Tibetan purity; Pangboche and its yeti scalp; Namche Bazar where lowland Nepalis and Sherpas meet at the gateway to Tibet; and for

---

THE ASCENT BEGAN with a climb up a vertical slab of rock. The track went up in steep zigzags, obstructed by bamboos, dead tree-trunks and trees which straggled over the path in an attempt to reach the light; the air was damp and heavy. [Jean] Couzy and I embarked on a long discussion: we had got as far as Bergson and Junger when we came upon a delightful meadow bright with snowdrops and a variety of other flowers.

"It was here that [Dr. Jacques] Oudot, [Marcel] Schatz and I bivouacked on April 27," said Couzy. Mountaineers are great lovers of habit, so we had lunch there. Tubes of condensed milk were passed round. Those who weren't sick of this form of nourishment sucked concentrated fruit tablets, and while the last of the sweating porters were still arriving, the smoke curled up from our cigarettes. Couzy had grown meditative as a result of our discussion, and [Gaston] Rebuffat thought of his little Dominique, of whom he had received no news. Resuming our march, we suddenly found ourselves at a turning of the path, in a grove of trees resplendent with brilliant colored flowers whose names I did not know. No vaulted cathedral roof could have been more magnificent. The track went on across a beautiful clearing. Round us was a cemetery of charred deodars whose trunks rose well over a hundred feet high, and giant rhododendrons bordering out path hung out great clusters of pink and red flowers.

the fitter members of the trip, Pheriche village and Tabhouche Hill with its renowned vistas—it's all there for you to experience. Don't leave Nepal without the luxury and thrill of an Everest trek.

ITINERARY: Day 1: Kathmandu to Lukla. Days 2-7: On trek. Days 8-9: Kathmandu. Day 10: Return.

🚶 ☕   Class III   **Moderate**
August-May
Sobek Expeditions   AS80

ARUN TO EVEREST

TAKE THE ROAD less traveled by to the world's summit, journeying up the scenic and cultural wonderland of the Arun Valley toward Mt. Everest. Challenge the heart of Nepal's great mountain range, with time to visit its famous Sherpas, its warrior Gurkhas, and the Limbu people whose culture is unique among the diverse inhabitants of Nepal. Our route takes us through the rarely-trekked and scenically diverse Arun Valley, a region characterized by sweeping vistas and isolated mountain villages, all beneath the towering summit of

MOUNTAIN WHEAT   Liz Hymans

Makalu, world's fifth highest peak. We share mugs of *tongma* with the Nepali villagers, listen to local legends of the surrounding peaks, and cross a final pass to Everest Base Camp, historic end-point of the trek. Finally we ascend Kalipatar, an 18,000-foot peak nearby from whose summit the pinnacle of Everest rises a mere 11,000 feet above! A high-altitude trek for the hardy, but worth every breath you take.

ITINERARY: Day 1: Kathmandu. Days 2-28: On trek. Days 29-31: Kathmandu. Day 32: Return.

🚶 ☕   Class IV   **Moderate**
December
Sobek Expeditions   AS106

MACHAPUCCHARE TREK

A JOURNEY SET IN the glorious crown of Nepal's most spectacular scenery, Machapucchare is an exquisite mountain, a near-perfect pyramid of snow and ice soaring 6000 meters above the surrounding countryside. From bustling markets to isolated pinnacles, past timeless villages and ever changing landscapes, our itinerary traverses the spectrum of historic and cultural Nepal. We follow a seldom-used trail from Pokhara to a hanging glacial lake on the south face of Machapucchare, a region so remote that it remains unnamed. An optional climb to the 4000-meter level of this compelling massif provides a unrivaled view of the Himalaya, a brilliant vision of vertiginous escarpments and vast snowfields sparkling in the rarefied alpine atmosphere. Past glaciers and moraine, through forests of oak and rhodedendron and across meadows carpeted in flowering daphne, our leisurely trek passes villages of the Gurung tribe, to whom music and dancing are an integral part of daily life. Beneath the towering peaks of Annapurna, Lamjung, Manaslu and Himalchuli, each a legend in its own right, we relax in the warm hospitality of the Gurung people while participating in their festive ceremonies. A final descent through the Marsyandi River valley brings us back to the main Kathmandu road where we begin immediately to yearn for a return to the beauty of Machapucchare.

ITINERARY: Days 1-2: En route. Day 3: Kathmandu. Day 4: Bus to Pokhara, begin trek. Days 5-23: On trek. Day 24: Kuringhat to Kathmandu. Days 25-26: Kathmandu. Day 27: Return.

🚶 ☕   Class IV   **Moderate**
September-May
Australian Himalayan Expeditions   AS83

THE EVEREST TREK

THE DAZZLING SPECTACLE of Mt. Everest can be fully appreciated on this shorter trek, designed for those without the time to attempt the more rugged trip to Everest Base Camp. Although the high point is below 4600 meters, we still view the glaciers of Everest to feel the Goddess Mountain's chilly breath. From the famed airstrip at Lukla in the Himalaya, we follow the Dudh Kosi Gorge to Namche Bazar in the Sherpa Khumbu region. This important market village is a traditional meeting point for lowlanders and Sherpas, and the gateway to the ancient yak trade route to Tibet. Sir Edmund Hillary's hospital and school at Khunde is on our route to two of the most fabled monasteries of Buddhism in Nepal: Thyangboche, a colorful complex surrounded by a splendid ring of Himalayan giants, and Pangboche, home of the famous (and controversial) yeti scalp. From Pheriche village, a scramble up Tabhouche Hill leads to humbling views of the Khumbu glacier, Mt. Everest and its surrounding peaks. The vision is, in understated terms, simply astounding.

ITINERARY: Days 1-2: Kathmandu. Day 3: Lukla. Days 4-14: On trek. Day 15: Lukla. Days 16-18: Kathmandu. Day 19: Return. Available in combination with Annapurna Trek as *Everest/Annapurna* (AS105).

🚶 ⚙️   Class III   **Moderate**
September-May
Australian Himalayan Expeditons   AS1

TIBETAN TRADER   Gary Bolton

CLASSIC EVEREST

THE ORIGINAL EXPEDITION route to Everest is retraced on this classic trek, venturing east from Jiri and across two major passes to the Dudh Kosi Valley. Along the route are delightful villages in the picturesque Solu Valley, reminiscent of European alpine vales. The Dudh Kosi's icy waters lead us north through the Sherpa villages, past Thyangboche Monastery for the final push up to Everest Base Camp and Kalipatar. Kalipatar (5545 meters), a rocky outcrop in the Everest basin, affords the finest views of Everest short of that from the moun-

---

ON THE THIRD OF JUNE, 1950, the first light of dawn found us still clinging to the tent poles at Camp V [at 24,600 feet]. Gradually the wind abated, and with daylight died away altogether. I made desperate attempts to push back the soft, icy stuff which stifled me, but every movement became an act of heroism. My mental powers were numbed: thinking was an effort, and we did not exchange a single word.

What a repellent place it was! To everyone who reached it, Camp V became one of the worst memories of their lives. We had only one thought — to get away. [Louis Lachenal and I] should have waited for the first rays of the sun, but at half-past five we felt we couldn't stick it any longer.

Which of us would have the energy to make tea? Although our minds worked slowly we were quite able to envisage all the movements that would be necessary — and neither of us could face up to it. It couldn't be helped — we would just have to go without. It was quite hard enough work to get ourselves and our boots out of our sleeping-bags — and the boots were frozen stiff so that we got them on only with the greatest difficulty. Every movement made us terribly breathless. We felt as if we were being stifled . . .

We went outside and put on our crampons, which we kept on all day. We wore as many clothes as possible; our sacks were very light. At six o'clock we started off. It was brilliantly fine, but also very cold. Our super-lightweight crampons bit deep into the steep slopes of ice and hard snow up which lay the first stage of our climb.

tain's own flanks. The magical lure of the Goddess Mountain, the earth's highest point, is never more magnetic than in the footsteps of the great adventurers who dared her icy slopes—some winning, some losing. The gamble is not so great for us, but the rewards are many.

ITINERARY: Days 1-3: To Kathmandu. Day 4: Kathmandu. Days 5-24: Trekking. Days 25-26: Kathmandu. Day 27: Fly out. Day 28: Return.

🚶 ☕ Class IV **Moderate**
September-June
Australian Himalayan Expeditions AS3

EVEREST/ARUN VALLEY

Only a very few have stood acrest the world's highest peak, yet trekking to the flanks of Mt. Everest is an adventure of the highest order that many can share. A trek to Everest Base Camp spans the entire scenic and cultural range of Nepal, from game-rich jungles of the Terai to the glaciers of Everest, with plenty of time betwixt for acclimatization, photography,

and searching out little-known faces and facets of the Himalaya. From Dharan, a market town in easternmost Nepal, we cross the Mahabharat range to the Arun River Valley, peopled by ex-Gurkha soldiers and Tibetan expatriates as well as its traditional Limbu inhabitants. Then it's up, rising through the wild and broken country of the middle hills to enter the first mountain villages, and finally reach the homeland of the Sherpas. We acclimate among the Sherpas under the spell of the earth's loftiest peaks, preparing for our final push to Everest Base Camp (5400m). Those who wish can ascend Kalipatar, a rocky outcrop in the Everest basin, for an unparalleled view of The Big One. A dramatic flight back to Kathmandu from Lukla leaves a hawk's-eye view in our minds that lasts as long as the Himalayan snows.

ITINERARY: Day 1: En route. Days 2-3: Kathmandu. Days 4-29: Trek. Day 30: Lukla. Days 31-33: Kathmandu. Day 34: Return.

🚶 ☕ Class IV **Moderate**
October-April
Australian Himalayan Expeditions AS2

BEHIND ANNAPURNA   Liz Hymans

ANNAPURNA SANCTUARY

PICTURE THIS: a 360-degree view of no fewer than five massive mountains in the heart of the Himalaya, all but one well above 7000 meters, and that — Machapucchare (6997m) — one of the most spectacular mountains in the world. This is the Annapurna Sanctuary, a beautiful meadowed uplands almost without parallel in the known world. Our journey into this uplifting region begins from the Pokhara, a trekker's trailhead whose views of the Annapurnas, Machapucchare and Manaslu are enough to boggle the most jaded mind. Along the Kaski Ridge we trek until we reach Ghorapani Pass (2895m), then we turn northward toward the Sanctuary itself. We rise up the steep gorge through thickets of bamboo, changing to coniferous forest, finally breaking into the alpine grassland of the sanctuary at the Machapucchare base camp. Several days are spent in this incredible interior, wandering from view to vista to vision until our entire perspective changes, from one of wonder and disbelief to one of pure, simple acceptance. That's just the way it is in Nepal.

ITINERARY: Day 1: En route. Days 2-4: Kathmandu. Day 5: Pokhara. Days 6-17: On trek. Days 18-19: Kathmandu. Day 20: Return.

🥾   Class IV   **Moderate**
September-May
Australian Himalayan Expeditions   AS8

AROUND ANNAPURNA

A MONTH OF MAJESTY among the high peaks of the Annapurna Massif, one of Nepal's most scenically impressive regions. The 23-day trek begins with leisurely days ambling up rhododendron-lined trails, following ancient footprints which rise ever deeper between towering peaks. The pace picks up as the passes are surmounted, each successive day reaching new plateaus of altitude and appearance, until the wild and veering landscape of Thorong La surrounds the trekker at the 18,000-foot level. From here we look north toward the mysterious land of Tibet, and south toward the 8000-meter peaks of Annapurna. Our return takes us along the precipitous Kali Gandakhi Gorge, where Dhaulagiri casts its shadow into the deepest regions of Nepal's secrets, four full miles below the sky-scraping peaks. By the time we reach Pokhara, and from there drive on to Kathmandu, the scenic splendor of Annapurna has penetrated our souls, even as we have pierced the cloud-draped curtains of the Himalaya.

ITINERARY: Days 1-2: Kathmandu. Day 3: To Pokhara; begin trek. Days 4-25: On trek. Days 26-27: Kathmandu. Day 28: Return.

🥾 🛶   Class IV   **Moderate**
November
Sobek Expeditions   AS107

SOMETIMES THE HARD CRUST bore our weight, but at others we broke through and sank into soft powder snow which made progress exhausting. We took turns in making the track and often stopped without any word having passed between us. Each of us lived in a closed and private world of his own. I was suspicious of my mental processes; my mind was working very slowly and I was perfectly aware of the low state of my intelligence. It was easiest just to stick to one thought at a time — safest, too. The cold was penetrating; for all our special eiderdown clothing we felt as if we'd nothing on. Whenever we halted, we stamped our feet hard. Lachenal went as far as to take off one boot which was a bit tight; he was in terror of frostbite.

"I don't want to be like Lambert," he said. Raymond Lambert, a Geneva guide, had to have all his toes amputated after an eventful climb during which he got his feet frostbitten. While Lachenal rubbed himself hard, I looked at the summits all around us; already we overtopped them all except the distant Dhaulagiri. The complicated structure of these mountains, with which our many laborious explorations had made us familiar, was now spread out plainly at our feet.

The going was incredibly exhausting, and every step was a struggle of mind over matter. . . . I began to be seriously worried. I realized very well the risk we were running; I knew from experience how insidiously and quickly frostbite can set in if one is not extremely careful. Nor was Lachenal under any illusions. "We're in danger of having frozen feet. Do you think it's worth it?"

ANNAPURNA CIRCUIT

THE CLASSIC NEPAL TREK routes up rhododendron-lined trails and along ancient foot-paths to the edge of the wild desert country of Tibet. For centuries the circum-Annapurna trail has linked isolated Buddhist communities nestled in the Himalaya with commercial centers as far away as Ceylon (Sri Lanka) and Singapore. Through Gurung villages and the pastures of Namun ridge, we branch off the main trail to Dudh Pokhari, for an eyrie-like view of the infinite foothills of the Himalaya. From Thorong Pass (5395m) we gaze across the wide, barren Tibetan Plateau to the north, while behind us rears the head of the Annapurna massif. The trail continues down into the Kali Gandaki Gorge, where Dhaulagiri and the Annapurnas tower four full miles above this plunging valley, deepest on earth. Surrounding us, an expanse of 360 of the most scenic degrees, and kilometers, the world has to offer!

ITINERARY: Day 1: En route. Days 2-4: Kathmandu. Days 5-24: On trek. Days 25-26: Kathmandu. Day 27: Return.

🚶 ⛺   Class IV   **Moderate**
March-April, September-November
Australian Himalayan Expeditions   AS7

EVEREST/ANNAPURNA

THE DYNAMIC DUO OF TREKKING in Nepal are the towering peaks of Everest and Annapurna. Everest is the world's highest peak (29,028 ft., 8853m), and Annapurna became the first 8000-meter mountain ever climbed (26,502 ft., 8083m), making these both monuments to mountaineering as well as spectacular trek routes in their own right. Alphabetically and in this adventure, Annapurna is first; we start with a ride to Pokhara in central Nepal, and follow the world's deepest canyon, the Kali Gandaki Gorge, on our penetration deep into the wilderness of the Annapurna Massif. From there we head for the lowland as an intermission, spending three days in Chitwan National Park enjoying the diverse wildlife and strange pleasures of an elephant-back safari. Thereupon we head once more into the hills, flying to Lukla to start our trek up the classic approach to Chomolungma, Mt. Everest. Thyangboche with its spectacular setting, surrounded by the sunlit summits of the highest Himalaya, is our destination on this eight-day venture up the ancient yak trading route across the mountains. From native markets and bazaars to views that

HIMALAYAN SUNSET   Liz Hymans

will etch themselves on your memory for life, these twin peaks promise—and deliver—the magnificence of Nepal.

ITINERARY: Days 1-2: Kathmandu. Day 3: Lukla. Days 6-10: Everest trek. Days 11-12: Kathmandu. Days 13-15: Chitwan. Day 16: Pokhara. Days 17-24: Annapurna trek. Day 25: Kathmandu. Day 26: Return. Annapurna trek available separately; 13-day itinerary.

🚶 ⛺   Class III   **Moderate**
September-May
Australian Himalayan Expeditions   AS105

SUN KHOSI RAFT EXPEDITION

NEPAL IS MORE than just mountains — ice and rivers carved these peaks, and the Sun Khosi and its tributaries adorn their flanks like a necklace of purls. From its headwaters in the dramatic high Himalaya to the broad tropical valleys of the Terai, the Sun Khosi slices through a cross-section of Nepal: the tortured gorges, the isolated retreats of *rishis,* the cobbled squares of Newari villages, the graveled spills of side canyons and the raging rapids of the river itself, all linked by suspension bridges an eon old. We challange the great whitewater of the upper and lower Sun Khosi after a short and easy trek to our put-in at Dolalghat. And as everywhere in Nepal, the constantly changing views of towering mountains turn every day into eternity, and infinity into every flower.

ITINERARY: Day 1: En route. Days 2-3: Kathmandu. Days 4-12: Rafting. Days 13-15: Kathmandu. Day 16: Return.

🚣 ⛺   Class III   **Moderate**
December, March
Australian Himalayan Expeditions   AS15

DARJEELING MONASTERY   Richard Bangs

TREKKING AMA DABLAM   Chris Baker

NEPAL FAMILY TREK

THE ENCHANTING HELAMBU region north of Kathmandu provides the setting for this low-altitude trek designed especially for families. Now children have the opportunity to share with parents in the excitement and cultural vitality of Nepal, a profoundly educational experience in a country where most people live with few luxuries in an environment of unsurpassed wonder. Traveling at a leisurely pace, we cover a total distance of approximately 130 kilometers in 15 days, pausing often in the villages to meet the Tamang and Newar people and enjoy their folk songs and dances. Our wanderings take us onward to the region of the Helmu people, Buddhists of Tibet origin, where we relax in the village of Tarke Gyang while getting to know our hosts. One of the finest panoramas of Nepal is just outside of Tarke Gyang: the Langtang Range and the massive peaks from Annapurna to Gauri Shankar which spread in luxuriant legion. From wildflower meadows to pine-fringed slopes and dense rain forests, this family outing provides an unforgettable experience for all ages.

ITINERARY: Days 1-2: En route. Day 3: Kathmandu. Day 4: Bus to Sundarijal, begin trek. Days 5-17: On trek. Day 18: Panchkal to Kathmandu. Day 19: Kathmandu. Day 20: Return.

🐫 🥾   Class III   **Medium**
December
Australian Himalayan Expeditions   AS86

LACHENAL APPEARED TO ME as a sort of specter — he was alone in his world, I in mine. But — and this was odd enough — any effort was slightly less exhausting than lower down. Perhaps it was hope lending us wings. . . . We looked down upon precipitous ridges which dropped away into space, and upon tiny glaciers far, far below. Familiar peaks soared arrow-like into the sky. Suddenly Lachenal grabbed me:

"If I go back, what will you do?"

A whole sequence of pictures flashed through my head: the days of marching in sweltering heat, the hard pitches we had overcome, the tremendous efforts we had all made to lay siege to the mountain, the daily heroism of my friends in establishing the camps. Now we were nearing our goal. In an hour or two, perhaps, victory would be ours. Must we give up? Impossible! My whole being revolted against the idea. I had made up my mind, irrevocably. Today we were consecrating an ideal, and no sacrifice was too great. I heard my voice clearly:

"I should go on by myself."

I would go alone. If he wished to go down it was not for me to stop him. He must make his own choice freely.

"Then I'll follow you."

BRIDGING THE STREAM   Kebos

LANGTANG VALLEY

DUE NORTH OF KATHMANDU, pressed against the final pitch of mountain that leads to Tibet, Langtang National Park is a practically un-visited wilderness of tiny villages of Sherpas and Tibetans, surrounded by glaciers and gorges. We trek from Trisuli north along the Trisuli River to the village monastery at Gat-lang, then cross the river to climb into the beautiful forests of Ghora Tabela. Into the high Langtang Valley, where clouds scud at eye level to crash softly into the main chain of the Hima-laya, we visit villages, genuflect at *gompas,* and find — at the high outpost of Kyangjin — a Swiss yak cheese factory. The region is one of the least explored in Nepal, with glaciers and canyons to the north and south so rugged the natives find no reason to enter them. The trek is moderately difficult, with the high point being the gentle Gosainkund Pass at 4600 meters. Nearby is the holy lake of Gosainkund, where thousands of Hindu pilgrims come each October. Join them then, or enjoy the riot of colors of springtime Nepal.

ITINERARY: Days 1-2: En route. Days 3-4: Kath-mandu. Days 5-18: On trek. Day 19: Kathmandu. Day 20: Return.

🚶 🏺   Class IV   **Moderate**
September-May
Australian Himalayan Expeditions   AS9

KANGCHENJUNGA

THE MOST MAGNIFICENT TREK in all Nepal may well be the approach to Kangchenjunga — at 8598 meters the world's third highest peak. Although the mountaineers' base camp is the destination of the trek, it is not just the moun-tains that make this a connoisseur's trip. Vast, terraced hillsides, villages prosperous and small, and rarely-visited people complement the glaciers, ridges and peaks of the northeastern Himālaya. From the tea-growing regions of Ilam near India's Darjeeling, across the hillside farms of the Rai and Gurkha, into the mountain country, the images of Nepal constantly shift and expand. No less than three major routes can take us toward Kangchenjunga: up the Milke Danda Ridge between Kanchenjunga and Makalu; along the ancient trading route through the Kumbakarka Basin, or up the Yalung Glacier to the southwestern base camp. Even if you have trekked in Nepal before, the impact of this scenery is incomparable.

ITINERARY: Days 1-2: En route. Days 3-4: Kath-mandu. Day 5: Dhankuta. Days 6-30: On trek. days 31-33: Kathmandu. Day 34: Return.

🚶   Class IV   **Moderate**
September-April
Australian Himalayan Expeditions   AS13

GAURI SHANKAR TREK

THE FLUTED PEAKS of Gauri Shankar and Melungtse shimmer over the sacred valley of Rolwaling, an icy and isolated alpine wilder-ness. We follow in the footsteps of Sir Edmund Hillary from the villages of Barabhise as we walk along rice-terraced hillsides spilling over with forests of rhododendron and pine. Past the low-lying villages of the Tamang, Newar and Chetri peoples, we climb through an ever-changing spectrum of cultures to remote Sherpa communities. Here squat stone houses dot the valley floor, dwarfed by the glassy escarpments of giant peaks. We pause to acclimate in the village of Beding, visiting its well-preserved monastery; then on we press to the glaciers surround Gauri Shankar. The Sherpas believe the Rolwaling valley to have been carved by their demi-god Padmasambhava and consider it one of the holiest places on earth, a natural shrine where no animals may be killed. Our 15-day trek is an opportunity to share their reverence for this special place of peace and beauty.

ITINERARY: Day 1: En route. Days 2-3: Kathmandu. Days 4-18: On trek. Day 19: Kathmandu. Day 20: Return.

🚶 ⛺   Class III   **Moderate**
May, October
Australian Himalayan Expeditions   AS82

HELAMBU TREK

SHORT BUT SPECTACULAR, this five-day trek in the Helambu is a five-star introduction to trekking in Nepal. Northeast of Kathmandu lies this land, bounded by a wall of 5000-meter peaks and inhabited by the Sherpa of mountain lore. This is the closest area to Kathmandu that boasts a large population of Tibetan descent. Add to this the enchanting alpine scenery, rhododendron forests and Buddhist monasteries of the region and you find a short trek which has it all. Altitudes average between 2000 and 3000 meters, but our crow-close approach to the high and remote Langtang Valley is the kind of experience worth crossing the globe to find. Savor the whole Himalayan Range, from Annapurna to Everest in the distance, underscored by the spectacle of sunrise and sunset that accents the jagged ridgelines. For the beginner or the trekker with little time, nothing could be finer than a week in Helambu.

ITINERARY: Days 1-2: En route. Days 3-4: Kathmandu. Days 5-9: On trek. Day 10: Return.

🚶 ⛺   Class III   **Medium**
September-May
Australian Himalayan Expeditions   AS72

HIMALAYAN FOOTHILLS

WINTER IS AN IDEAL TIME to trek in the subtropical mountains of the Himalaya. The weather is at its most pleasant, and the people more friendly as their harvests are in and time is free. Even up in the higher hills it is the dry season, and crystal-clear panoramas confront you at every switchback. Beginning with Dhaulagiri in the west, past the summits of the Annapurna massif to Lamjung Himal, Manaslu and Himalchuli, a stacked deck of seven- and eight-thousand meter peaks is dealt. This trek takes us through numerous tiny hamlets off the main trekking path, including the hill towns of the Ghurkas who united many local fiefdoms into modern Nepal. Rarely ascending above 3000 meters, we take a leisurely path that includes visits to Trisuli Bazar, the slopes of Lamjung Himal, and Gurung towns of Ghanpokhara and Siklis on our portal-to-portal path to Pokhara. A highly-recommended introduction to trekking in Nepal.

ITINERARY: Days 1-2: En route. Day 3: Arrive Kathmandu. Day 4: Kathmandu. Day 5: To Trisuli Bazar; begin trekking. Days 6-17: On trek. Days 18-19: Pokhara. Days 20-21: Kathmandu. Day 22: Return.

🚶 ⛺   Class III   **Moderate**
December-February
Himalaya   AS6

I FELT AS THOUGH I were plunging into something new and quite abnormal. I had the strangest and most vivid impressions, such as I had never before known in the mountains. There was something unnatural in the way I saw Lachenal and everything around us. I smiled to myself at the paltriness of our efforts, for I could stand apart and watch myself making these efforts. But all sense of exertion was gone, as though there were no longer any gravity. This diaphonous landscape, this quintessence of purity — these were not the mountains I knew: they were the mountains of my dreams.

The snow, sprinkled over every rock and gleaming in the sun, was of a radiant beauty that touched me to the heart. I had never seen such complete transparency, and I was living in a world of crystal. Sounds were indistinct, the atmosphere like cotton wool.

An astonishing happiness welled up in me, but I could not define it. Everything was so new, so utterly unprecedented. It was not in the least like anything I had known in the Alps, where one feels buoyed up by the presence of others — by the people of whom one is vaguely aware, or even by the dwellings one can see in the far distance.

This was quite different. An enormous gulf was between me and the world. This was a different universe — withered, desert, lifeless; a fantastic universe where the presence of man was not foreseen, perhaps not desired. We were braving an interdict, overstepping a boundary, and yet we had no fear as we continued upward. . . .

HINKU REGION   Nigel Dabby

MAKALU BASE CAMP

THE ARDOUS ASCENT to the rarely traveled regions of Makalu, the world's fifth-highest mountain, begins in Dharan and follows the narrow trails of the Arun River Valley along ever-steepening cliff faces. High above the river we climb, crossing the 4312-meter Barun La into the Barun Valley, last lowlands before the steep trail over rugged moraines to Makalu Base Camp. Our efforts are rewarded by fantastic views of the rarely seen *Kangshun* (northeast) face of Mt. Everest in Tibet, the steepest and probably most difficult approach to the world's highest summit. Weather permitting, we remain at the Makalu camp for several days to explore the surrounding slopes, glaciers and valleys, and visit areas where few travelers have been or will ever be. Our return route takes us through a region of remote mountain fastness and unspoiled alpine scenery, past lonely Sherpa villages to the tiny Tumlingtar airstrip on the river terraces of the Arun. A remarkable journey that combines exciting trekking with isolated Nepalese scenery.

ITINERARY: Day 1: En route. Days 2-3: Kathmandu. Day 4: Dhankuta. Days 5-30: On trek. Day 31: Fly Tumlingtar to Kathmandu. Days 32-33: Kathmandu. Day 34: Return.

☈ Class IV **Moderate**
March, April, September
Australian Himalayan Expeditions   AS84

HIGH ALTITUDE TREK

THE CHALLENGE AND ADVENTURE of the high Himalaya await on this month-long journey over some of the world's loftiest trekking passes. We set off from Kirantichap on the classic Everest expedition route, climbing in the shadow of the high northern peaks to Namche Bazar, our base for the ascent by the trails of Sherpa herdsmen to the beautiful alpine lake in Gokyo Valley. A formidable climb over 5460-meter Nymgawa La to Lobuje Village is rewarded by breathtaking views of the west ridge of Mt. Everest. On to Kalipatar and Everest Base Camp, where we rope up for the difficult ascent of 5510-meter Kongma La. The south face of Lhotse, one of the world's great unmet climbing challenges, looms overhead as we descend into the Chukung Valley. From here, experienced and well-acclimated climbers can attempt the ascent of Island Peak (6189m), a spectacular climb even among the imposing summits of Lhotse, Everest, Cho, Oyu, Gauri Shankar and the other Himalayan giants of the Everest-Lhotse basin. This trip includes some rock and ice climbing, and requires extensive outdoor experience and excellent physical condition.

ITINERARY: Days 1-2: En route. Day 3: Kathmandu. Day 4: Kathmandu to Kirantichap, begin trekking. Days 5-30: On trek. Day 31: Fly Lukla to Kathmandu. Days 32-33: Kathmandu. Day 34: Return.

☈ ⚔ Class V **Moderate**
March, April, September
Australian Himalayan Expeditions   AS85

INDIA

ABODE OF THE GODS

GARWHAL: HOME OF THE GODS. Mist-shrouded valleys walled in by steeply spectacular peaks seem a perfect setting for the gods of the Hindus. A few days in the Garwhal may make a believer out of you! Rishikesh, the sacred city where the Ganges leaves the mountains and brings its life-giving waters to the parched plains, is a lodestone for devout Hindus. Thousands of scantily-clad *saddhus*, or Hindu holy men, populate the town, some sitting in one spot for years of devotion without moving. We drive from Rishikesh to Soneprayag in the Himalayas to begin the trek to Gangotri, another magnet for pilgrims. Our route takes us through towns, forests, meadows, and across a glacier to the foot of Shivaling, the goddess Shiva's mountain. A jutting triangular peak of riveting beauty, it calls to pilgrims searching for the source of the Ganges. We return by bus to Delhi via Uttarkashi and Mussoorie, two enchanting hill towns. Pines, peaks and pilgrims: a memorable Himalayan encounter!

ITINERARY: Day 1: En route. Day 2: Delhi. Day 3: Rishikesh. Days 4-17: Trekking. Days 18-19: Mussoorie. Day 20: Delhi. Day 21: Return.

🚶 🛶　　　　Class IV　　**Moderate**
May, October
Australian Himalayan Expeditions　　　　AS114

GANGES HOLY MAN　　Richard Bangs

GANGES RIVER

THEY CALL IT "GANGA," one of the most celebrated of all the world's waterways. From its headwaters in the Garwhal region, where its source is honored by the devotion of pilgrims, to its outflow at the enormous delta on the Bay of Bengal, the Ganges is the major artery for northern India's millions. We explore its upper reaches along the Bhagarati tributary, which links with the Alaknanda at Deoprayag to form the Mother River of India. Then our route continues through narrow canyons, down 50-foot-per-mile drops into the land of the Bengal tiger

---

LIFTING OUR EYES occasionally from the slope, we saw the couloir opening out on to . . . well, we didn't quite know, probably a ridge. But where was the top — left or right? Stopping at every step, leaning on our axes we tried to recover our breath and to calm down our racing hearts, which were thumping as though they would burst. We knew we were there now — that nothing could stop us. No need to exchange looks — each of us would have read the same determination in the other's eyes. A slight detour to the left, a few more steps — the summit ridge came gradually nearer — a few more rocks to avoid. We dragged ourselves up. Could we possibly be there?

Yes!

A fierce and savage wind tore at us.

We were on top of Annapurna! 8,075 meters, 26,493 feet . . .

The summit was a corniced crest of ice, and the precipices on the far side which plunged vertically down beneath us were terrifying, unfathomable. There could be few other mountains in the world like this. Clouds floated halfway down, concealing the gentle, fertile valley of Pokhara, 23,000 feet below. Above us there was nothing!

Our mission was accomplished. But at the same time we had accomplished something infinitely greater. How wonderful life would now become! What an inconceivable experience it is to attain one's ideal and, at the very same moment, to fulfill oneself. I was stirred to the depths of my being. Never had I felt happiness like this — so intense and yet so pure. That brown rock, the highest of them all, that ridge of ice — were these the goals of a lifetime? Or were they, rather, the limits of a man's pride?

TONS RIVER   Mike Boyle

beyond our sandy beach camps. There's time too to see the cultural highlights of these Indian mountain communities as well as Delhi, fascinating capital of ancient India. Bathe in Shiva's dripping hair—ride the Ganges and its waters of eternity!

ITINERARY: Days 1-2: Delhi. Day 3: Rishikesh. Day 4: Deoprayag. Day 5: Theri. Days 6-12: On the river. Day 13: Rishikesh. Days 14-15: Delhi. Day 16: Return.

⚓ 🛶   Class IV   **Premium**
October
Sobek Expeditions   AS109

MAGICAL KULU

A PASTORAL IDYLL in the wondrous valleys of Himalchal Pradesh, high above the old British summer capital of Simla. We drive from Simla, where the Raj lives on, to the eminently liveable town of Manali whose perfect climate and relaxed life-style continue to attract a substantial European population. Then on to the flower-filled meadows of Kulu. The Gadi nomads are the only inhabitants of this lovely realm, and their simple Hindu customs stand in fascinating contrast to the ways of the Gujars of Kashmir and the Buddhists of Ladakh, making this an ideal add-on option to many trips to northern India. While camping in the scenic Kulu Valley, our days are made even more interesting by optional treks into the surrounding landscape. A week of mountain magic.

ITINERARY: Day 1: Chandigarh to Simla. Day 2: Simla. Days 3-4: Manali. Days 5-6: Kulu Valley. Day 7: Chandigarh. Day 8: Return.

🛶 🐎   Class II   **Moderate**
May-July, August-October
Australian Himalayan Expeditions   AS113

TONS RIVER

MORE THAN JUST countless Class III-V rapids, most of them as yet untamed. More than a scenic wonderland rising from every vantage, soaring to the skies of northern India. More than the cultural encounter of a lifetime, as cults, tribes and villages pass by with every river mile. The Tons River is a revelation in river-running, beginning at 5,000 feet elevation (1525m) in the beautiful evergreen forests of the Himalaya. From there we run rapids the equal of any found on the Bio-Bio or Çoruh, riding the chilly snow-melt of springtime. The scenery is endlessly rewarding, but what makes the trip a special journey is the variety of cultures we encounter. At put-in there are the polyandrous Garhwali natives, their traditional culture still secure. They practice a rare form of Hinduism, with influences not only from the recent Buddhist belief, but traces of pre-historic magic as well. Downstream, we come to the villages of Sherpas, far from their traditional homeland, the most recent immigrants to the area. Nomadic Muslim tribes watch from the hills above as we end our nine days on the river, journey to Mussoorie, and reluctantly make a memory of the magic.

ITINERARY: Days 1-2: En route. Day 3: Arrive Delhi. Day 4: To Mussoorie. Day 5: In Mussoorie. Days 6-13: On the river. Day 14: Dehradun. Day 15: To Delhi. Day 16: Return.

⚓ 🛶   Class IV   **Medium**
April-May
White Magic Unlimited   AS74

BEST OF INDIA

THE HUMAN PAGEANT is on display in India as it is nowhere else in the world, alive in an everyday setting brimming with the traditions and temples of millennia-old culture. To feel the richness of this world, one must get out amongst the people. What better way to do this than with the modern and traditional modes of transport in India—the camel, the sailboat and the bicycle? We cycle from the Taj Mahal to Jaipur past the legendary city of Fatehpur Sikri, a spectacular ghost town abandoned for lack of water, where temples and fort stand as a monument to Indian splendor. Thence to the immense bird-filled marshes of Bharatpur, one of Asia's finest bird parks. An interim among the pink palaces of Jaipur prepares us for a camel trek across the vast Rajasthan desert—a voyage into another time. Ancient customs and ghostly caravanserai are the signposts back to the days when camels carried the trade, a time alive with cacaphony and color. Back to the future of the 19th century, as the Maharajah's railway whisks us on to Delhi and the Ganges, India's holiest current. We sail downriver on local boats, marveling as India unfolds in all her majesty along the teeming shoreline. Finally we debark at Varanasi, which abounds with pilgrims and temples, reveling in venerable traditions that refuse to yield to the passing centuries. See the entire spectrum of Indian life or choose a partial itinerary that explores the side of India most intriguing to you.

ITINERARY: Days 1-2: To Delhi. Day 3: Agra. Days 4-7: Cycle. Days 8-9: Jaipur/Jodhpur. Days 10-13: Camels. Day 14: Train to Jodhpur. Day 15: Delhi. Days 16-20: Ganges. Day 21: Varanasi. Day 22: Delhi. Days 23-24: En route home.

🐫 🚲 ⛰   Class III   **Moderate**
October-April
Australian Himalayan Expeditions   AS111

RAJASTHAN CAMEL

CONTRAST IS THE LAW of the land in Rajasthan, where a once-warlike people create delicate works of art, where wild landscapes wrap India's most beautiful city, where the fabric of history remains untorn by the modern age. In this remarkable domain of western India, the story of Rajasthan's bloody past is told in the crumbling forts beneath rocky ridges, drifted over by the shifting sands. We visit the historical highlights of Udaipur, the Maharaja's Palace in Jodhpur, and the walled city of Jaisalmer before journeying to Pushkar. Here, the annual Camel Fair sets the mood — with some 200,000 people and 50,000 camels — for a four-day camel trek across flat desert sands in the company of the region's garishly-garbed villagers and the full moon. Accommodations range from the spartan to the regal, sights from the extraordinary to the amazing.

ITINERARY: Day 1: En route. Days 2-3: Delhi. Day 4: On train. Day 5: Bikaner. Days 6-24: Camel trek. Days 15-16: Jaisalmeer. Day 17: On train. Day 18: Jodhpur. Days 19-21: Jaipur. Day 22: Agra. Days 23-24: Delhi. Day 25: Return.

🐫 🐫   Class III   **Medium**
December
Australian Himalayan Expeditions   AS25

CYCLE INDIA

"GO TO THE VILLAGES, that is India; therein lies the soul of India." The Mahatma's dictum for discovery holds as true now as it did in his

---

LACHENAL WAS ALREADY FAR BELOW; he had reached the foot of the couloir. I hurried down in his tracks. I went as fast as I could, but it was dangerous going. At every step one had to take care that the snow did not break away beneath one's weight. Lachenal, going faster than I thought he was capable of, was now on the long traverse. It was my turn to cross the area of mixed rock and snow. At last I reached the foot of the rock-band. I had hurried and I was out of breath. I undid my sack. What had I been going to do? I couldn't say.

"My gloves!"

Before I had time to bend over, I saw them slide and roll. They went further and further straight down the slope. I remained where I was, quite stunned. I watched them rolling down slowly, with no appearance of stopping. The movement of those gloves was engraved in my sight as something irredeemable, against which I was powerless. The consequences might be most serious. What was I to do?

"Quickly, down to Camp V."

Rebuffat and [Lionel] Terray would be there. My concern dissolved like magic. I now had a fixed objective again: to reach the camp. Never for a minute did it occur to me to use as gloves the socks which I always carry in reserve for just such a mishap as this.

own time, and we follow Gandhi's credo in our cycle tour of this vastly complicated country. Beginning in Delhi, where the Moghul and modern India meet, we pedal past rice and mustard fields to the holy city of Mathura, then on to the Taj Mahal to see its fabulous palaces. Past ancient towns, bird sancturies, camel fairs and giant fortresses, we ride aboard Indian-made "Atlas" bicycles along a flatland course. Our route parallels misty rivers, crosses quiet fields and enters fascinating villages and their bustling bazaars. Highlights include the "Pink City" of Jaipur; the deer, boar and tiger of Sariska Game Sanctuary; and the impressive ghost town of Fatehpur. The greatest variety of people found anywhere on earth await our visit on this memorable tour in the footsteps of the Mahatma.

ITINERARY: Day 1: En route. Days 2-3: Bombay. Days 4-16: Cycle tour to Goa. Day 17: Fly to Delhi. Day 18: Delhi. Day 19: Agra. Days 20-23: Cycle tour to Jaipur. Day 24: Jaipur. Day 25: Return.

🚴 ♨   Class III   **Moderate**
December
Australian Himalayan Expeditions   AS65

HIMALAYA EXPLORATORY SKI

SKI WHERE NO ONE has skied before on a cross-country expedition in Himalchal Pradesh: the experience of a lifetime for the fit cross-country buff. Manali, a lovely town where the forest and fields will be awakening to the onset of spring, is the base for the expedition. We head up to the snow and start skiing through forests and peaks. Supplies stockpiled in the summer await our arrival at small settlements along our journey's route. Beyond the last village we head out into the snowy wilderness, aiming for the heights of Bara Lapcha (5182 meters). Surrounded by Himalayan towers, Bara Lapcha is a pass with few peers: northern vistas reveal the high peaks of the Kashmir Himalaya, while to the south lies the Mukhila Range for a full panorama of snow and ice. To the best of our knowledge, the 1986 exploratory expedition will be the first group to ski this area.

ITINERARY: Day 1: En route. Day 2: Delhi. Days 3-5: Manali. Days 6-22: Ski expedition. Days 23-25: Manali. Days 26-28: Delhi. Day 29: Return.

⛷ ♨   Class V   **Moderate**
March
Australiàn Himalayan Expeditions   AS116

KASHMIR/ LADAKH

TRANS-HIMALAYA TREK

THE CLASSIC KASHMIR TREK includes the stark lunar panoramas of the Zaskar Range and the rich alpine regions of Kashmir, as well as native villages, Buddhist *gompas* and glacial wilderness. This extended trek has a little bit of everything and a great deal of the best. Walk in wonderment across Margan Pass (3500m) into the untrammeled Warwan Valley, past rough-hewn timber houses, to the foot of the Bhoktol Glacier (4420m). Following this serpentine river of black ice and rock, we crest the Punjab Himalaya beneath the towering twin peaks of Nun Kun (7135m). But there's more — our highest point is over Kanji La (5180m) into the moonland of Ladakh, well above all vegetation to a riot of colors and shapes like nowhere else on earth. Take tea with monks in hidden monasteries, look down on uninhabited and uninhabitable regions, and wonder if perhaps there's not something extra in the rarefied atmosphere we breathe.

ITINERARY: Days 1-2: En route. Day 3: Delhi to Srinagar. Days 4-5: Srinagar. Day 6: Pahalgam. Days 7-23: Trek. Day 24: Alchi. Days 25-27: Leh. Day 28: Kargil. Days 29-31: Srinagar. Day 32: Return.

🚶 ♨   Class IV   **Moderate**
July, August
Himalaya   AS29

LADAKHI LADY   Jim Slade

VALE OF KASHMIR

FROM THE LUXURIOUS COMFORT of floating houseboats in Srinagar to the splendor of alpine valleys and glacial lakes, this beginner's trek winds leisurely through the cultural contrasts and paradisiacal beauty found only in Kashmir. We relax in the style of raj and royalty among the floating gardens of Dal Lake, amble through pine forests and flowering meadows, and camp amidst the towering Himalaya. By day we visit Gujar nomads as they graze their flocks in the high pastures, and at night our gregarious guides regale us with tales of yak traders on the silk route to China. Optional day trips can be made to the impressive slopes of Kolahoi and the serene shores of Tarsar Lake. From the Kashmir Valley we fly on to Leh, capital of the Buddhist region of Ladakh, where the forbiddingly stark surrounding mountains have earned it the name of "Little Tibet." From Hemis, an impressive 16th century monastery where the monks practice under an incarnate Lama, we take day trips into the deep gorges of the Stok region, and spend our evenings basking in the warm hospitality of local villagers. There's also time to explore the Moghul Garden and lily-covered waters of the fabled Kashmir lakes, or to shop for intricate carpets, wood carvings, and other crafts in the markets of Kashmir.

ITINERARY: Days 1-2: En route. Day 3: Arrive Srinagar. Days 4-5: Srinagar. Day 6: Phalgam. Days 7-11: Hiking or trekking. Day 12: Srinagar. Days 13-17: Leh. Days 18-19: Srinagar. Day 20: Return.

🛥 🚶   Class II   **Moderate**
May-August
Australian Himalayan Expeditions   AS95

KASHMIR ALPINE TREK

MANY WHO'VE SEEN HER agree: Kashmir represents the ultimate alpine walking experience, with its verdant meadows, pristine lakes, and glacial valleys set among the towering peaks of the Himalaya. It is a land where every month offers new surprises of unforgettable beauty. June is springtime, when the receding snows reveal a burst of greenery and Gujar shepherds drive their flocks to the high pastures. Summer begins in July as the brilliant sun silhouettes the distant peaks and lifts ethereal mists from the lower valleys. August heralds in a rainbow eruption of wildflowers, followed by the golden tones of September that signal herdsmen to return to the lower valleys. We begin our trek in Pahalgam and follow the pine-scented Lidder Valley to the slopes of Mt. Kolahoi, walking beneath ever-changing mountain vistas. From our camp alongside a serene glacial lake we may spot brown bear, Hangul deer, hyrax, and eagles soaring high above the surrounding crags. Crossing 4354-meter Yemnher La, we enter the picturesque Sindh Valley, with its breathtaking panorama of Nanga Parbat and the Karakoram framed by the snowy peaks of the Pir Panjal. We cross three more 4000-meter passes into the heart of the Haramukh Range, climaxing our trek with a visit to the mirror-like waters of Lake Gangobal.

ITINERARY: Days 1-3: En route to Srinagar. Day 4: Srinagar. Day 5: To Pahalgam, begin trek. Days 6-21: On trek. Day 22: To Srinagar. Days 23-26: Srinagar. Day 27: Return.

🚶 🥾 🛥   Class III   **Moderate**
June-September
Australian Himalayan Expeditions   AS93

THE CLOUDS GREW THICKER and came right down over us; the wind blew stronger, but I did not suffer from the cold. Perhaps the descent had restored my circulation. Should I be able to find the tents in the mist? I watched the rib ending in the beak-like point which overlooked the camp. It was gradually swallowed up by the clouds, but I was able to make out the spearhead rib lower down. If the mist should thicken I would make straight for that rib and follow it down, and in this way I would be bound to come upon the tent.

Lachenal disappeared from time to time, and then the mist was so thick that I lost sight of him altogether. I kept going at the same speed, as fast as my breathing would allow. . . .

The ground was broken; with my crampons I went straight down walls of bare ice. There were some patches ahead — a few more steps. It was the camp all right, but there were two tents!

So Rebuffat and Terray had come up. What a mercy! I should be able to tell them that we had been successful, that we were returning from the top. How thrilled they would be!

I got there, dropping down from above. . . . I tripped over one of the guy-ropes of the first tent; there was movement inside, they had heard me. Rebuffat and Terray put their heads out.

"We've made it. We're back from Annapurna!"

ZASKAR PUT-IN   Jim Slade

ZASKAR RAFT EXPEDITION

SHEER CLIFFS OF AMBER ROCK rise thousands of feet from the water's edge, merging into snowy peaks above and plunging the canyons below into permanent shadow. Brilliant white beaches provide campsites along gorges of awesome beauty, and rapid-fire rapids of world-class whitewater set the pace for nonstop action. This is the Zaskar River in the high ranges of Ladakh. Combining the supercharged Zaskar with almost 200 kilometers of exploratory trekking over seldom traveled trails and passes makes this expedition an awesome challenge. After acclimatizing among the forests, pastures and Hindu villages of the Kulu Valley, we cross the Rothang Pass to Darcha and begin our trek on ancient trade routes, climbing in the company of yak trains over 5322-meter Shingo La. A long descent to the Zaskar valley takes us to the village of Kargya along the Tsarap Chu river, where we take time to relax and explore the surrounding glaciers and slopes. The final leg of our trek follows the Tsarap Chu downstream to Padam where it joins the Doda Chu to form the Zaskar River. Then it's into the rafts for an eight-day rush over high-octane hydraulics to the mighty Indus River. Top it all off with three days of idyllic luxury on a houseboat among the floating gardens of Srinagar, and your wildest expectations will be exceeded on an adventure unlike any other.

ITINERARY: Day 1: En route. Day 2: Delhi. Days 3-4: To Manali. Day 5: Manali. Day 6: To Darcha, begin trek. Days 7-17: On trek. Days 18-25: On river. Day 26: Leh. Day 27: To Srinagar. Days 28-30: Srinagar. Day 31: To Delhi. Day 32: Return.

⚹ ✈ ⛑   Class IV   **Moderate**
August
Australian Himalayan Expeditions   AS92

TRANS-ZANSKAR TREK

THE WESTERN HIMALAYA encompasses some of the most challenging and rewarding trekking terrain in the world. Among the formidable folds of mountains in the Great Himalaya and Zaskar ranges, Buddhist nomads still herd their flocks to high summer pastures, yak trains still tred little-known passes, and the king still holds court in the tiny medieval kingdom of Zangla. We begin our trek in the market of Stok, setting off over the Ganda pass for our first glimpse of the challenge that lies ahead. Several days are spent traversing Ruberung La and climbing through awesome canyons before crossing Chacha La to Zangla. Here we relax and absorb the antique atmosphere of this time-locked kingdom, where a visit to the modest palace may result in an impromptu invitation to dine with the king himself. From Zangla we follow time-worn trails to Phuktal, one of the most isolated Buddhist communities in the world. Our traverse of the Great Himalaya is completed as we cross Shingo Pass and descend to Darcha Village and the first roadway seen in weeks. It's all capped off with a well-deserved rest among the pine forests of Manali, a time to refine memories of a grand expedition.

ITINERARY: Day 1: En route. Day 2: Arrive Delhi. Day 3: To Srinagar. Days 4-5: Srinagar. Day 6: Fly to Leh. Day 7: Leh. Day 8: To Stok; begin trek. Days 9-29: On trek. Days 30-33: Manali. Day 34: Delhi. Day 35: Return.

⚹ ⛑   Class IV   **Moderate**
June-September
Australian Himalayan Expeditions   AS94

SRINAGAR STREET   Inge Martin

TIBETAN CHARACTER   Jim Slade

HEMIS FESTIVAL

AN ANCIENT MONASTERY four miles high is the site of one of Buddhism's most durable festivals, the summer celebrations at Hemis in Ladakh. Known as "Little Tibet," Ladakh is an extension of the Tibetan Plateau in northwest India, where the rich traditions of Mahayana Buddhism still flourish in their purest surviving form. This month-long expedition includes a 12-day trek in the awesome and forbidding terrain of Ladakh, and visits to *gompas* at Thiksey, Shey, and Leh as well as Hemis. We join the colorful crowds journeying toward Hemis, a swelling stream of villagers arrayed in beautifully woven clothes and turquoise-heavy hats, to witness the festival. Lamas dressed in fantastic masks and costumes portray demons, spirits and bodhisattvas, dancing and dramatizing the age-old myths of Buddhism — all to the music of 14-foot trumpets, huge cymbals and hand-wrought drums. A wealth of Ladakhi antiques and jewelry entices us, the great paintings and sculpture of Alchi Gompa impress us, and the comfortable houseboats of Srinagar relax us.

ITINERARY: Days 1-2: En route. Day 3: Delhi to Srinagar. Day 4: Srinagar. Day 5: Kargil. Day 6: Alchi. Days 7-9: Leh. Days 10-11: Hemis. Day 12: Stok; begin trek. Days 13-18: On trek. Days 19-20: Leh. Days 21-22: Srinagar. Day 23: Delhi. Day 24: Return.

🏺 🚶   Class III   **Moderate**
June
Himalaya   AS28

WORDS FAILED ME. I had so much to say. The sight of familiar faces dispelled the strange feeling that I had experienced since morning, and I became, once more, just a mountaineer.

Terray, who was speechless with delight, wrung my hands. Then the smile vanished from his face: "Maurice — your hands!" There was an uneasy silence. I had forgotten that I had lost my gloves: my fingers were violet and white and hard as wood. The other two stared at them in dismay — they realized the full seriousness of the injury. But, still blissfully floating on a sea of joy remote from reality, I leaned over towards towards Terray and said confidentially, "You're in such splendid form, and you've done so marvelously, it's absolutely tragic you didn't come up there with us!"

"What I did was for the Expedition, my dear Maurice, and anyway you've got up, and that's a victory for the whole lot of us."

I nearly burst with happiness. How could I tell him all that his answer meant to me? The rapture I had felt on the summit, which might have seemed a purely personal, egotistical emotion, had been transformed by his words into a complete and perfect joy with no shadow upon it. His answer proved that this victory was not just one man's achievement, a matter for personal pride; no — and Terray was the first to understand this — it was a victory for us all, a victory for mankind itself.

KASHMIR/LADAKH PANORAMA

THE WESTERN HIMALAYAN wonderland reveals itself along footpaths and river runs in the near-mythical lands of Kashmir and Ladakh. The Vale of Kashmir is a fabulously fertile province of India with a history as rich as its soil, a tradition of generous hospitality, and a *mise en scene* of palaces adrift and flower-draped gardens. Ladakh is a striking contrast — a spartan land known as "Little Tibet," peopled by Buddhist monks and mountain tribes who have only encountered Westerners in the last decade. An eight-day trek takes us up to the Kolahoi Glacier and across Yemnher Pass for sweeping Himalayan views, then into the scented pine forests of the Sindh Valley. The ancient face of Ladakh lives in the smiles of 100 monks at Hemis, a 16th century *gompa*, before we set out on the swirling waters of the Indus River. Our descent takes us through gorge country where even the hearty Ladakhis have been unable to construct trails. The winding mountain road out of Ladakh leads back to Srinagar, where we unwind in idyllic Kashmir.

ITINERARY: Days 1-2: En route. Day 3: Arrive Srinagar. Days 4-5: Srinagar. Day 6: Phalgam. Days 7-13: On trek. Day 14: Kargil. Day 15: Drive to Leh. Days 16-17: Leh. Day 18: Hemis. Days 19-20: Rafting. Day 21: Leh. Days 22-23: Drive Leh/Srinagar. Days 24-26: Srinagar. Day 27: Return.

🌋 🚶 ✈   Class III   **Moderate**
June-September
Australian Himalayan Expeditions   AS27

NEPALI GIRL   Jim Slade

POWDER AND PINES

SKI HIMALAYAN SNOWS on a cross-country adventure for experienced skiers. The little-tracked powder of Kashmir offers some of the world's finest cross-country skiing, so we ski the Lidder Valley from a base camp above Pahalgam, and strike out as deeply into the snow-blanketed peaks and forests as our skills will take us. Some may wish to stay within a day's tour of our hut (provisioned in the summer months to see us through the winter); others may want to try out snow camping for two or three days. Remote magnificent scenery and wonderful snow will be the delight of all. After a week of this winter wonderland, we return to Pahalgam and drive to Gulmarg, India's premier ski resort. Here we stay in a comfortable old world hotel, a delightful haven after a day's skiing. Discover the slopes of another world!

ITINERARY: Days 1-2: To Delhi. Days 3-4: Srinagar. Days 5-11: Lidder Valley ski tour. Days 12-15: Gulmarg skiing. Days 16-19: Srinagar. Day 20: Delhi and return.

⛷ 🌋 🦆   Class III   **Moderate**
March
Australian Himalayan Expeditions   AS115

KASHMIR/LADAKH BY JEEP

FROM THE POSH COMFORT of floating Victorian houses on Dal Lake to the cliff-clinging monasteries at Thiksey, this jeep-trek trundles through a caper of contrasts across the Zanskar Range into Ladakh. Here we visit the great monasteries and villages of the upper Indus Valley, exploring Shey, Thiksey and Hemis *gompas*. Our guides are native Ladakhis whose insight into the religion, history and culture of this Buddhist region is instinctive. At Leh, Ladakh's capital, we browse though the highest marketplace in the world, looking high and bidding low for material proof of our presence in "Little Tibet" — a region only opened to trekkers in the last decade. Our route then takes us back to the legendary Vale of Kashmir for several days of individual exploration, *shikhara* boating, and Kashmiri cuisine.

ITINERARY: Days 1-2 En route. Day 3: Delhi to Srinagar. Day 4: Srinagar. Days 5-12: Jeep trek. Day 13: Arrive Srinagar. Day 14: Srinagar. Day 15: Return.

🌋 🚙   Class II   **Medium**
June-August
Himalaya   AS30

COMBINATIONS

HIMALAYA END-TO-END

SHIKARA, DAL LAKE   Pam Roberson

YOU CAN HAVE IT ALL. The complete Himalaya from Kashmir in the west to Bhutan in the east offers up a lavish sampling of varied and intriguing adventures—even for the non-trekker. Try the enchanting Vale of Kashmir, with its sumptuous houseboats, serene lakes, gardens and handicraft shops. Or Simla, summer capital of British India, with its deodar and pine trees, lush tea plantations and the indelible imprint of the Raj. Sample the cities of Delhi, Agra and Jaipur, treasure chests of Indian culture, architecture and history; or the ancient towns of Patan, Kathmandu and Bhaktapur, and take an overflight of Mt. Everest. At Pokhara, some of the Himalaya's finest scenery, including the peaks of Annapurna and Machapucchare, are reflected in Phewa lake. A safari to Chitwan Park, a drive along the bottom of Nepal to Siliguri, the "toy train" to Darjeeling—whose tiny engine pulls four coaches up an amazingly steep gradient past Kanchenjunga, the world's third highest peak—all these treats await you. There's also Bhutan, the living Shangri-La, where we spend a week in cliff-perched monasteries in a magical countryside to conclude this fairy-tale tour. Not everyone has six weeks to see the Himalaya, though, so we offer partial itineraries: *Himalayan Environments* and *East from Annapurna*.

ITINERARY: Days 1-2: To Srinagar. Days 3-5: Srinagar. Day 6: To Chandigarh. Days 7-9: Simla. Day 10: Delhi. Day 11: Agra—Taj Mahal. Days 12-14: Jaipur. Days 15-16: Delhi. Days 17-20: Kathmandu. Days 21-23: Pokhara. Days 24-26: Royal Chitwan National Park. Day 27: To Siliguri. Days 28-30: Darjeeling. Day 31: Kalimpong. Days 32-33: Gangtok. Days 34-35: Jaldapara Game Reserve. Days 36-42: Bhutan. Day 43: To Calcutta. Day 44: Return.
[Note: *Himalayan Environments* (AS11) Days 1-26; *East of Annapurna* Days 17-44, plus international flying time]

🚙 🛶 🦆   Class I   **Moderate**
October–June
Australian Himalayan Expeditions   AS110

"HI! HELP! HELP! . . . Still half intoxicated and remote from reality I had heard nothing. Terray felt a chill at his heart, and his thoughts flew to his partner on so many unforgettable climbs; together they had so often skirted death, and won so many splendid victories. Putting his head out, and seeing Lachenal clinging to the slope a hundred yards lower down, he dressed in frantic haste. . . .

He spotted him through a rift in the mist, lying on the slope much farther down than he had thought. Terray set his teeth, and glissaded down like a madman. How would he be able to brake without crampons, on the wind-hardened snow? But Terray was a first-class skier, and with a jump-turn he stopped beside Lachenal, who was suffering from concussion after his tremendous fall. In a state of collapse, with no ice-axe, Balaclava, or gloves, and only one crampon, he gazed vacantly around him.

"My feet are frost-bitten. Take me down . . . take me down, so that Oudot can see to me."

"It can't be done," said Terray sorrowfully. "Can't you see we're in the middle of a storm . . . it'll be dark soon."

But Lachenal was obsessed by the fear of amputation. With a gesture of despair he tore the axe out of Terray's hands and tried to force his way down; but soon he saw the futility of his action and resolved to climb up to the camp. While Terray cut steps without stopping, Lachenal, ravaged and exhausted as he was, dragged himself along on all fours. . . .

For our comrades it was a tragic moment: Annapurna was conquered, and the first eight-thousander had been climbed. Every one of us had been ready to sacrifice everything for this. Yet, as they looked at our feet and hands, what can Terray and Rebuffat have felt?

SRINAGAR SQUASH VENDOR   Pam Roberson

HIMALAYAN ENVIRONMENTS

TRAINS AND BOATS AND PLANES, with an elephant safari thrown in, make this four-week-long excursion to India and Nepal a tempting travel potpourri. The excursion includes an elaborate 14-course Kashmiri feast in Srinagar, center of the Vale of Kashmir, and small *shikhara* boats that float the outlying lakes of this Indian garden spot. The narrow-gauge railway leading from Chandigarh to Simla, the summer capital of British India, spirals up through terraced hillsides. From the Kathmandu Valley we wing past the mammoth peaks of Everest and the central Himalaya. A jungle safari through the Royal Chitwan National Park brings us into the homeland of the one-horned rhino, the sloth bear, the dolphin of the Ganges, and some 300 bird species. The Taj Mahal, Pokhara in the Annapurnas, the "Pink City" of Jaipur — there are more faces of India and Nepal than you ever dreamed possible.

ITINERARY: Day 1: En route. Day 2: Delhi. Days 3-5: Srinagar. Day 6: Chandigarh. Days 7-9: Simla. Day 10: Delhi. Day 11: Agra. Days 12-14: Jaipur. Days 15-16: Delhi. Days 17-18: Kathmandu. Days 19-21: Pokhara. Day 22: Kathmandu. Days 23-25: Royal Chitwan. Day 26: Kathmandu. Day 27: Return.

🐚 🦢 🚙   Class I   **Moderate**
January-April, October-December
Australian Himalayan Expedtions   AS11

ADVENTURE SMORGASBORD

IF YOUR TASTE IS FOR adventure, this expedition is a seven-course meal sure to satisfy the most gluttonous gadabout. By cycle, camel, train and elephant, with more traditional means of transport thrown in for contrast, we concoct a spicy feast of Indian delights. First up is Delhi, of course, with the appetizing Taj Mahal; then a bike ride through the villages of India en route to the "Pink City" of Jaipur. Following a colorful train ride to Jodhpur, we board camels for a trek across the Rajasthan desert, an event sure to leave you thirsty for still more. More there is: bird sanctuaries and wildlife parks, tea plantations and wildlife, to say nothing of a hill safari in the back country of scenic Sri Lanka. Then it's time to relax: a dessert in the Maldives, India's tropical paradise, where we bask in the delights of indolence, an indulgence we all deserve.

ITINERARY: Day 1: Delhi. Day 2: Agra. Days 3-6: Cycle tour. Day 7: Jaipur. Day 8: Train to Jodhpur. Days 9-11: Camel trek. Day 12: Jaisalmeer. Day 13: Jodhpur. Day 14: Delhi. Days 15-16: Corbett National Park. Day 17: Delhi. Day 18: Fly to Sri Lanka. Day 19: Colombo. Days 20-25: Hill safari. Day 26: To Male. Days 27-33: Maldives sailing. Day 34: Male and return.

🐫 🚲 ⛵   Class III   **Medium**
October-March
Australian Himalayan Expeditions   AS90

TOP OF THE WORLD

ACROSS THE LAST FRONTIER, the all-but-forgotten trek route from Tibet to Nepal. Now Sobek becomes among the first to offer this ultimate adventure high, following the age-old trading paths from the Buddhist capital of Lhasa on the Tibetan Plateau to the rarified passes of the Himalaya en route to Nepal and, beyond, the Indian subcontinent. Our adventure begins in Beijing, then by plane continues to Chengdu and Lhasa as we penetrate ever deeper into the mysterious East. Several days in Lhasa, the remarkable center of Tibetan Buddhism with its famous Potala Palace, allow us time to adjust to the rare climate, both atmospheric and cultural. Then aboard coach for the journey higher and farther into the Himalaya, past ragged peaks and rugged valleys, to the long-sealed Tibet/Nepal border town of Khasa. We pause here, to savor the historic moment; then continue to Kathmandu, bustling capital of the mountain kingdom of Nepal. Sightseeing with expert guides and a Mt. Everest fly-over highlight our days here, prior to our return flight to Hong Kong and journey's end.

ITINERARY: Days 1-2: Beijing. Day 3: Chengdu. Day 4: Arrive Lhasa. Days 5-7: Lhasa. Day 8: Gyantse. Day 9: Xigatse. Days 10-11: Khasa. Day 12: To Kathmandu. Days 13-14: Kathmandu. Day 15: Hong Kong. Day 16: Return.

🚐 🛶   Class III   **Premium**
October
Sobek Exeditions   AS108

OCEAN TO SKY

THE THREE JEWELS OF ASIA are the Maldive Islands, Sri Lanka and the mountain kingdom of Nepal. We link them together in a necklace of mountain scenery and action that takes us from the limpid waters of the Bay of Bengal to the heights of the Himalaya. Our trip starts out with the high notes, as we trek through the Annapurnas for eight days, wending our way along the Kali Gandaki Gorge to the Trisuli River. Then we descend the Trisuli River for three days, riding the musical waves, until we reach Chitwan National Park. Here we take a day-long safari to view the celebrated game of the Terai region, including the rare one-horned Indian rhino, from the vantage of an elephant's back. After a couple days to explore the sights of Kathmandu, we fly to Colombo, our introduction to Sri Lanka. A six-day "hill safari" on bicycle and foot-trails takes us behind the screens of the island nation known until recently as Ceylon. Finally we head for the Maldives,

---

EDITOR'S NOTE: The four climbers spent the night of June 3 in the tent at Camp V, at 24,600 feet; the next day they became lost in the first storm of the monsoon, and spent the night in a crevasse just 30 yards from Camp IV, at 23,500 feet. On the morning of June 5 fellow mountaineer Marcel Schatz found the party, all of whom were by now partially or completely snowblind, and shortly thereafter four Sherpas joined them. At midday, an avalanche swept Herzog and two Sherpas 500 feet down into a serac field, which fortunately arrested their fall. It wasn't until late that afternoon that the climbers rejoined their companions, including expedition physician Jacques Oudot, at the well-equipped Camp II, at 19,350 feet.

Yet in 1950, the slopes of Annapurna were even more isolated than they are today. A long descent to below snow level, to the rocky region of shepherds and isolated villages, led only to the steep gorges of the Miristi Khola, a tributary of the Kali Gandaki. It was not until July 4 — a month and a day after Maurice Herzog and Louis Lachenal reached the summit of Annapurna — that the expedition returned to the relative civilization of Nepal's capital, Kathmandu. Both Herzog and Lachenal lost several fingers and toes, amputated on the long march by Dr. Oudot. Nonetheless, Maurice Herzog concludes his account of the expedition not with self-pity or regret, but with the following words:

One always talks of the ideal as a goal towards which one strives but which one never reaches. For every one of us, Annapurna was an ideal that had been realized. In our youths we had not been misled by fantasies, nor by the bloody battles of modern warfare which feed the imagination of the young. For us the mountains had been a natural field of activity where, playing on the frontiers of life and death, we had found the freedom for which we were blindly groping and which was as necessary to us as bread. The mountains had bestowed on us their beauties, and we adored them with a child's simplicity and revered them with a monk's veneration of the divine.

Annapurna, to which we had gone emptyhanded, was a treasure upon which we should live the rest of our days. With this realization we turn the page: a new life begins.

There are other Annapurnas in the lives of men.   ▲

and sail for a week in the Bay of Bengal. It's all packed into 33 days of wonderment, a wonder that's meant for you.

ITINERARY: Day 1: Arrive Kathmandu. Day 2: Kathmandu. Days 3-6: Trisuli River. Days 7-9: Elephant safari. Day 10: Pokhara. Days 11-17: On trek. Day 18: Kathmandu. Day 19: Fly to Colombo. Days 20-25: Hill safari. Day 26: To Male. Days 27-32: Maldives sailing. Day 33: Male and return.

🦆 ✈ 🚲   Class III   **Moderate**
October-March
Australian Himalayan Expeditions   AS58

INDIA AND THAILAND

ASIA'S TEMPLES AND PALACES are eloquent testimony to the flourishing cultures of past and present. En route to our Nepal adventure (*AS78*) we offer a 12-day opportunity to sample two of the world's great cities and thrill to some of mankind's finest architectural achievements. Bangkok's superb silk and handicrafts, legendary nightlife and pulsating streets, are just the backdrop for her true treasures, the *wats* or temples. The Emerald Buddha, Wat Arun (Temple of the Dawn), Wat Po (Reclining Buddha Temple), and Wat Saket (Golden Mount) are just a few of the sites of Thai Buddhism in Bangkok. Then on to Delhi for museums, the Red Fort and an urban beehive of alleys and marketplaces. It's all a fitting prelude to the eternal majesty of man's greatest monument to woman, the Taj Mahal. Our swing through India continues from Agra on to Jaipur and Udaipur, while the list of masterpieces lengthens: Agra Fort, Sikandra, the Rose Palace, the Amber Palace, the Temple of Kali, the Peacock Courtyard. Nights are in first-class hotels, and tours are by commercial bus with knowledgeable guides. A shorter 6-day introduction to the cultures of Asia is possible as a post-trip extension to *Gateway to Nepal*, with four days in Delhi and the nearby Taj Mahal, and two days in Bangkok. Either itinerary gives you a taste of the best of Asia.

PRE-TRIP ITINERARY: Day 1: Depart U.S. Days 2-3: Bangkok. Days 4-5: Delhi. Day 6: Taj Mahal. Days 7-8: Jaipur. Days 9-10: Udaipur. Day 11: Kathmandu. Day 12: Join *AS78*.

POST-TRIP ITINERARY: Day 1: Kathmandu from *AS78*. Days 2-3: Delhi. Day 4: Taj Mahal. Day 5: Bangkok. Day 6: Return.

🐘   Class I   **Moderate**
October-May, August
Sobek Expeditions   AS81

TRISULI RIVER   Liz Hymans

GRAND ADVENTURE

PLAY WITH THE PLAYERS in the world's finest combination of adventure travel dramatics, ranging from the comedy of camel driving to the theatrics of trekking. Nepal, India, Sri Lanka and the Maldives are the stages as we sail, raft, cycle, safari and trek with princes and monarchs in the swelling scenes of modern India. The curtain opens on Delhi, where we fill the proscenium with the domed vault of the Taj Mahal before ringing in the bicycle's bells as we tour the villages of India, from Jaipur to the thousand cranes of Bharatpur National Park. Act II finds us aboard the ships of the desert, as we ride camel-back across the sandy routes of Rajasthan to Jaisalmeer, to the haunting music of the camelteer's pipes. The plot thickens with Act III, as we head to the Himalaya—the markets of Kathmandu, whitewater on the Trisuli and the wildlife of Elephant Camp, all to the ever-present backdrop of the great range. With the fourth act, we enter that range, and trek into the rarefied air of the Annapurnas to witness the gargantuan giants from a closer vantage. Finally the fever-pitch breaks: we retreat with Act V to the tea fields of Sri Lanka, touring its lush coast by bus and bike, and finally a week of sailing among the palm-pricked Maldives. Comes down the curtain, and the adventure begins to live anew in the medium of memory.

ITINERARY: Day 1: Delhi. Day 2: Agra. Days 3-5: Cycling. Days 6-7: Jaipur. Day 8: Jodhpur. Days 9-11: Camel trek. Day 12: Jaisalmeer. Day 13: Return to Jodhpur. Day 14: Delhi. Days 15-16: Kathmandu. Days 17-19: Trisuli River. Days 20-22: Elephant Camp safari. Day 23: Pokhara. Days 24-30: Annapurna trek. Days 31-32: Kathmandu. Day 33: Colombo. Days 34-39: Sri Lanka hill safari. Day 40: Male. Days 41-47: Maldives sailing. Day 48: Male. Day 49: Return. Also available as *Sea Sand Snow* option, 42-day itinerary excluding Sri Lanka; and as *Ocean and Desert*, 29-day itinerary excluding Nepal and Sri Lanka.

⋔ ✈ ⚲   Class III   **Moderate**
October-March
Australian Himalayan Expeditions   AS56

HOMAGE   Liz Hymans

INTRODUCTION TO EXPEDITION TRAVEL

SAMPLE THE EXCITEMENT and variety of expedition travel on this far-ranging adventure through an ever-changing spectrum of transport and terrain. By camel, elephant, bike, river raft, and foot we journey from the plains of India to the mountains of Nepal, from desert to jungle to alpine passes, from the solitude of the wilderness to the bustle of ancient cities. The expedition begins in Delhi with a visit to the Taj Mahal, then we board bicycles and wheel south through the villages to Jaipur and Jodhpur.

CHITWAN ELEPHANT RIDE   Liz Hymans

Here we trade our two-wheelers for the humped mounts of camels, and drift across the plains and shifting sands of time to Jaisalmeer. Brief sojourns in Delhi and Kathmandu are followed by three days of whitewater rafting on the Trisuli River, then a visit to the forests of southern Nepal for an elephant-back game safari. Then we trek along the towering Annapurna Range of the Himalaya, where we climb to the top of Poon Hill and peer down into the spectacular Kali Gandaki Gorge. After this adventure in transportation—bikes to camels, elephants to rafts, footpower to jets—simple locomotion will never be the same.

ITINERARY: Day 1: Delhi. Day 2: Agra. Days 3-5: Cycling. Days 6-7: Jaipur. Day 8: Jodhpur. Days 9-11: Camel trek. Day 12: Jaisalmeer. Day 13: Jaisalmeer/Jodhpur. Day 14: Delhi. Days 15-16: Kathmandu. Days 17-19: Trisuli River rafting. Days 20-22: Elephant Camp. Day 23: Pokhara. Days 23-30: On trek. Days 31-32: Kathmandu. Day 33: Return.

🐘 🐫 ⚲   Class III   **Medium**
October-March
Australian Himalayan Expeditions   AS89

CHINA

CHINA BICYCLE

AN OLD WAY TO SEE A NEW COUNTRY, bicycling through China allows the Western tourists the same pace of daily life that their hosts share, and we see China as through Chinese eyes. While it is a customary way for the people of the country to travel, our plainly different reasons attract their attention and welcome. Clusters of village children giggle as they gather round. We jostle for space with pointed-capped peasants, dodge shoulder-poles and lumbering buffalo. Stopping when we like, where we like, we pass through the heart of Old China — from Macau to Guangzhou (Canton), 650 miles of daily adventure away. Ancient pagodas rise out of the misty lakes, limestone crags loom in the pale gloom high above the Seven Star Crags; factories flex, temples hum, and bazaars buzz; and our comfort is assured in local hotels and at local tables. Guandong Province is our pedalling-grounds, as we pass through Foshan, Shichinsand, and Zaonghua Hot Springs, where our road-sore muscles seem a dynasty away. A side trip to Beijing, capital of ancient as well as modern China, is on the itinerary for most departures.

ITINERARY: Day 1: En route. Day 2: Hong Kong. Day 3: Macau. Days 4-17: Bicycle tour. Day 18: Guangzhou to Beijing flight. Days 19-21: Beijing. Day 22: Guangzhou. Days 23-24: Hong Kong. Day 25: Return. *Extended tour:* Days 22-28: Guilin region cycling. Day 29: Hong Kong. Day 30: Return.

🚴 🐣 🐤   Class III   **Medium**
August-May
Australian Himalayan Expeditions   AS63

TIBET TREK

LONG A FORBIDDEN LAND, Tibet today beckons to the most adventurous of adventure travelers. It has it all: an ancient culture, a mystical tradition, soaring mountains that crest with the world's own summit, and a fascinating *frisson* of contrast between the Tibet of old and the new China. After entering China by way of Hong Kong, we fly to Chengdu, then travel on to Lhasa, capital of Tibetan Buddhism. We spend a few days here acclimating to the altitude, while visiting the Dalai Lama's retreat and the other monasteries and temples of this sky-high community. Then off we go, heading across the wild Tibetan Plateau for the ruins of the Rongbuk Monastery, not far from the base camp for today's summit attempts

DRESSED UP IN TIBET   Jim Slade

on Everest. Our trek route takes us up the Rongbuk Glacier to the mountaineer's Camp III — at 21,300 feet (6500m), the highest goal of any trek in the world. From here, we work our way regretfully back to the low country, ending our journey with several days in Beijing. A last look at the Great Wall, the Ming Tombs, the bicycles in the streets and the centuries-old traditions of China seal our impressions of Tibet, the Forbidden Land.

ITINERARY: Day 1: Guangzhou. Day 2: Chengdu. Days 3-6: Lhasa. Days 7-8: Xigaze. Day 9: Xegar. Days 10-19: On trek. Day 20: Xegar. Day 21: Xigaze. Day 22: Lhasa. Days 23-24: En route. Days 25-27: Beijing. Day 28: Return.

🚶 🐤   Class IV   **Premium**
May, September
Australian Himalayan Expeditions   AS64

TIENSHAN SILK ROUTE

THE SILK ROUTE WAS MORE than just a highway for materials and spices; it was also an avenue of ideas, carrying the traffic of religious beliefs and the concepts of whole civilizations from east to west and back. This month-long program is an immersion in the sights and sensations of the Silk Route as it traverses the great girth of China. We take a short trek to Mt. Bogda, allowing pack animals to carry our gear from camp to camp; but for the most part we stay in hotels and palaces, worthy of the royalty whose caravans crossed these endless expanses. Highlights include Tienshe Lake and the mountains of Tienshan, the southern reach of Sibera; Kazakh nomads who serve yoghurt and flatbread in their yurts; the Turfan oasis in the heart of the Gobi desert; the 10,000 Buddhas of

Dunghuang, and the ancient walled city of Xian, the piquant cuisine of Xichuan Province, the Ming Tombs and, of course, the Great Wall of China. Ancient relics, timeless scenery, and modern squares and museums combine to give us a deep and lasting portrait of China's culture, history, and hopes.

ITINERARY: Day 1: En route. Days 2-3: Beijing. Days 4-5: Urumqi. Day 6: Tienshe Lake. Days 7-12: On trek. Day 13: Urumqi. Days 14-15: Tulufan. Days 16-17: Dunghuang. Day 18: On train. Days 19-20: Xian. Day 21: Beijing and return.

🚙 🛶 🥾   Class III   **Premium**
July-August
Australian Himalayan Expeditions   AS101

MONGOLIAN OVERLAND

THE MONGOLIAN EMPIRE was once the largest in the world, spreading behind the armies of the Great Khan from the Mediterranean to the Sea of Japan, from Vienna to Vladivostok. For the past several decades, it has been all but inaccessible. Now it is open to visitors, and its rolling grasslands, virgin forests, isolated people and ancient capital can once more be appreciated. On this well-appointed itinerary we take in the highlights of China, including the Great Wall and the Ming Tombs, before venturing across the breadth of the Gobi desert on a remarkable train ride to Mongolia. Our travels take us north to Terelj, where yurts dot the valley floors and fermented mare's milk is the campfire aperitif. We head down to Ulan Bator, fly on to Khujirt, visit the ruins of Karokorum and explore a 16th-century Buddhist monastery surrounded by 108 *stupas*. After the gold of Mongolia, all else seems dross.

ITINERARY: Day 1: To Beijing. Days 2-4: Beijing. Day 5: On train. Days 6-7: Ulan Bator. Days 8-12: Terelj trek. Day 13: Ulan Bator. Days 14-15: Khujirt. Day 16: Ulan Bator. Days 17-20: Gobi trek. Day 21: Ulan Bator. Day 22: On train. Days 23-24: Beijing. Day 24: Return.

🚙 🥾 🛶   Class II   **Medium**
June, July, September
Australian Himalayan Expeditions   AS98

MONGOLIAN PANORAMA

SELDOM-VISITED INNER MONGOLIA opens up to our inquiring eyes as it never has before on this trek, horseback, camelback and cycle trip through its many wonders. We pay homage to the classic attractions of the Beijing area before flying north to Hohhot, the capital of Inner Mongolia. Our cycles await us there, and we set the wheels a-spinning en route to Siziwangqi, at the edge of the vast Mongolian grasslands. From the village of Wangfuedui, where we overnight in yurts, the vast expanse of the steppes beckons, and horses are made ready to bear us into the vastness in proper style. At last we dismount and travel by foot to the ruins of an ancient temple, where Tibetan was spoken thousands of miles from the center of Buddhism. Then on to Baotou for a trek to another ancient lamaserai, and across the Yellow River to the village of E Mong. A camel trek to nomadic yurt camps is our next pleasure, the adventure completing an all-around appreciation of Mongolia.

ITINERARY: Days 1-2: To Beijing. Day 3: Fly to Hohhot. Days 4-6: Cycling to Wangfuedui. Days 7-13: Horse trek. Day 14: Train to Baotou. Day 15: Trek to Wundangzhou. Days 16-17: Camel trek. Days 18-19: En route. Days 20-21: Beijing. Day 22: Return.

🥾 🚲 🐫 🛶   Class III   **Premium**
August-October
Australian Himalayan Expeditions   AS117

CENTRAL ASIA TREK

TREK TO THE END of the Great Wall, and continue into the heartlands of central Asia, where the snow-capped peaks of the Pamirs rise over the barren deserts to western China. Using Bactrian camels as pack support, we venture into the remotest provinces of China for views that few have enjoyed before us: the heights of Mt. Kongur, of Muztagata, and the circle of giant peaks that affords us views into the Soviet Union. After our trek we gasp as Kirghiz nomads, whose expertise with wild horses is the stuff of legend, play a rough game called *buz kazi* with up to 50 players, no rules, and some survivors. Those who resist the temptation to join the game fly back to Urumqi and drive to the fir trees and lush meadows of the Tienshan Mountains, whose glaciated slopes contrast with the deserts of the Pamirs. We trek to the "Mountain of God," Bogda (5534m), highest peak of the range. This survey of the extremes of China will not soon pass from the mind's eye.

ITINERARY: Day 1: Arrive Beijing. Days 2-3: Beijing. Days 4-6: Urumqi. Days 7-8: Kashgar. Day 9: Kal Qoli Lake. Days 10-16: On camel trek. Days 17-18: Kashgar. Day 19: Urumqi. Days 20-24: On trek. Day 25: Urumqi. Days 26-27: Beijing. Day 28: Return.

🥾 🛶   Class IV   **Medium**
June, August
Australian Himalayan Expeditions   AS99

PAKISTAN

HINDU KUSH AND HUNZA

TWO OF THE WORLD'S GREAT mountain ranges meet in a mass of serrated ridges in northern Pakistan. Walk in the valleys of the Hindu Kush and the Karakoram, enjoying the peoples and places of both. Afghanis, Persians, Macedonians, Indians and Europeans have passed through the Kalash Valley on their way from India to Europe, and each has left a bit of themselves behind. It's easy to see why some chose to stay: bubbling streams flow down from the glaciers to support verdant fields and woods of silver birch beneath the peaks of the Hindu Kush. After a week's idyllic walking here, we take one of the world's classic mountain drives across the high passes to Gilgit and the Hunza Valley. Rakaposhi (7708 meters), queen of the Karakoram peaks, dominates this valley. A short trek takes us past glaciers and peaks to the villages of the long-lived Hunzakots, a people as rugged and enduring as the mountain ranges. Perhaps we will discover the secret of their longevity in the crisp surround of meadow and mountain.

ITINERARY: Days 1-2: To Lahore. Day 3: Lahore. Day 4: Train to Peshawar. Day 5: Peshawar. Days 6-13: Chitral; Hindu Kush trek. Days 14-15: Drive to Gilgit. Days 16-21: Hunza trek. Day 22: Islamabad. Day 23: Fly home.

🚶 🚙 ⛴   Class III   **Medium**
June-July
Australian Himalayan Expeditions   AS19

LUNCH, BALTORO GLACIER   Skip Horner

GOATSKIN RAFT, INDUS RIVER   Jim Slade

MARCO POLO SILK ROUTE

RETRACE THE FABLED JOURNEY of the 13th-century Italian explorer through the Chitral and Hunza region of northern Pakistan. The romance of Polo's passage through the unknown lands of the Middle East and China is the stuff that dreams are made of. His feat cannot now be duplicated, but the lands at which he marveled, with much of their beauty and charm retained, can be visited by modern-day Marcos with a minimum of fuss and hardship. For two full weeks we shop bazaars in the Hindu Kush, jeep above precipitous gorges in the Yarkhun Valley, ferry across the Ghizar River on inflated goatskins, witness the Kalash Kafir dances, and ascend the Karakoram Highway into the rarefied atmosphere of the Hunza, the ageless land.

ITINERARY: Days 1-3: Rawalpindi. Days 4-6: Chitral, Hindu Kush. Days 7-8: Yarkhun Valley, Mastuj. Days 9-11: Karakoram, Gilgit. Day 12: Hunza. Day 13: Rawalpindi. Day 14: Taxila. Day 15: Home.

🚙 ⛴   Class II   **Premium**
May
Silk Road Expeditions   AS16

K2 TREK

SPECTACULAR IS THE WORD for this expedition to the world's second highest mountain, K2 in Pakistan's Karakoram Range. Just as 8611-meter K2 is more difficult to climb than the taller Everest (8848m), so the K2 Trek is more demanding than that to Everest Base Camp. But the rewards are correspondingly greater, including the incredible experience of spending three weeks on glaciers in absolute wilderness. Surrounded by the sublime snowscapes of Masherbrum, Hidden Peak, Gasherbrum and K2 itself, camped beneath a solid canopy of brilliant stars, hearing only the sounds of living glaciers – these are sensations only a few will ever know. Three days of trekking through Balti villages, then we leave behind contact with inhabited lands for 20 days and 200 kilometers. Our route takes us up the Baltoro Glacier to Concordia, where six peaks over 8000 meters create a reality that is spectacularly surreal.

ITINERARY: Day 1: En route. Day 2: Arrive Islamabad. Day 3: Islamabad. Day 4: Skardu. Day 5: Dassu. Days 6-28: On trek. Day 29: Return to Skardu. Days 30-31: Skardu. Day 32: Gilgit. Days 33-34: Islamabad. Day 35: Return.

🚶 🐫   Class V   **Medium**
August
Australian Himalayan Expeditions   AS18

BHUTAN/ SIKKIM

CHOMOLHARI BASE CAMP

LAND OF THE DRAGON is the name the Bhutanese use for their remote Himalayan kingdom, Druk-Yul. Years of stout defense of Druk-Yul and a cautious tourism policy have preserved this jewel for the few who venture into her interior. Trekking here is like trekking in Nepal 25 years ago, an ancient land discovered anew. The hike to Chomolhari base camp is one of Bhutan's finest, with stupendous mountain scenery and the chance to see Himalayan wildlife such as musk deer and blue sheep that simply no longer exist elsewhere. Nor do we neglect the Buddhist spirit of the nation, as we visit the cliff-clinging lamaserai at Taksang as well as several lesser temples and fortresses. Villages dot our route, and their ubiquitous offerings of *chang* (millet beer) encourage our interaction with people whose exposure to the outside world has been slight. The highest pass crossed is just under 16,000 feet (5000 meters), and the yak pastures and inhabited valleys are welcome respites from the ups and downs of Himalayan hiking. Capture the spirit of the real Himalaya in the land of the dragon.

ITINERARY: Days 0-2: To Delhi, Bagdogra and Bhutan. Days 3-5: Paro Valley. Days 6-15: On trek. Day 16: Thimpu. Day 17: To Delhi. Day 18: Home.

🚶 🐫   Class IV   **Premium**
May, September
Exodus   AS120

MAGICAL KINGDOMS

THE EAST HIMALAYAN KINGDOMS of Bhutan and Sikkim and the tea country of Darjeeling are the highlights of this lofty tour for non-trekkers. We kick off with a train ride to Darjeeling, on the narrow-gauge "toy train" that rides impossible switchbacks to the tea-rich plains fronting the Himalaya. This former British hill station is a look at the old days of colonialism, with the sun rising over Everest not so very far away. Then we jeep to the capital of Sikkim, Gangtok, and its quaint kingdom only recently accepted into the fold of Mother India. After a full day at the Jaldapara Game reserve, where we ride elephants and view rhino, tiger, and bird on the wing, we tour Bhutan — a land lost in time, nestled in the Himalaya. Masked dancing, cliff-hanging monasteries, and the surrounding peaks make this the photogenic focus of our tour. For the experienced Himalaya traveler, this could be something new; for the newcomer, it is a perfect introduction.

ITINERARY: Days 1-2: En route. Day 3: Arrive Siliguri. Day 4: Train. Days 5-6: Darjeeling. Day 7: Kalimpong. Days 8-9: Gangok. Days 10-11: Jaldapara Game Preserve. Day 12: To Bhutan. Days 13-18: Bhutan tour. Day 19: Siliguri and return.

🐫 🐘 🚙   Class I   **Medium**
March-May, October-January
Australian Himilayan Expeditions   AS66

HIMALAYAN SPRINGTIME   Liz Hymans

ORANGUTAN & FRIENDS   Michael Nichols

SOUTHEAST

ALAS RIVER

THE RIVER OF THE RED APE, the Alas, spits and smokes through the heart of one of Asia's largest wildlife areas, home of rhinos, leopards, tigers and the "wild man of Borneo" himself, the orangutan. First explored by Sobek in 1984, the Alas is a classic river experience for the true adventure lover, with Class III rapids and world-class scenery at every bend, and the rare opportunity to penetrate the orangutan's homeland. These huge yet gentle beasts are thought by some primatologists to be among mankind's closest relatives, though they remain little understood. On the island of Sumatra the Indonesian government has guaranteed their protection in Gunung Leuser National Park, and has instituted a "rehabilitation" program to reintroduce domesticated apes to the wild. After a visit to this center at Bohorak, we float and splash down the Alas for nine days, ending with a short stop-over at Lake Toba—a unique alpine resort in the mid-tropics. If the river and wildlife haven't sated your appetite for travel, Medan, Sumatra's capital, offers the best connections to Bali in the Far East. Be among the first to appreciate the Alas!

5-DAY ITINERARY: Day 1: Medan, Sumatra. Days 2-4: On the river. Day 5: Return.

14-DAY ITINERARY: Day 1: Medan. Day 2: Bohorak Research Centre. Day 3: Berstagi. Days 4-10: On the river. Day 11: Gelombang. Day 12: Lake Toba. Day 13: Medan. Day 14: Return.

✈ 🦆 🏺   Class III   **Premium**
April-October
Sobek Expeditions   AS77

BHUTAN AND SIKKIM

TWO HIDDEN KINGDOMS in the Eastern Himalaya, each rife with spectacle and ripe with culture, are the backdrops for twin treks. Comparing the isolated mountain-folk of Bhutan with the more exposed Sikkimese gives us a parallax view of modern Asia. From Bhutan's capital, at Thimphu, we hike along the Ningula Ridge, where herdsmen graze their yaks in the shadows of Chomolhari. At Taksang Monastery, clinging to a cliff at the head of the Paro Valley, the ancient traditions of Tibetan Buddhism breathe with life. On the Sikkim trek, we pass beneath Kangchenjunga, the third highest peak on earth, down into the tea-growing regions of Darjeeling. At this enchanting old British hill station, tea is still taken promptly at 3 each afternoon. One lump or two?

ITINERARY: Day 1: En route. Day 2: Arrive Siliguri. Day 3: To Thimpu. Days 4-7: Bhutan trek. Day 8: Paro. Days 9-11: Darjeeling. Days 12-18: Sikkim trek. Day 19: Siliguri and return.

🏺 🚶   Class III   **Medium**
April, September
Australian Himalayan Expeditions   AS35

DRAGONS & DEMONS

VIRGIN RAIN FOREST, Komodo dragons and Balinese dance dramas are three fruits of the Indonesian cornucopia, a small sample of its bountiful provender. With so much bounty in a 3200-mile archipelago of 150 million people, our trek zeroes in on the fauna and flora of the national parks, the lightly peopled wildernesses. The turquoise seas, elegant religious dances and Hindu temples are the background for a trek into the heart of wild Indonesia on Lombok Island and a traditional fishing boat sail around Komodo. On Lombok, the rain forest of Gunung Rinjani National Park is our home for six days packed with superb views, village encounters, active volcanoes, crater lakes and hot springs. A final descent down the northern slopes of Mt. Rinjani takes us to the fishing village of Bayan, where boats then become our primary mode of transport. We visit the attractive little island of Gili Air with its remarkable tall houses, the wildlife reserve of Pulao Moyo and finally Komodo, where unique lizards grow to 12 feet long and a diversity of sea life underscores the wonder of intriguing Indonesia.

ITINERARY: Day 1: En route. Days 2-3: On Bali. Days 4-5: Lombok. Days 6-11: Trek. Day 12: Gili Air. Days 13-14: Pulao Moyo. Days 15-17: Komodo. Day 18: Bali. Day 19: Home.

🚶 🐚 🐟   Class III   **Medium**
June-October
Exodus   AS121

ISLAND EXPLORER

THE FACES OF INDONESIA say it all. Diversity, both cultural and physical, is the only constant on an exploration of some of the 23,677 islands that together form this archipelago nation. Temple festivals in Bali, traditional textile weaving villages in the lesser Sunda islands, Dayak longhouses in Borneo, the matriarchal societies of West Sumatra, primitive Asmat tribes on Irian Jaya, colorful tropical reefs of the Flores and Banda seas, the world's greatest concentration of active volcanoes, lush tropical rain forests and secluded sandy beaches are the things dreams—and Indonesia—are made of. These abundant wonders are revealed from the luxury of the *Island Explorer,* a 36-person Norwegian cruise ship built to the finest international standards. Most cruising takes place at night to allow days for island expeditions: lunch with Komodo dragons, horse rides into the hills, volcano climbs or a stalk of the rare white rhino—each port-of-call brings another rare and wondrous experience. You can choose from packages as short as a five-day cruise out of Bali to full three-week land/cruise packages. Each itinerary is as varied as the islands themselves.

SAMPLE ITINERARY: *Islands East of Bali* Days 1-4: To and in Hong Kong. Day 5: Bali. Days 6-10: Cruise Komodo, Flores, Sumba and Lombok. Days 11-13: Bali. Day 14: Home.

🚢 🐚   Class I   **Premium**
Year-round
Salen-Lindblad Cruising   AS125

MALAYSIA & BORNEO

FROM THE WILDS OF BORNEO to the wisdom of ancient cultures, the Malaysian peninsula and nearby island of Borneo are living museums ripe for research. Along with contemporary crafts and culture, we step back into the prehistory of Borneo as we visit Niah Caves, where excavations date man in Borneo back 40,000 years. On the banks of the Skrang River, we overnight in an Iban longhouse after navigating the river in traditional wooden craft. But it is the "wild man of Borneo," the orangutan, that steals the scene as we wind up our Borneo visit

KOMODO DRAGON   Bart Henderson

in a sanctuary at Sepilok. History, modern life and nature continue to blend smoothly in Malaysia, where a six-day stay is highlighted by Kuala Tahan National Park. Jungle river trips, an overnight in a blind to observe tapir, deer, scladang, wild buffalo or tigers, and short treks to caves and hillside observation points present us with the fundamental lessons of jungle flora, fauna and survival. Nothing can top the medieval moods and animal adventures of Borneo and Malaysia, but our final two days in Singapore are not without adventures of their own.

ITINERARY: Days 1-2: En route. Day 3: Singapore. Day 4: Kuching. Days 5-6: Skrang River. Day 7: Miri. Day 8: Sandakan. Day 9: Orangutan sanctuary. Day 10: Singapore. Day 11: Malacca. Day 12: Kuala Lumpur. Days 13-16: Kuala Tahan National Park. Days 17-18: Singapore. Day 19: Home.

⚱ ☚   Class II   **Premium**
Year-round
Safaricentre   AS122

SOUTHEAST ASIAN ENVIRONMENTS

FROM THAILAND TO CHINA, the hills and jungles teem with colorful people and ancient civilizations, the foci of this tour of the Golden Triangle. Thailand is first: We visit Chiang Mai and Chiang Rai, homelands of hill tribes that include the Meo, Karen and Akha people. Impressive handicraft and a traditional flavor little-diluted by Western incursions highlight this encounter. Then Burma: Rangoon, Pagan, and Mandalay. Pagan is a wonder where thousands of Buddhist *stupas* cover a 40-square-kilometer site, testimony to the religious fervor of the Burmese. Mandalay, the former royal capital of Burma on the banks of the Irrawaddy River, contrasts colorful pagodas with remnants of British colonial grandeur. We return to the modern capital of Rangoon for the flight to China, where the "stone forest" of Kunming awaits our arrival with silent patience. Guilin, famous for its majestic limestone hills and jagged lake scenery, is viewed from on deck as we cruise into the heart of its brush-stroked beauty. The final stop on this cultural caravan is Hong Kong, a fitting close for our royal Asian suite.

ITINERARY: Day 1: To Bangkok. Day 2: Bangkok. Days 3-4: Chiang Mai. Days 5-6: Chiang Rai. Day 7: Bangkok. Days 8-9: Rangoon. Day 10: Pagan. Days 11-12: Mandalay. Day 13: Rangoon. Days 14-16: Kunming. Days 17-19: Guilin. Days 20-22: Hong Kong. Day 23: Return.

⚱ ☚   Class I   **Medium**
September-January
Australian Himalayan Expeditions   AS118

ARCHES, THAILAND   Liz Hymans

MALDIVES SAILING

COCONUT COVERED ATOLLS scatter across the Indian Ocean, the exposed tops of a submarine ridge. Shallow coral surrounding every island creates a reef fantasia of color and texture. Arab *dhonies* slice across the waters, their triangular sails arched in the wind. Sailing and diving in the Maldives combine in an aquatic odyssey of pleasure, from the snorkel explorations of reefs that rank among the world's finest, to the catching of barracuda and collection of coconuts for delicious fresh meals in this tropical paradise. The heritage of the natives (the islands were settled by Asians who were then converted to Islam in the 12th century, and influenced by Europeans from the 16th century on) adds a cultural resonance to our sea-faring sojourn. The Maldivians say, "Here the world ends and paradise begins." We think a sail among the atolls will make you agree!

ITINERARY: Day 1: Arrive Male. Days 2-7 or 2-14: Sail. Day 8 or 15: Return.

▲ ⚑   Class II   **Moderate**
Year-round
Australian Himalayan Expeditions   AS39

THAI HILLS

THE HILL TRIBES OF THAILAND are a fascinating counterpoint to the Sherpas of the Himalaya, for they are in fact more closely related to one another than they are to the Nepalese or other Asians. Trekking from the Mae Kok River into the rolling hill country, we visit villages of the Lahu, Lisu and Karen, sleep in local houses and enjoy traditional hospitality in the pleasantly mild climate. There's also time to explore the bustling market of Chiang Mai and the cosmopolitan pleasures of Bangkok. This trip is available as an extension to Nepal and India trip schedules.

ITINERARY: Day 1: Bangkok. Day 2: Chiang Mai. Days 3-5: Trek. Days 6-7: Chiang Mai. Day 8: Return.

⚊   Class III   **Moderate**
Year-round
Australian Himilayan Expeditions   AS49

LISU MOTHER   Michael Ingram

THAI BEACHES

A WEEK OF SUN, sand and surf on some of Thailand's best beaches. After any of our Bangkok-based trips we offer a week of relaxation—sit on the beach, snorkel, dine on superb sea food and soak up the sun. We bus down the neck of Thailand to Phuket, the emerald Thai countryside and its small villages flying past our windows, then board a boat out to Raya Island. This is your base for the next few days, a comparatively unspoilt beach resort that ranks as Thailand's finest. This beach option is unescorted, so the days at Raya are free to explore the neighboring villages and countryside or just to idle on the sweeping beaches, using your time as you see fit. Whether on your way home from Nepal

SRI LANKAN FISHERMAN   Richard Bangs

or back from Burma, this idyll will provide a happy ending to your adventure.

ITINERARY: Day 1: Bus Bangkok to Phuket. Days 2-6: Raya Island. Day 7: Fly Phuket/Bangkok. Day 8: Return.

⚊   Class I   **Moderate**
Year-round
Australian Himalayan Expeditions   AS112

HILLS OF SRI LANKA

THE COOL UPLAND HILLS of Sri Lanka are a green trove of ancient cities, sacred summits, craft centers and rolling plains. From the capital city of Colombo we drive to Polonnaruwa, a fascinating ancient settlement, then on to Sigiriya, the "Lion Rock." These scenes prepare us for Kandy, the old capital of Ceylon, where you can purchase some of Asia's finest handicrafts and gemstones while awing at the temples and buildings. We continue up through misty tea plantations to Adam's Peak surmounted by the footprint of humanity's first father. The British influence can be seen as clearly in the graceful tea plantations as in the names of the Horton Plains, in Sri Lanka's center. Ancient pathways score the spectacular countryside, enriched by both history and the tropical sun. This is a wonderful contrast to the tropical coast, particularly recommended in combination with *Maldives Sailing,* or as an option to our Indian adventures.

ITINERARY: Day 1: Arrive Colombo. Days 2-6: Hill safari. Day 7: Colombo. Day 8: Return.

⚊   Class I   **Moderate**
Year-round
Australian Himalayan Expeditions   AS40

THAILAND ADVENTURE

THE GOLDEN TRIANGLE LINKS China, Burma, and Thailand in a colorful and distinctive region tailor-made for trekking. Lush vegetation and a good climate support several traditional tribes, including the White and Red Karen, the Meo and the Laku, each with their own distinctive dress, language and religion. We join the people of this region in their own milieus as we ride elephants through extensive teak forests and build bamboo rafts to float down the Chomtong River. We interact with the hill farmers informally, making friendships that do not interfere with their traditional values. There are other faces of Thailand, too—the Prisoner of War Museum on the Kwai River, jungle houseboating, and snorkeling on Raya Island in the Andaman Sea.

ITINERARY: Day 1: Bangkok. Days 2-3: Chiang Mai. Day 4: Mae Hong Sorn. Days 5-10: Trek. Day 11: Chiang Mai. Days 12-14: River trek. Day 15: Chiang Rai. Day 16: Bangkok. Day 17: Kangchanburi. Day 18: River Kwai. Days 19-22: Raya Island. Day 23: Bangkok. Day 24: Return.

🚶 ☕ 🚣   Class III   **Moderate**
December-March
Australian Himalayan Expeditions   AS47

SINAI SIREN   Ben Yosef

☕ 🚶 🐫   Class III   **Moderate**
Year-round
Jabaliya   AS54

MIDDLE EAST

HIGH SINAI CIRCUIT

SPLENDOR, SOLITUDE AND HISTORY combine in the Sinai to form landscapes of barren majesty and people of austere dignity. Where massive granite peaks rise high above deep dry gorges, the Bedouin Moslems tend isolated orchards and hire out their services as camel drivers. We use their skills and knowledge of the mountains of the High Range of the Sinai, as we explore the unique cultural treasures of the Spring of Moses, the Monastery of Santa Katarina, and spartan Bedouin encampments. The awesome landscape has been inspiration for profound spiritual experiences from the time of Moses through Christian hermits of the third century to the present day; now it's our turn to become initiated to its mysteries.

ITINERARY: Day 1: Eilat to Santa Katarina. Days 2-5: Camel trek. Day 6: Santa Katarina. Day 7: Cairo or Eilat, Israel.

DESERT EXPLORER

THE NEGEV DESERT is a vast triangle of deep canyons, steep peaks and fantastic sandstone bluffs—all carved by a system of stream beds that may remain dry for decades. Most striking of all are huge craters formed by erosion, geological windows into the depths of the earth's crust. Hike through these canyons, descend into these craters, and be witness to the age-old struggle of the region's inhabitants against both the desert winds and the winds of change. We overland from oasis to oasis, seeing gazelles, ibex and hydrax by day, and hearing jackals, hyenas, wolves and leopards at night. Our route takes us from modern Jerusalem to ancient Byzantine ruins at Avdat to the salt wedge of Mount Sodom on a lively journey into legend.

ITINERARY: Day 1: Jerusalem to Judean desert. Day 2: Massada. Day 3-4: Hiking. Day 5: Jerusalem.

🚙 ☕   Class II   **Moderate**
Year-round
Jabaliya   AS53

ISRAELI HIDEAWAY   Timi Ben-Yosef

THE SOUTHERN SINAI

Follow in the footsteps of Moses through the rugged mountains which lie between the Gulf of Suez and the Gulf of Agaba—one of the most striking realms of desert in the world. Due to its complex geological structure, a unique variety of landscapes congregate in this, the southern tip of the Sinai: sharp, black mountains of metamorphic rock, deep and narrow canyons of colorful walls, Sahara-style sand dunes, and huge sandstone blocks—all braced by the breezy blue beaches of the bifurcating gulfs. Our overlanding tour of this fascinating region takes us along the Sinai coast to Santa Katarina Monastery, where we hike up nearby Jabel Musa (2285m)—the Mount Sinai of myth. Then into the Bronze Age, as we visit the burial structures at Nawamis, and visit with the Bedouin population of this sandy quarter. After a full day of swimming and snorkeling along the coral reefs of Dahab, we return to Tel Aviv via Eilat and Jerusalem for a final farewell to the Middle East, and the nearest reach of Asia.

ITINERARY: Day 1: Meet in Tel Aviv; transfer to Eilat, begin tour. Day 2: Santa Katarina. Day 3: Nawamis. Day 4: Dahab. Day 5: To Tel Aviv and return.

🚙 🏺   Class II   **Moderate**
Year-round
Jabaliya   AS76

GRAND SINAI SAFARI

Into the mystic lands of the Sinai, where legends survive the harsh landscape and mysteries erupt from the desert sands. This in-depth tour of the Sinai takes us by four-wheel drive through the Arabian landscape, from oasis to oasis, down wadis and up dunes, from the present into the past. We take in the medieval monastery of Santa Katarina, climb the holy heights of Mt. Sinai (Jabal Musa, 2285m), visit the petrified Forest of Pillars and the sanctified tomb of Sheikh Ukhbus. Then we descend: down into the turquoise mines of Sarabit el Khadim, where the sky-blue stone was extricated to make jewelry for Hathor, Egyptian goddess of the sky, who has a temple near the site. This camping tour shows us the best and most notable of Sinai's many attractions, in ways only the adventurous traveler can discover.

ITINERARY: Day 1: Eilat to Canyon of Colors. Day 2: Santa Katarina. Day 3: Mt. Sinai; on to El Andar Oasis. Day 4: Forest of Pillars; Sarabit el Khadim. Day 5: To Cairo and return.

🚜 🏺   Class II   **Moderate**
Year-round
Jabilaya Trekking   AS55

JAPAN

JAPAN CYCLE

Traditional Japan is a world vastly different from ours — and from the rest of modern Japan. From architecture to etiquette, Japan has long seemed a cipher to the Western mind. We experience the old ways as we bicycle for ten days on the island of Kyushu in the south. Night stops will be in *minishukus* (guest houses) and *ryokans* (inns), where we sleep on tatami mats, take hot sand baths, and enjoy the warmth and politeness of our hosts. We also stay in mountain resorts and at Ibesuki, a popular Japanese hot springs where our fellow guests will be workers from the "new Japan" to the north. Close looks at the smoking Sakasrujima volcano, the wooden temple of the Shogun and Nara, and the famous *Shinkansen* (bullet train) round out our immersion in another way of life.

ITINERARY: Days 1-2: Tokyo. Day 3: Huga. Days 4-12: Cycle tour. Day 13: Kagoshima. Days 14-17: Kirishima. Day 17: Osaka. Day 18: Kyoto. Days 19-20: Nara. Day 21: Tokyo and return. *Hokkaido Extension:* Day 21: Tokyo. Days 22-23: Hakodate. Day 24: Niseko. Days 25-26: Sapporo. Day 27: Tokyo. Day 28: Return.

🚲 🏺   Class III   **Medium**
April-May, September-October
Australian Himalayan Expeditions   AS42

JAPANESE ALPS

THE JEWELS OF JAPANESE mountains are the Kita Alps, rising more than 3000 meters from sea level in the northern reaches. Trekking for nine days through this mountain marvel, we climb steeply through low-elevation forest along rocky, narrow trails to the peaks themselves. Easing the strain of our day-time exertions, the nights are spent Japanese-style in mountain huts, soaking weary bones in communal hot springs. Our only companions here are likely to be Japanese mountain enthusiasts, since few Westerners are familiar with these alpine trails. We also spend four days in Kyoto, ancient capital of Japan, and explore the many temples and museums that make the city a living museum of Japanese culture, art, and history.

ITINERARY: Day 1: Departure. Day 2: Arrive Tokyo. Day 3: Tokyo. Day 4: Train to Nakabusa. Days 5-7: Kyoto. Day 8: Train to Nagoya. Day 9: Mt. Ontake. Day 10: Takayama. Days 11-18: Trek. Day 19: Tokyo. Day 20: Return.

⚞ ⚱   Class IV   **Medium**
August
Himalaya   AS41

HOKKAIDO CYCLE

JAPAN'S NORTHERN ISLAND, Hokkaido, is a wild and strange mixture of scenic spectacle, cultural anomaly, gracious cities and windswept coasts. While much of Japan has accelerated in pace and population in recent decades, Hokkaido still preserves the qualities of life that makes a cycling/hiking tour of Japan an endeavor to remember. We begin with a day of acculturation in Tokyo, after which the ferry ride to Noboribetsu on the southern coast of Hokkaido is like a passage into the past. Here we begin our 9-day cycle tour of Hokkaido with a traverse of Shikotsu National Park around Lake Toya, the watery caldera of an extinct volcano; then pump on to the scenic Shokotan Peninsula with its exceptional scenery and sparse settlements; and end our two-wheeler tour in Sapporo with a shopping spree in its underground shops. Along the route we visit the last remaining Ainu village, peopled by the Mongoloid natives of the north island who are slowly being assimilated into the Japanese mainstream, but still retain their cultural and genetic heritage to this day. A final ferry ride takes us out to Rishiri Island, to the far north of Japan's domain, where a climb up Rishiri Mountain affords us a peek across the La Pérouse Strait to the trailing edge of the Soviet Union. A two-week option on Kyushu, Japan's southern island, is available as an extension (see *AS42*).

ITINERARY: Days 1-2: Tokyo. Day 3: Ferry. Day 4: Noribetsu; begin cycle. Days 5-11: Cycle tour. Days 12-13: Sapporo. Day 14: To Tokyo and return.

⚲ ⚱ ⚞   Class III   **Medium**
May, June, August
Australian Himalayan Expeditions   AS43

MISTS OF THE ORIENT   Bart Henderson

TURKEY

MOUNT ARARAT TREK

JOURNEY UP THE SLOPES of the Flood's first island, following the original mountaineer, Noah, to its 17,010-foot (5185m) summit. Located in eastern Turkey near the Russian and Iranian borders, Ararat is a dormant volcano whose last eruption was in 1840. Today, the upper third of the mountain is covered with snow year-round, and the last hundred yards around the summit have turned to ice, the beginnings of a glacial system. An ascent to its top—higher than any point in Europe—is a wondrous journey through a landscape ravaged by the ages and volcanic activity, yet pulsing with the lure of legend. Along the route to Ararat, we take time to visit the ruins of ancient towns, colorful Erzurum, exotic castles at Hosap, and the sights of Istanbul, one of civilization's most central cities.

ITINERARY: Day 1: Istanbul. Day 2: Erzurum. Day 3: Dogubeyazit. Days 4-8: Ararat trek. Days 9-10: Van. Days 11-12: Istanbul. Day 13: Return.

⚐ ☖   Class III   **Moderate**

March-December
Trek Travel   AS124

TURQUOISE COAST

THE TURQUOISE COAST of Turkey, with its wooded inlets and islands, beautiful Greek and Roman ruins, and charming villages, is one of the few places left in the modern world that is at once both unspoiled and civilized. We board the *Kaptan*, our 21-meter motor-sail yacht, on the characteristically Greek island of Rhodes and set sail on an argonautical journey into the wilderness coves and blue-green waters of the Aegean and Mediterranean. On the water we swim, snorkel, windsurf and fish; when we drop anchor in any of the many isolated coves that decorate the region, we hike up pine-scented hills to wildflower meadows, and clamber around the great stone ruins of long-eclipsed empires: Lycian, Carian, Grecian, Roman, Byzantine and Ottoman. Turkish villages on many of the islands extend their hospitality when we shop for locally-crafted carpets, brasswork and embroidery. Finally we return to the fabled Isle of Rhodes, passing through the harbor mouth the great Colossus once straddled, back to the modern world that has descended from the Aegean heritage.

ITINERARY: Day 1: Athens. Days 2-3: Rhodes. Days 4-13: Sailing. Day 14: Return.

▲ ☖   Class II   **Medium**

September, May
Sobek Expeditions   AS51

CAMEL BOY, YEMEN   Jim Slade

TAURUS AND CAPPODOCIA

THE RUGGED RANGE OF the Taurus Mountains, a limestone massif on the southern coast of Turkey, possesses an almost mystical beauty. A complex system of spires, peaks and ridges created by the easily-erodable sedimentary rock creates a landscape of spectacular scenery, surmounted by three 12,000-foot (3650m) summits. The denizens of the region use these remote canyons and high valleys for pasturage during the summer, herding their sheep and goats amidst the splendid and dramatic scenery. We trek in this unique region for six full days, enjoying the views and the inhabitants' hospitality, bathing in clear waterfalls, and climbing to the summit of the high peaks. Along the way to the Taurus we visit Cappodocia, one of the world's most bizarre ruins: an underground city of rock churches, monasteries, dwellings and theaters lacing through elevated mounts of stone. Other sights en route include Tarsus, birthplace of St. Paul; Cennet Chennem (the Caves of Heaven and Hell); the minarets and tombs of Konya; and the bazaars and mosques of Istanbul. A Turkish treat for the intrepid trekker.

ITINERARY: Day 1: Istanbul. Day 2: To Cappodocia. Day 3: Cappodocia. Day 4: To Taurus. Days 5-10: On trek. Day 11: Karsanti. Day 12: Tarsus and Mersin. Day 13: Konya. Day 14: Ankara. Day 15: Istanbul. Day 16: Return.

🚶 🛶 🚙   Class III   **Moderate**
June-October
Trek Travel   AS123

NORTH YEMEN

THE TIBET OF THE MIDDLE EAST is a mountainous marvel with a history stretching back 2,500 years. Stone castles up to ten stories high perched on mountain tops; miles of stone terraces surrounding medieval walled castles; friendly people decked out in robes, turbans and bejewelled daggers preening and posing for the cameras; the semi-arid plain by the sea; and the ancient ruin-filled Red Sea ports are some of Arabia Felix's attractions. We drive to the principal cities and sites of North Yemen, taking day-long side hikes to reach the more remote castles and mosques. This scenic and historic gem is one of the best-kept secrets of the travel world—for natural and architectural beauty it is unsurpassed.

RICHES OF TURKEY   Jim Slade

ITINERARY: Day 1-3: Sanaa. Day 4: Wadi Dahr. Days 5-6: Sadah, Bhamas hot springs. Day 8: Ibb, Taiz. Days 9-11: Red Sea coast. Days 12-13: In the mountains. Days 14-15: Sanaa. Day 16: Return.

🚙 🛶   Class I   **Medium**
January
Silk Road Expeditions   AS52

ÇORUH RIVER

TURKEY'S WHITEWATER SURPRISE has all the perks and requisites of a great river. The rapids are fast and furious, swelling and boiling in rapid-fire display of all the hydrotechnics that make river running the sport it is. We never lack for excitement, nor do we suffer a dearth of other stimulants. The forested vertical gorge, rising to a backdrop of snow-capped peaks poking the clouds, is a visual delight. Seljuk and Byzantine castles perch on rock ramparts above the river. Mix the above with several parts of local color and ageless village life, a high waterfall, and pleasant hot springs, and you know you've got one of the greats. We encourage active, experienced participants ready for big whitewater and possible portages to challenge the Çoruh.

ITINERARY: Days 1-3: Ankara. Day 4: To the river. Days 5-13: The Çoruh. Day 14: Artvin. Day 15: Erzurum. Day 16: Return.

🛶 🛶   Class IV   **Medium**
May, June
Sobek Expeditions   AS50

Wild Places of Indonesia

Photography by Michael Nichols

Here Nature was lavish with her paint.

Wooded folds of mountain twine for miles, silent, motionless, a green tapestry stretching to the horizon, into the next world, slightly blurred by the heat. Coffee-colored waves of the rivers tear through the jungles, wild to get to the sea. Helmeted hornbills swoop like pterodactyls. Waterfalls make a tremendous fuss of their descents, leaping in flashes so white the clouds seem as soiled as last week's linen.

It is Java, Sumatra, Bali, Kalimantan, Sulawesi, New Guinea and thousands more, stretching like a string of emeralds for 4,000 miles along the Equator. It is a medley of rare and endangered wildlife, from the carpet-covered, red-chocolate, button-eyed orangutans, to the elusive elephants who can disappear into the jungle in a twinkle; from the Godzilla-like Komodo dragons, to the lime-green pit vipers, and on . . .

It is a land with an uncertain border between the temporal and the spiritual; the world's most populous Muslim nation, but with a legacy of frontier Hinduism blended with aboriginal animism, mixed with every faith ever flowered.

With an absence of subtlety, with crude, accurate coloring, it breathes a freedom from unnecessary detail, like a Chinese painting: high, indigo peaks suspended in cloud; gigantic white masks of mists; marching volcanoes; orange flame trees; dark and luxuriant forests that seem to pant for release.

It is the finest celebration of nature ever known on this planet, and this is a bite-sized, bantam tribute to a rich banquet of wildness that is nearing, too soon, its final course.

— Richard Bangs
All photos Michael Nichols/Magnum

ALPINE FREEDOM   Chris Noble

EUROPE

SCOTLAND   Tom Gilmore

NOT SO FAR: A EUROPEAN JOURNEY

by Jan Morris

*T*he farm dog leapt from the gate and snapped enthusiastically at my hub caps. Somebody waved goodbye, teacup in hand, from the Parrys' front window. I met the postman in his van halfway up the lane, and through his window he passed me an electricity bill, a notice about next week's bring-and-buy sale at the village hall, and three chances to win £50,000 in a Reader's Digest Prize Draw. There was snow on the high summit of Moel Hebog, the hefty bald mountain in front of me; behind my back the Irish Sea lay silent beneath a cold and western sheen.

I was leaving on a European journey: from this far Welsh corner of the continent, looking across to Ireland, to Montenegro on the other side of it, looking down to Albania. I was about to cross, not just a geographical conglomeration, or a historical expression, but a civilization: between these two extremes some 200 million people, whether they admit it or not, live to a common heritage and a more or less common set of values. This is the ghost of the Roman Empire, still perceptible after so many centuries of exorcism: if the Irish in the West were never subject to the Roman order, and have consequentially lived in tumultuous distemper ever since, the Albanians in the East have long disowned the patrimony, and live in a state of chill and utter isolation, the only people on earth among whom all forms of religion are strictly prohibited.

The rest of us along the route, Welsh, English, French, Italian, Swiss, Yugoslavs, are members really, for all our political styles, of the same spectral commonwealth. The great motorways which now criss-cross all Europe are only late successors to the high roads of the legions. The gradual weakening of nationality in western Europe, the blurring of frontiers, the mixing of languages, even the universal acceptance of bank and credit cards, which means I could really travel from Caenarfon to Cetinje without a solid penny in my pocket — all these phenomena of the 1980s are only returns to the imperial conveniences of Rome.

From *Journeys* (Oxford University Press), copyright © 1984 by Jan Morris. First published in *Encounter*, London.

THE ALPS

HIKING THE SWISS ALPS

IN THE MOSAIC OF SWISS CANTONS the Valais stands out as spectacular. It harbors one of the most isolated districts of the Alps, the Upper Rhone Valley from the vercorin to Haute-Nendaz. We hike a portion of this valley through chalet-studded mountain landscapes under a sky of Mediterranean clarity. We cross glaciers, follow wild mountain valleys, and view panoramas of alpine lakes and meadows. Our nights are spent in comfortable lodges and huts. We top it all off a farewell dinner which includes the famous cheese specialty of the Alps, Raclette. An unforgettably pleasant week.

ITINERARY: Day 0: Arrive Zurich or Geneva. Day 1: Sion to Vercorin. Days 2-6: Hiking. Day 7: To Sion and return.

🚶	Class III	**Moderate**
May-September		
Forum Travel	EU7	

ALPINE SKIING

IT'S ALL DOWNHILL FROM THE TOP. The ultimate in wilderness skiing awaits those who take their skiing to extremes on the other side of the Alps. The French call it *ski-sauvage*— skiing beyond designated trails into sanctuaries of natural snow surrounded by immense glaciers and rugged peaks. The finest certified guides and the world's most extensive network of lifts take you past the boundaries of the ski areas to an untouched winter magnificence, where steep chutes lead between rocky ridges to large, open bowls. Escorted by chamois, marmots, foxes, ptarmigans and eagles, you can ski a labyrinth of national park-lands from France to Italy—on a single run! Daily expeditions are based out of the finest resorts in the Alps—Val d'Isere, Chamonix, and Zermatt— with all the creature comforts and after-dark excitement you'd expect. And for the ski mountaineer, two-week springtime adventures use a system of mountain refuges for inter-resort expeditions that combine the best of cross-country and downhill. *C'est formidable!*

IT IS AS THOUGH THE BRITISH Isles are tilted permanently to one corner — the southeast corner, bottom right, where London stands seething upon the Thames. Everything slithers and tumbles down there, all the talent, all the money, and when I got on to the M4 motorway that morning I felt that I was being swept away helter-skelter, willy-nilly across the breadth of England. Around me all the energies of the place seemed to be heading in a single direction — the trucks from Cornwall and South Wales, the tourist buses, the ramshackle No Nuclear estate cards, the stream of expense-account Fords, their salesmen drivers tapping their steering-wheels to the rhythm of Radio One. London! London! shouted the direction signs. London! . . .

Mrs. Thatcher's Britain is an uneasy kingdom, a kingdom of anomalies. It is poor but it is rich. It is weak but it is resilient. It is very clever in some ways, thick as mutton in others. It wins more Nobel Prizes per capita than any other nation, yet it can hardly keep its head above bankruptcy. It is socially at loggerheads with itself, but is united in a sentimental passion for the charade of monarchy. Even the sensations of a motorway drive like ours are muddled and puzzling, as we pass out of the poor wild mountains of Wales, where there are far more sheep than humans, so swiftly into the most thickly populated and intensely developed landscape in Europe. The road is bumpy and often interrupted by desultory road works, there being not enough money to maintain it properly; yet beside it the lovely manor houses stand serene as ever in their old walled gardens, the villages cluster cosily around, the cows are plump, the meadowlands green and rich.

ITINERARY: Day 1: Arrive Chamonix, Val d'Isere or Zermatt. Days 2-7: Adventure skiing. Day 8: Depart.

🎿   Class IV   **Medium**
January-April
Le Grand Ski   EU35

SWISS DAY HIKES

THE MAJESTIC GRANDEUR of the Swiss Alps need not be an unapproachable one. You can hike the high trails overlooking the quaint villages, breathe the frost-cleansed air, and feast your eyes on the panoramic vistas of peak and valley—while still enjoying the amenities of a 4-star hotel. Choose between spacious accommodations at resorts in Saas Fee beneath the icefalls of Switzerland, Pontresina with its invigorating climate and meadows and mountains of magnificence, and the world-famous village of Zermatt at the base of the monarch of the Alps, the Matterhorn. All hotels feature Old World flavor and savory dining, full breakfast and dinner included. Meanwhile the call of the wild lures us onto secret trails of easy-to-difficult hiking, depending on your own preference. Hikes range between 6 and 15 miles a day, and an optional climb of a 10,000-foot peak is included. Regardless of the difficulty of the hikes you choose, or of the village resort hotel where you enjoy each night's rest, you will experience the grandeur of the Alps and the tranquility of its valleys with fellow hiking enthusiasts from around the world.

ITINERARY: Day 1: Depart U.S. Day 2: Arrive Geneva or Zurich; transfer to hotel. Days 3-6: Hiking. Day 7: Transfer to Geneva/Zurich. Day 8: Return. *Note:* 16-day itineraries at two resorts possible.

🥾   Class I   **Medium**
June-September
Ryder/Walker Alpine Adventures   EU44

RIVERS OF SWITZERLAND

RIVER FEVER has spread to Europe! Three-, four- and seven-day whitewater packages are now possible on the finest streams Switzerland offers. These trips are designed for whitewater beginners, including a day of flatwater instruction, but this is a necessary prelude to the Class II-IV excitement that follows. The Aare is an easy 16 miles in the Bernese Alps with scenery to delight the eye; the Reuss is another easy one-day on Europe's most attractive stretch of river amidst huge rocks deposited by an ancient glacier. An eye-opener in the lower Alps, the Thur boasts wild and wooded pre-alpine valleys and moderate rapids, while the Upper Rhine roars through an imposing gorge with bizarre rock towers of white limestone. Other rivers

ITINERARY: Departures from Zurich for camping/rafting trips of 3, 4, or 7 days.
✈   Class III   **Moderate**
June-September
Eurotrek   EU38

LAKE GENEVA CYCLE

PADDLE ACTION   Pam Roberson

PICTURESQUE VILLAGES, historic cities and the backdrop of the perennially snow-capped Mont Blanc mark our path around the perimeter of Lake Geneva. Five days of easy cycling on Swiss-made 10-speeds take us through France and Switzerland, from Lausanne to Geneva and back, via Evian-les-Bains and Montreux to Lausanne. Our longest stage is just 31 miles (50km), an easy distance to cover at an unhurried pace. Combine superb alpine scenery and delicious regional cooking with accommodation in tourist-class hotels, spice with vineyards, Roman ruins, fishing villages and the fresh, clean air of mountains, and the ingredients concoct a mountain holiday par excellence. Cycle a circular route 'round Lake Geneva for a world-class feast of fun and fitness.

ITINERARY: Day 1: Lausanne. Day 2: To Nyon. Day 3: To Geneva. Day 4: To Evian-les-Bains. Day 5: To Montreux. Day 6: To Lausanne. Day 7: Return.
🚴   Class III   **Moderate**
May-September
Forum Travel   EU28

include the Sense's tricky rapids near Bern; the Simme's picture postcard view of Switzerland with two miles of uninterrupted whitewater to challenge the enthusiast; the deep V-shaped gorge of the Saane, concealing violent waters; the Moësa, Class III rapids in the Italian-flavored Ticino region, and the Inn, Europe's *pièce de résistance*, a three-day battle through narrow gorges and classic alpine scenery. Catch the fever and ride the first wave of riverine enthusiasm with the Swiss.

A BOAT FOR FRANCE! There is always a boat for France. Night and day for a thousand years or more, if you turn up at Dover you will find a boat for France. The English Channel here is the busiest waterway on earth, and in the high summer season there is a car-ferry out of Dover every ten minutes. Whenever I looked out of the Free Enterprise's *windows, as dusk fell over the sea, somewhere out there another ferry was stubbing its bows into the swell: and once I saw, a weird black shape half-hidden by flying spray, the whirring scudding passage of a hovercraft in the grey.*

The car was clamped below decks, towered over by the mighty juggernaut trucks, German, Dutch, French, British, Italian, even Bulgarian or Rumanian, which are the colorful familiars of modern Europe. Upstairs the ship had apparently been hijacked by demoniac schoolchildren. They clustered in mobs around the Space Invaders machine. They stormed the souvenir shop. They experimented with foreign currencies in the coffee machine. They tripped up passing stewards. They shouted hilarious insults at each other. They lurched in screaming phalanxes up and down stairs.

Some were British, some French, some Italian, some Finnish for all I know, but physically they were indistinguishable. As we approached the French coast they were marshalled into some sort of discipline by pimply bearded schoolteachers, and I left them standing there waiting for the gangplank to go down in a condition of sullen suppression, interspersed now and then with giggles and belches. Their teachers surveyed them with distaste. A few elderly tourists stood warily around their flanks. The ship docked with a bit of a bump, and faintly above the roar of the starting engines, from far below on the car deck, I heard their eldrich shrieks.

WESTERN

WHITEWATER FRANCE

NOT FAR FROM the fashionable beaches of St. Tropez, the southern Alps boast beautiful and impressive river valleys where untamed rivers watered by snow-covered mountains and the glaciers of Haute Savoie flow under warm Mediterranean skies. For nine days we navigate the waters of four rivers, beginning with the Argens, a new discovery that snakes through forested wilderness with surprises at every bend. The Durance is next, with powerful branching waters, eroded precipices, poplar-punctuated river meadows, and large shady campsites; then the Grand Canyon of the Verdon, with challenging whitewater and natural wonders reminiscent of its American namesake. Finally the Var, where a wide, unspoiled mountain valley leads into the Gorges de Daluis: deeply fissured red rock walls encasing raging whitewater and brief intervals of lush greenery. Pack your bags for a whitewater holiday, found on the rivers of southern France.

ITINERARY: Day 1: Zurich; by coach to France. Day 2: The Argens. Day 3: Hike the Grand Canyon of the Verdon. Days 4-5: The Verdon. Days 6-7: The Var. Day 8: Côte d'Azur. Day 9: To Zurich and return.

✈	Class III	**Moderate**
April-July		
Eurotrek	EU39	

FRANCE BY CANOE

THE INDIAN CANOE is not much used by its originators today, but it is still the ideal craft for river travel. It is roomy, with plenty of space for two paddlers and their gear, it doesn't capsize easily and it can tackle stretches of moderate whitewater comfortably. And it's at home almost everywhere—even in France, on the waters of the Ardèche and the Gardon. The Ardèche gorges are Europe's best-known stretch of wild river, with a lovely juxtaposition of wilderness scenery and man-made sights. Erosion has created fantastic sculptures over millions of years, including the Pont d'Arc, a 65-foot natural bridge over the river, or the Cirque de la Madeleine, where the river is trying to force its way through to create another span. Take your time to hear the nocturnal song of the nightingales, to savor the soft hiss of the river along its confining walls, and to admire the towering pinnacles of rock isolated high above the river by the last red rays of the evening sun. Then move onto the quieter but more isolated waters of the Gardon, and float beneath the famous Roman viaduct of Pont du Gard. You'll get to know the wild side of France in harmony with its countryside, its people and its hidden places. A 14-day canoeing holiday on the Loire, Dronne and Tarn is also available; see itinerary below.

ITINERARIES: *Ardeche Gorge:* Day 1: Zurich to the Ardèche. Days 2-3: Introduction to canoeing. Days 4-5: Ardèche gorge. Day 6: Rest day; optional excursions to Avignon and Nîmes. Days 7-8: The Gardon. Day 9: To Zurich. *Loire/Dronne:* Day 1: Basel, France. Days 2-4: The Loire. Days 5-6: Castle Tour. Days 7-10: The Dronne. Days 11-13: The Tarn Gorge. Day 14: En route. Day 15: Basel and return.

⚊⚊	Class III	**Moderate**
April-October		
Eurotrek	EU40	

STREETS OF FRANCE   Renée Kramer

HOUSEBOAT FRANCE

A CRISS-CROSS NETWORK of canals, some centuries old, intertwine across the face of France. Before traffic began to be transferred to the roads these canals were of major importance moving people and merchandise around the country. Canal barges still ply these waterways, far removed from the noise and bustle of auto traffic. In the south of France the Rhone canal is a delightful waterway that is ideal for a rediscovery of Europe. The canal flows to the most beautiful beaches of the Mediterranean as it meanders through tree-lined countryside, small towns and villages, and wine-growing regions. The climax of the trip is Carcassone, the medieval fortified city. A second barge journey is offered on the Saône, which served the trading centers of Burgundy in ancient times. On the Saône we make the gradual transition from north to south, with clearly demarcated climate and architectural changes. The famous wine-growing regions of Beaune, Mâcon and Beaujolais are strung along the river's course, and there's always plenty of time allowed for forays into the vineyards and villages. Our boats are 80-100 feet long, fully equipped barges accommodating as many as 20 guests; surf boards, canoes and bicycles are also aboard for the passengers' use. Float into the heart of France in traditional style—with a difference.

ITINERARY: Day 1: Zurich to embarkation point; begin float. Days 2-3: On the Saône *or* Days 2-6: One week Rhone canal trip; *or* Days 2-13: Two week Rhone canal trip. Day 4, 7, or 14: Return Zurich.

⚓ 🕸   Class I   **Moderate**
June-September
Eurotrek   EU41

SPANISH LINTEL   Karen Petersen

TOUR DE FRANCE

A CYCLIST'S PARADISE: A dense network of well-kept backroads which few cars travel, with villages, history and natural delights including fine food and, of necessity, wine. This dictionary

---

HIGH IN THE ROCKFACE above Chamonix, a huddle of brownish structures, a mesh of steel girdering, a great hole in the mountainside — the Mont Blanc Tunnel. The road winds heavily out of the Chamonix valley to reach it, and the effect is Wagnerian. The white massif looms operatically high above; the great trucks lumber around the horseshoe bends like so many giants; what dread enchantment, you may wonder, dwells within that hole, what fancy Grimm or Tolkien, what Worm of the Alps?

They tell me that when the tunnel was first opened migrating swallows used it to save themselves a flight over the mountains; and for people of the cold north, like me, it offers an almost symbolic transference to the warm south of our profoundest desires. No birds could fly through it now, for it is a tube heavy always with fumes and chemicals, but still as I climbed up to it that day I felt a bit like a swallow myself, genetically impelled toward the sun. The valley behind me, playing up to the allegory, was thick with grey mist, and the peaks above swirled with cloud: but at the other end of that noxious worm-hole, surely the sparkle awaited me.

And so, magically, it proved. The bare dank rock of the tunnel swept by me in the darkness, the illuminated signs kilometer by kilometer, the little sheltering alcoves with the emergency telephones, and presently far in the distance I saw a tiny circle of bright yellow light, hardly bigger than a pinhead. Like a bird I pursued it, and larger it grew, and brighter, and yellower, and presently it lost its outline, and came flooding into the tunnel to greet me, and dazzled me with its splendor — and it was the sunshine of Italy, on the warm side of the Alps!

definition applies to France, where we cycle as far as we wish each day, unencumbered by extra weight as a coach follows our treads. Burgundy, the Auvergne, the Dordogne and Perigord Noir, the Dronne and Perigord Vert, the Atlantic Coast and the castles of the Loire—our route cuts east to west across the center of France and back. We start in the vinous land of Beaune, Pommard, Volnay, Meursault and Nuit-St-Georges, with an obligatory visit to one of the wine cellars. Then the volcano-dominated landscape of Auvergne, with its houses built of dark volcanic stone and the Chaine des Puys, a chain of extinct cones. On to the cultural treasures of the Dordogne valley including countless castles and fortifications, medieval towns, and the prehistoric paintings at Les Eyzies' caves. Small towns, unspoiled countryside and rich menus highlight the next stage, leading to the piney woods and sandy dunes of the Atlantic. Then north and east to the Loire castles—Chenonceaux, Chambord and more. After two weeks of two-wheel wonders, we train back to Basel with a treasure chest of memories in tow.

ITINERARY: Day 1: Meet in Basel: train to Nuit-St-Georges; cycle. Day 2: Burgundy. Days 3-5: The Auvergne. Days 6-9: The Dordogne. Days 10-11: The Dronne. Days 12-13: The Atlantic Coast. Days 14-15: Loire castles. Day 16: To Basel.

🚴 ♓   Class III   **Moderate**
July-September
Eurotrek   EU45

SUNNY SIDE OF THE PYRENEES

SAY OLÉ TO THE SIGHTS and sounds of Spain on this tempting combination of the highest peaks in the Pyrenees and the frenzied "running of the bulls" in Pamplona. Sightseeing in Barcelona prepares us for the Old World atmosphere of the Pyrenees villages. We hike eastward past wildflower-dotted alpine meadows and crisp, clean lakes flanking the peaks of the Andorra region, including an optional ascent of Pic des Bareytes. We stay in the simple hotels of small mountain hamlets, and some nights mountain *refugios* provide the roof over our heads. Spanish hut attendants regale us with the local stories and satiate us with local cuisine. And that is far from all: three days of hiking in the National Park of Aigues Tortes, as lovely a mountain area as the world has to offer; the Festival of Montgarri, rarely witnessed by

outsiders; and the grand finale in Pamplona where we flee in the footsteps of Hemingway, complete our spicy Spanish stay. The carnival atmosphere of the running of the bulls contrasts sharply with the peace of the Pyrenees, but both extremes are guaranteed to leave a pleasant panorama of memories.

ITINERARY: Day 1: En route. Day 2: Barcelona. Day 3: To Andorra. Days 4-6: Andorra; optional Pic des Bareytes climb. Days 7-9: On trek. Day 10: Drive to Plaza de l'Artiga. Days 11-12: On trek. Days 13-15: Pamplona. Day 16: Return.

🚶 ♓   Class III   **Moderate**
June
Above the Clouds   EU29

BRITAIN

THE LAKE DISTRICT

FROM SHAP IN THE EAST to Ravenglass in the west, the Lake District of northwestern England echoes with the songs and sonnets inspired by its beauty. Haweswater, Thirlmere, Coniston, Derwent, Windermere — with names as ethereal as the country itself, this is a land of grand castles and quaint villages, sheer cliffs and quiet valleys, mountain screes and grassy moors. We hike for five days in this historic high country, squeeze in a trip by small steamer on

ENGLISH PONY   Eurotrek

Lake Ullswater, and ride on a miniature railway along the Eskdale Valley. Nights are spent in country inns and hotels where our gear is shuttled each day, so our limbs are light for day hikes through hill and dale. Shorter weekend walks on the Pilgrim's Way along the Dorset Coast, on the South Downs and other tracks can also be arranged. Experience the greatness of Britain, from its Roman fortresses to its everyday folk.

ITINERARY: Day 0: Arrive London. Day 1: Train to Oxenholme, begin walking. Days 2-6: Walking tours. Day 7: Train back to London; return.

⚐ ☕   Class II   **Moderate**
April, July
Escapade   EU14

SCANDINAVIA

TREKKING NORWAY

Mountains and fjords laced with waterfalls have made Norway justly famous. To appreciate its diversity, we travel by foot, railroad and ship to the coasts, to the mountains, and to the arctic tundra. From the Mediterranean climate of the western fjords to the harsh glaciers of Jotunheimen, we see it all, and by stay-

I ALWAYS FEEL HAPPY on the Dalmatian coast of Yugoslavia. It suits me. I like its mean between simplicity and sophistication, between communism and capitalism, between the local and the national. I like to go into a supermarket and find it moderately, temperately stocked, without that vulgar profusion of choice which makes the modern Western store seen a little obscene to the traveler, without the boorish austerity of your whole-hog Soviet Grocer No. 4. I like the sense of wry comradeship which, with an almost universal flashing of lights and comical gestures, warns you that there is a speed trap down the road. I like the ships which are always in sight, fishing boats loitering among the green islets, tall white ferry-streamers chugging into port, tankers in dry docks up unexpected creeks, motor torpedo-boats in grey clusters at their moorings, hydrofoils flashing off for Venice — ships always and everywhere along that incomparable coast, pervading every image and crossing every vista.

It is the sexiest of coasts, the most virile, the lustiest. Bold are its men, brave its women, doggedly its children hold back their tears; Tito would be proud of them still. I drove over from Split one day to buy a bottle of black wine from a country homestead, and wonderfully earthy and organic was the domestic hierarchy I discovered inside the house: a brawny stubbly farmer-husband, a tough buxom wife, a one-eyed cat, a sprightly terrier, and in a steamy scullery behind the kitchen, the Wine-Mother herself in the fullness of her years, stirring and tasting and stirring again — "Good health, good luck," cried these amiable bucolics as they filled my glass, and bonk, when I returned to the car I tripped on a stick, and went back to town dripping thick black country wine all over the bonnet, as though I had been baptized by the gods of revelry.

ing in huts and hotels we make this an ideal program for the less rugged. Our first three days are spent out walking through the Hardangervidda and the wildly romantic Aurland. Then we bus and train to the coast for an unforgettable cruise through Sogne fjord, where superb contrasts of land and sea sear into our souls. Mt. Fannaraken, Lake Bygden and a variety of glaciers and peaks enrich our hours on foot in the Jotunheimen, "home of the giants." Finally north by ship, past the Seven Sisters waterfalls and on to Trondheim, to end a mythic journey to the northwestern edge of Europe.

ITINERARY: Day 1: Oslo. Days 2-4: Hiking. Day 5: Bergen. Day 6: Sogne fjord. Days 7-9: On trek in Jotunheimen. Day 10: Lom. Day 11: Hellesylt. Day 12: On ferry. Day 13: Trondheim. Day 14: Oslo and return.

🚢 🚶 🚙   Class II   **Moderate**
July-August
Eurotrek   EU37

GREEK DANCE   Pam Roberson

SOUTHERN

THE MOUNTAINS OF GREECE

GREAT LIMESTONE CRAGS and the chasms of the Pindos Mountains march to the sea from the northwest corner of Greece, creating a buffer that has isolated the centuries from this region. Little has changed here since King Phillip of Macedonia, and even the tourist industry has ignored the area and left it peacefully alone. The landscape is awe-inspiring; peaks cluster here, Smolkas and Gamila and Vasslitsa scalloping the 2500 meter range; sheer cliffs stretch thousands of feet to the bottom of massive gorges; beech and fir blanket the hills. Although we stay in inns and huts, we carry our own gear into the wild heights, visiting neat villages surrounded by terraced hillsides, glimpsing the graceful grecian goats, and ascending to the summits if our enthusiasms so carry us. Then take it easy — the soft coast at Parge waits to soothe your weary legs, the Mediterranean sun to warm your tired bones.

ITINERARY: Day 1: Arrive in Corfu, ferry and bus to Ioannina. Day 2: Ioannina. Days 3-11: Mountain hiking. Day 12: Ioannina. Days 13-14: Parga. Day 15: Return.

🚶 🏔   Class III   **Moderate**
June-September
Exodus   EU25

CORSICA TREK

THE CORSICAN HINTERLAND boasts hidden marvels reachable only on foot: gentle grazing land where isolated alpine dairies offer the hiker the chance to fortify himself with fresh milk and goat's cheese; crystal clear streams and distant vistas of peaks and forest that bring a sigh of surprise after the rocky coastline of the island; and the wild mountains themselves, stony spine of the island. The trek begins in fragrant woods, over pleasant elevated plateaus laced with little streams and lakes, and past an array of alpine inns. As the elevation increases, the trails narrow and steepen; a rest day is spent in the pools and waterfalls of Manganello gorge, a refreshing interlude before our ascent of Mont d'Oro (2390m) and its magnificent overview of the island. We then descend to the coast for three days of seaside diversions, resting our weary limbs in preparation for our trek in the Bavella Range. Curious statue-like rock formations, oak forests, the slopes of Monte Incudine, vegetation fragrant with thyme, and small Corsican villages under Mediterranean skies enliven our trek, after which we relax a night on the Corsican coast.

ITINERARY: Day 1: Depart Zurich to Bastia. Day 2: Bastia to trek point. Days 3-6: Trekking central highlands. Days 7-9: At the coast. Days 10-12: Trekking the Bavellas. Day 13: Bastia to La Spezia or Livorno. Day 14: Return to Zurich.

🚶 🐟   Class III   **Moderate**
June-October
Eurotrek   EU36

TARA RIVER

THE MONTENEGRIN HINTERLAND of Yugoslavia is rugged mountain country where the Tara carves its steep canyon through the Dinaric Alps. Clear water spills over dozens of exciting rapids, and small farms and shepherd villages complement the wildness of this rare corner of Europe. But first the scenery of the quiet Drina River and the wilderness of Durmitor National Park compete to introduce marvelous Montenegro. Only Yugoslavia could offer a package like this, with the best of a Europe no longer rich in wilderness: quiet countryside, a national park, four days on the rapids of the trackless Tara Gorge, and finally the more traditional flavors of the Atlantic Coast. No trip to Eastern Europe is over without seeing Dubrovnik, the Pearl of the Adriatic, relaxing on its beaches and immersing in the Old World culture of Yugoslavia.

ITINERARY: Days 1-3: Zurich to Sarajevo by coach. Day 4: Rafting the Drina. Day 5: Durmitor National Park. Days 6-9: The Tara. Days 10-12: Adriatic Coast and Dubrovnik. Days 13-14: To Zurich. (Also available with flights to/from Zurich, leaving two days later and returning one day earlier.)

✈ ⛵   Class III   **Moderate**
June-September
Eurotrek   EU12

TRANSYLVANIAN ALPS

OF ALL THE MOUNTAINS in Europe, none are more shrouded in mystery than the Translyvanian Alps. The Bran Castle, home of Dracula, drapes an unearthly aura over the rugged Romanian terrain of misted lakes and barely believable wildlife. We take two weeks to traverse the entire length of these Alps (traveling only by daylight), highlighted by an easy ascent of Mt. Moldoveanu (2543m), highest in Romania. Accommodations will be in selected mountain chalets, where the cuisine reeks of the protective "stinking rose," garlic. The July departure features the annual folk festival at Durau, and two days of trekking in the Ceahlu Mountains, while on the October trip we spend the full moon at Dracula's castle. Anything can happen in Transylvania, so be prepared for the experiences of this lifetime — or the one beyond.

ITINERARY: Day 1: Bucharest. Day 2: To Busteni; begin trek. Days 3-14: On trek. Days 15-16: Sibiu. Days 17-19: Curau folk festival (July); or Bran Castle (September). Days 20-21: Bucharest. Day 22: Return. *Note:* Shorter 17-day itinerary also available.

🚶 ☕   Class III   **Moderate**
July-September
Above the Clouds   EU23

CYCLING EASTERN EUROPE

EVERYDAY LIFE BEHIND the Iron Curtain receives little attention here in the United States. What do the people there do, talk about by day and night, say in the streets or over a beer? What does a Slovak village look like? How does the goulash taste in Hungary? What secrets are waiting to be discovered in Transylvania? We follow up on these questions by avoiding the familiar tourist routes and making for the countryside. Using a comfortable passenger coach to cover the long distances, and cycles to venture off at each stop, we make contact with everyday life in the East. A circular route traces a path from Vienna across Czechoslovakia into the Tokay region of Hungary, across the Carpathian mountains into Rumania and Transylvania, and even to Dracula's castle. We swing back to Budapest and the sophisticated south of

---

"BACK AGAIN," SAID THE MAGNIFICO at the café on the road into the Black Mountains, on the last ridge before Cetinje and the heart of Montenegro. We had met before, you see. He is always there, it seems, summer or winter, like a major-domo of these uplands, or a Chief of Protocol. He wears black breeches, and a wide belt like a cummerbund, and he stands about seven feet tall, and speaks in a basso profondo, and tosses slivovic back like lime juice, and is in fact in all respects the very model of a modern Montenegrin.

With this splendid fellow at my side, kneading his moustaches, I sat down on the bench outside the café, and looked back, far down the corkscrew Kotor road, far up the glittering Dalmatian coast, along the way I had come. I had journeyed from one extremity to another, over the shifting and anxious face of western Europe — a continent betwixt and between these days, a continent out of gear perhaps, rickety Britain with its fairy fantasies, young France, half macho, half poet-and-peasant, Switzerland of the fanatic roller-skaters, Italy of the sham horse and the real live monks, Yugoslavia with its lid tippling and clanking, like a kettle on the boil.

"Come far?" inquired the Montenegrin, lighting a short cigar. Not so far, I thought; but over the ridge before us, wrapped in their Godless silence, stood the mountains of Albania. ▲

Hungary, along the Danube and back to Vienna. Modern cities, historic castles, gentle countryside, collective factories, and vibrant traditions: the contrasts are everywhere as we delve deep into the lives of the real people of Eastern Europe.

ITINERARY: Day 1: Zurich to Vienna. Day 2: Coach to Czechoslovakia. Days 3-5: Slovak cycling. Days 6-8: Cycling the Hungarian Puszta. Day 9: En route. Days 10-13: Cycling Rumania. Day 14: Coach to Hungary. **Day 15: Cycling on the Theiss.** Days 16-17: Budapest. Days 18-19: The Danube. Days 20-21: Return by rail to Zurich.

⚙ 🚙 ⛴   Class III   **Moderate**
July-August
Eurotrek   EU43

YUGOSLAVIA NORTH AND SOUTH

THE MOST DIVERSE COUNTRY in Europe, Yugoslavia crowds East and West into its borders with a cluster of climates, cultures and terrains. We explore it in depth, from its highest peaks to the fabled Adriatic coast, trekking south from the Austrian border into the Kamnik and Julian alps. Although we spend our nights in mountain huts, our route takes us to the summits of mounts Grintovec and Triglav, which crown the two ranges. Then down to the sea we go, to explore the Adriatic coast—the walled city of Dubrovnik, the spectacular bays, the languid beaches, the surrounding mountains and the famous play of light and shade. As a final kicker, we become the first group ever to trek through the North Albanian Alps, where the clothing, architecture and faces display the Turkish influence of earlier rulers. A superior three-dimensional view of one of Europe's prize countries.

ITINERARY: Day 1: Zagreb. Day 2: Kravec and begin trek. Days 3-12: On trek. Day 13: Ljubljana. Day 14: Skopje. Day 15: Lake Ohrid. Day 16: Tetova. Days 17-20: North Albanian Alps. Day 21: Pec. Day 22: Kotor. Day 23: Dubrovnik. Day 24: Evening return to Zagreb. Day 25: Return.

🚶 🚙 ⛴   Class IV   **Medium**
July
Above the Clouds   EU24

GREEK ISLANDS SAIL

ISLAND-HOPPING BY YACHT in the Cyclades and Ionian islands is a dream shared by sailors, sun-seekers, swimmers and culture enthusiasts. A classic combination of good sailing, bathing in quiet bays, classical and modern Greece

add up to a full fix of fun. The sailing areas of the Ionians and Cyclades are famous for good wind conditions, warm southern climate and typical Greek hospitality. We have adapted our cruise schedule to allow for wind conditions and your wishes, concentrating on the Cyclades (Milos, Paros, Naxos, Santorini and many lesser-known isles) before and after the main season, and sailing the more-sheltered Ionian Islands (Kerkira, Lefkada, Ithaki, Kefalonia and Zakinthos) in the summer when the stormy *meltemi* wind blows its hardest. Our yachts are 35 ft. and 38 ft. in length, fully equipped for the cruise, with just 6-8 passengers per boat. Greek skippers handle the navigation; you can help out with the sailing and everyday tasks, though prior sailing is not necessary. Just bring your appetite for adventure and enjoy the fruits of the sun and the sea on a Mediterranean idyll.

ITINERARY: Day 1: Fly Zurich to embarkation point. Days 2-12: Sailing. Day 13: Return Zurich by air (flights included).

⛵   Class II   **Medium**
May-October
Eurotrek   EU42

CRUISE CUISINE   Liz Hymans

OCEANIA

NEW GUINEA COLOR   Judy Gordon

THE HIGH VALLEY

by *Kenneth E. Read*

*I*n 1944 I was living in a village called Tofmora in the Upper Markham Valley in New Guinea. I was a member of the Australian armed forces but was engaged in work that is also my civilian occupation, social anthropology. . . . The research involved gathering information on native reactions to the war and the Japanese occupation, a charge that necessitated a thorough enquiry into most aspects of the people's lives. Few members of my profession have been so poorly equipped for field research. Only the barest minimum of supplies necessary to support me and to further my work was available: writing materials, the normal issue of army clothing, two cases of canned corned beef, some flour, hard biscuits, and a small chest, or caddy, or trade tobacco. . . When I ran out of food, I existed for three months on whatever the villagers were willing to give me, for by then there was no money to buy the things I needed. Yet this was one of the happiest periods of my life.

PAPUA NEW GUINEA

KOKODA TRAIL

ONE OF THE WORLD'S GREAT walks was the scene of prolonged and bloody encounters between Allied forces and the Japanese Army just 40 years ago. Now the jungle has returned, concealing untold amounts of war relics, surrounding the warm villages of the Kaoiri tribes, bearing fresh fruit hanging over the cool pools of mountain streams. The Kokoda Trail winds 140 kilometers across the knife-edged ridges of the Owen Stanley Range in southwest Papua New Guinea, through deep jungle highlands surrounding Mt. Victoria (4076m, 13,363 ft.). Our ten day trek allows time enough to pursue our individual interests, such as photography, lolling in the mountain pools, searching for war relics, or bird and butterfly watching in the rain forest. At the end of each day, there are welcome smiles, fresh fruit and the comfortable houses of the Kaoiri to rest in, and wonder at how different it has all become.

ITINERARY: Day 1: Arrival in Port Moresby. Day 2: Port Moresby. Day 3: To Kokoda and begin trek. Days 4-13: On trek. Day 14: Port Moresby and return.

🚶 🥚 Class IV **Moderate**
Year-round
Pacific Expeditions OC53

IN RETROSPECT IT IS POSSIBLE to distinguish many reasons why the experience was so rewarding, though when living through it there was no time to examine my reactions, nor to ask myself why I seemed to move so effortlessly with the rhythm of the days rather than against them. I was fortunate in the physical location of the place where I had chosen to live. The valley of the Markham River runs inland from the Huon Gulf in a northwesterly direction; it is a broad expanse of open country flanked on either side by uninterrupted ranges, whose uppermost heights are veiled perpetually in clouds. . . .

The paths connecting inhabited sites ran through dense plantings of coconut palms whose fronds met overhead to form a vaulted ceiling thirty to fifty feet above the ground. Light penetrated only fitfully through this gently moving screen; even at midday the village was cool and shadowed, filled with a silence that seemed to ignore the crushing intensity of the sun vibrating in the open valley. Beyond the palms, groves of banana trees, a lighter more translucent green, encroached upon ochre-colored hills patched with scattered gardens of sweet potatoes, yams, and taro. These in turn gave way to tier upon receding tier of jungle-covered heights. The stream Burubward rose inside this mass of tangled vegetation, and, slipping through the folds of the hills, approached within two hundred yards of the village . . .

Returning from a day's walk in the ranges, tired, my skin inflamed and stiff from the sun, I often paused here to bathe my feet in the water. Gradually, my mind and body began to relax; and with the tension gone, the landscape rose toward me with the heart-catching loveliness of a distant cry. I was reminded of childhood times at the seaside when, standing on a bare reef, I had looked down into a pool and marveled at the gradations of color, the shades of jade, emerald, and cobalt; the miniature forests, lifting to the ocean's pulse; and the valleys of sand held in nets of suffused light. When I rose to continue my journey home the mood would not leave me. The day closed over my head as I began the descent, and thereafter I progressed through an unreal world where the ochre colors of grasslands and the varying greens of jungle and plantations flowed past me in gentle succession. . . .

SEAS AND SUMMITS

COMBINE THE GRANDEUR of Papua New Guinea's highest peak with an idyll on a tropical island, throw in a rafting trip on the Waghi River, and you have a potpourri of Papua that will provide the stuff of anecdote and amazement for years to come. We begin with a drive through the spectacular Gembogl Gorge to the Chimbu district, visiting native villages along the way. Then we tread through successive forests of tree ferns, beech and oak, and finally alpine meadows to the base of Mt. Wilhelm, at 4359 meters the country's highest mountain. As we climb to its summit, we gauge our altitude by the miles of still impenetrable wild that spreads in purple ridges below us. Back at more hospitable elevations, we fly to Madang's beautiful harbor, where a boat takes us to Manam Island off the north coast. A steaming volcano pins the island to the ocean floor, amid a world of colorful tropical fish, beautiful beaches and festive locals.

ITINERARY: Day 1: Port Moresby. Days 2-6: Mt. Wilhelm trek. Day 7: Waghi River. Day 8: Mt. Hagen. Day 9: Madang. Days 10-12: Manam Island. Day 13: Madang. Day 14: Port Moresby. Day 15: Return.

Class III   **Moderate**
Year-round
Pacific Expeditions   OC10

PAPUA PANORAMA

THE ULTIMATE NON-TREKKING adventure in Papua New Guinea highlights the vibrant art and culture of the Sepik River and the Highlands, both in deluxe style. From a fine hotel in the coastal city of Madang, we cruise in the first-class comfort of the *Melanesian Explorer* along the coast and up the Sepik River, with frequent village excursions to look over the famous arts of this culturally rich and diverse region. We top off the cruise with two nights at the Karawari Lodge, a truly luxurious property where some of the finest regional art and beautiful examples of the sweeping *Haus tamburan* architectural style have been gathered. Then by charter to the Highlands, where the eye-delighting spectacle of a lively *sing-sing* is but a prelude to a day of rafting through the Waghi Gorge, where birds of paradise fly amidst steep-walled scenery. A better exposure to the incredible profusion of life in New Guinea could not be imagined.

ITINERARY: Day 1: Port Moresby. Day 2: Madang. Days 3-6: Sepik River cruise. Days 7-8: Karawari Lodge. Days 9-10: Mt. Hagen, Tribal Tops. Day 11: Waghi River rafting. Day 12: To Port Moresby. Day 13: Return.

Class I   **Premium**
Year-round
Pacific Expeditions   OC52

PROM NIGHT, NEW GUINEA   Richard Bangs

villages, sing in the showers of tributary waterfalls, and pluck coconuts at the river's edge. The Watut is offered by itself or in combination with other aspects of the fascinating island.

ITINERARY: Day 1: Lae to river. Days 2-5: Watut. Day 6: End river in Lae.

⚞ ⚟ ⚙   Class III   **Premium**
April-November
Tribal Tops   OC1

WATUT RIVER

THE WILDEST RIVER RUN in the Pacific, brimming with bodacious rapids and rich in history and culture, the Watut drains the razorback peaks of central New Guinea. It begins with a deceptively hushed glide through gold country, then explodes into the Kuper Mountains, roaring through 100 major rapids for a water rodeo wrapped in glistening jungle. We visit native

SEPIK RIVER SAFARI

NEW GUINEA IS A RICH and raucous land, blessed with a blazing color-quilt of cultural enclaves. It is a prolific breeding ground of artistic expression, most clearly evidenced along the Sepik River and in the highlands. For art collectors, appreciators and admirers, we delve deep into the Upper Sepik region and its renowned wood carvings. We venture upriver in dugout canoes, visit the handcrafters of the Sepik in their homes and stay in native villages. An adventure miles from the mainstream of modern life.

ITINERARY: Day 1: Port Moresby to Wewak, PNG. Day 2: Murik Lake. Days 3-7: Sepik River safari. Day 8: Wewak. Day 9: To Port Moresby and return.

⚞ ⚟ ⚙   Class II   **Premium**
Year-round
Tribal Tops   OC6

THE FIRST FEW DAYS AT TOFMORA were among the most difficult I have faced, and even after several months I was often filled with despair. But gradually I began to respond to the villagers as individuals. It is not possible to say when this first occurred (perhaps when I found myself sitting with a man in the evening and realized that I had sought him simply for companionship and not because I wanted information), but the discovery has remained one of the most rewarding in my life.

I realize now that it is one of the benefits of my profession to experience this response to persons whose outlook and background could hardly be more dissimilar from my own. I can remember many of the villagers better than friends of only a short time ago; it is not necessary to try to recall their names. I was as much at ease with some of them as I have been with only a few other people. Yet I was not, and could never be one of them. Even in their midst, my life was entirely different from theirs, and I could not expect them to appreciate many of the things that concerned me deeply. Looking down on the village from one of the gardens, I visualized it in an aesthetic convention wholly foreign to the man who stood beside me with his arm around my shoulders; and though I might learn to see with his eyes, it was unlikely that he would ever see with mine. Yet this did not make the weight of his arm any less companionable; we did not have to be born in the same environment to like each other . . .

Looking back now, I believe I was permanently elated most of the time I was there. At least this is the only name I can give to a state of mind in which certainty in my own abilities and discovery of myself joined with a compassion for others and a gratitude for the lessons in acceptance that they taught me.

THE WAGHI RIVER

DEEP IN THE JUNGLES of the New Guinea highlands, a waterfall-laced gorge, resounding with the calls of birds of paradise, remained unknown into the 1980s. Then came Sobek: on its 1983 first descent of the Waghi River—filmed by the BBC for their "Great River Journeys" series—the bounteous beauties of the gorge were revealed to all. Tree ferns leaned over the limestone canyon; whitewater raced between the eroded walls like a freight-train to Eden; the refreshing spray of waterfalls leavened the air with good vibrations. This one-day trip is now available to all who venture into the culturally-rich highlands near Goroka, and begins at the comfortable Tribal Tops Lodge. For the casual visitor to New Guinea, or the explorer seeking respite from the trials of discovery, the Waghi River promises a taste of paradise.

ITINERARY: One-day trips meet at Goroka in the morning and return in the afternoon.

✈ 🛶   Class II   **Moderate**
April-October
Tribal Tops   OC55

TAGARI OVERLAND

EXPERIENCE THE WILDS of New Guinea, where jagged limestone outcroppings rise white and surreal, underground rivers bubble, and Simbu tribesmen don colorful and intricate headdresses woven from the plumage of the bird of paradise. From the comfort of a totally contained four-wheel drive vehicle, we wend our way over 9,000-foot mountain passes surrounded by cloud-silent forests, between upthrusts of jagged limestone through a karst land formation riddled with caves, sinkholes and subterranean rivers. Travel on through river valleys shadowed by mountains, and skim across a patchwork quilt of tea and coffee plantations. Evenings are spent at carefully selected inns or modern camping facilities. Papua New Guinea is alive with spectacle, color and excitement. Come and join the celebration!

ITINERARY: Day 1: Port Moresby to Goroka. Day 2: Keglsugl. Day 3: Tribal Tops. Day 4: Jimi. Day 5: Mt. Hagen. Day 6: Pangia. Days 7-8: Tari. Day 9: Mt. Hagen. Day 10: Port Moresby and return.

🚙 🛶   Class II   **Premium**
Year-round
Tribal Tops   OC52

HIGHLANDS HIGHLIGHTS

NATURE'S SPECTACLE—whitewater careering through stark rock gorges, bright orchids and darting butterflies splashed against the dark tropical forest—can be matched only by the splendid and unique artistry of man in the New Guinea highlands. We dance with the eerie mudmen of Asaro and attend the riotous festival known as the *sing-sing*, visit thatched villages sandwiched between cliffs ribboned with waterfalls, and catch a rare glimpse of the elusive and unforgettable bird of paradise at Baiyer River Sanctuary. This trip combines the cultural diversity of Papua New Guinea's rugged central mountains with a safe but exhilarating day on the scenic Waghi River.

ITINERARY: Day 1: Mt. Hagen. Day 2: Wabag. Day 3: Baiyer River Sanctuary. Day 4: Waghi River rafting. Day 5: Waghi Valley. Day 6: Mt. Wilhelm and Pari caves. Day 7: Port Moresby.

🛶 🛶 ✈   Class I   **Premium**
Year-round
Tribal Tops   OC4

BODY ENGLISH   Michael Nichols

SOLEMN HIGHLANDER   Jim Slade

YET MY MIND WAS NOT ALWAYS on my work and the people around me. Sometimes in the afternoon, wanting to be alone for a while, I left my house to walk a short distance into the grasslands. As I passed from the palm grove to the open country, the light struck my face a visible blow, forcing me to close my eyes. Brought to a sudden stop, I was overcome by a spinning darkness. When I was again able to look, the great valley seemed to billow into the distance like a russet sea breaking against the escarpment of the southern chain of mountains. It was the most dramatic part of the territory, more even than the green silence of the jungle, where the infrequent cry of a bird exploded like an arrow in the stillness. In that bowl of pulsing light I was more keenly aware of the whole country, second in size only to Greenland among the world's islands, and of the character of the life within it. The multiplicity of peoples, divided by language, belief, and custom, are fastened in remote regions whose only entrance passes through the clouds, or they spend their days in houses built above the sea, where the air is heavy with the smell of kelp and where a child's first sight of the world is the moving brightness of watery reflections on thatched roof and plaited walls. The valley also recalled the enmities and suspicions that further separated these groups from one another; for it was here, not so very long ago, that men from Tofmora and its sister settlements set out to raid and kill, moving downwind through tall grasses that concealed their approach from their victim.

EXPLORATORY TREK

PAPUA NEW GUINEA OFFERS more exploratory trekking than just about anywhere else in the world. It truly had, until recently, blank places on the map, marked "Unknown." Our exploratory expeditions trek into regions few outsiders have ever penetrated, offering pristine culture, wildlife, and scenery for the first group of commercial trekkers. One planned route is into the hidden villages of the Biami tribe, first contacted by Europeans just 15 years ago, where the appearance of white-skinned people is still a sensational event. The Biami are small, almost Pygmy-like in stature, and like the Pygmies they are seldom seen without the bows and arrows of their hunting economy. Farther into the Southern Highlands, the so-called "Tari Wigmen" are found, so named for their spectacular headdresses; we will try to join them for a real *sing-sing*, the traditional native festival as practiced here far from the tourist centers of Papua New Guinea's more visited areas. This is a tough and uncertain trek, for those in top physical and mental condition, able and willing to take a real expedition into one of the most primitive areas of the world. If that describes you, this is your ideal adventure.

ITINERARY: Day 1: Port Moresby. Day 2: Nomad, Western Province. Days 3-11: On trek. Day 12: Tari. Day 13: Port Moresby. Day 14: Return.

⚕ ⛺ 🐚   Class IV   **Medium**
June
Pacific Expeditions   OC50

LOST WORLD EXPEDITION

NATURE DOES NOTHING by halves on the rugged island of New Guinea, and we take full advantage of its exuberance on this trek through its most remote environs. We depart Mt. Hagen along New Guinea's mountain spine and follow the path of a fast-descending river through foothills and coastal plains until we reach the Bismarck Sea. From the spectacle of jagged mountains tearing their cloudy veil to white sands and azure water, our trek encompasses the spectacular variety of New Guinea's sights. But nature's is not the only artistry we encounter. Little-known Kunga and Bonmaku villages line our route through the Bismarck Range. With pride and care born of long tradition, many of the people we meet adorn themselves with fascinating arrangements of feathers, beads and natural dyes. Closer to the coast and its low-lying rivers, the people have created an array of sculpture and paintings that is bewildering in its complexity, artistic off-spring of a tribal world riotous in its expression. An ideal way to explore an island of captivating contrasts.

ITINERARY: Day 1: Fly Port Moresby to Mt. Hagen. Days 2-15: Trek Mt. Hagen to Wewak. Day 16: Wewak. Day 17: Wewak to Port Moresby.

⚕ ⛺ 🐚   Class IV   **Premium**
Year-round
Tribal Tops   OC57

SOUTHERN HIGHLANDS

STRAIGHT FROM THE HEART of the highlands to the tropical forests that surround Lake Kutubu, we will see, feel and taste the village life of the Huli and Foi cultures on this 12-day adventure. Each is distinguished by clothing styles, language, traditions and economy, yet both share the essential qualities of warmth and curiosity, and our trek among them will earn us many new friends and a portfolio of portraits. Sleep in the close, thatched huts of the villagers, and share their native cuisine of *mumu*, stone-cooked vegetables; voyage to a tropical island in the middle of Lake Kutubu in dugout canoes; and trek along the narrow pathways that serve as highways of trade. Our experience of village life extends even to Foi burial sites, where the skulls and bones of the dead are arranged geometrically on ledges overlooking the lake's expanse. Highlands wildlife is witnessed too, including the courting display of the handsome yellow and black bird of paradise that in the midst of his dance reveals a stunning spray of long red feathers. An invigorating, fulfilling and certainly different trek in the land that time forgot.

ITINERARY: Day 1: Port Moresby. Days 2-3: Huli villages. Days 4-6: Trek, ending in Tari. Day 7: Fly to Pimaga. Days 8-11: Day trips on Lake Kutubu. Day 12: Fly to Mendi. Day 13: Return to Port Moresby.

⚕ ⛺ 🐚   Class III   **Medium**
April-October
Pacific Expeditions   OC9

SOUTH PACIFIC

FIJI HIGHLANDS AND ISLANDS

POLYMORPHOUS POLYNESIA PRESENTS a cornucopia of color, myth, spirit and ceremony, nowhere better expressed than on the island of Fiji. We spend two weeks trekking into the interior of the main island, visit coconut-draped Motoriki and kick around a couple of nights in Fiji's capital of Suva. The pace is slow as we trek 40 kilometers between rocky hills, across upland grass meadows, through thick forests and across refreshing mountain streams, bound for the native villages scattered through the highlands. There we stay in thatched-roof houses, enjoying sumptuous meals of tropical fruit, wild pig, taro, yams, tapioca (as it was meant to be made!) and freshly caught fish. Then, over a large communal bowl of *yanggona,* we listen to many legends of Old Fiji—of tribal fighting and cannibalism, of spirits who inhabit the hills, of lovers who pursue each other to the underworld. Snorkeling, sunning, fishing and otherwise unwinding in Motoriki flesh out your fondest Fijian fantasy.

ITINERARY: Day 1: Nadi. Days 2-8: On Fiji trek. Day 9: Lautoka. Days 10-12: Motoriki. Day 13: Suva. Day 14: Nadi and return.

☻ ☙ 木   Class III   **Moderate**

May-October
Australian Himalayan Expeditions   OC24

POLYNESIA AND TONGA

ROMANCE, ADVENTURE and beauty are the beacons that call the traveler to the South Pacific. And nowhere do these three lights shine more brightly than on Tonga, the Friendly Island. Seven days of sailing aboard 44-foot (13-meter) sloops amongst the small islands of the Vava'u group, and a few days in Polynesia's only remaining kingdom exploring the palace of its monarchy, add up to two weeks of heaven on earth. Our South Pacific sojourn begins with arrival in Honolulu, where a casual evening of introduction prepares us for the pleasures of Polynesia. Then we wing across the broad blue to Pago Pago for two days and nights of hiking across the rolling hills and teeming forests of Samoa, or diving the polychromatic reefs in search of incandescent fish or life-encrusted wrecks. In Tonga, we visit the sights of the Kingdom before boarding our sloops for a full week of solitary pleasures in the company of friends. Riding the winds between isolated, reef-rimmed islands, we anchor off untouched coves, scuba or skin-dive on virgin reefs, fish for exotic fillets and engage in adventure travel's major pastime: the active pursuit of relaxation. If tropical treats like dazzling reefs, swaying palms and southern nights are your thing, then Tonga is your place.

ITINERARY: Day 1: Fly Honolulu to Tonga. Day 2: Nukualofa. Day 3: Vava'u. Days 4-10: Sailing. Days 11-12: Vava'u. Day 13: Return.

▲ ☻ ⚓   Class II   **Medium**

November
Pacific Quest   OC47

BUT THE QUALITY OF LIGHT was the most remarkable ingredient of all. It was difficult to tell where it came from. Every feature of the landscape seemed to be its own source of brightness, possessed of such dazzling clarity that I could not trust my judgment to the usual yardstick of reality. How far was it to the summit of the mountains in the south, where each tree was precisely etched against the sky? The gardens clinging to slopes below looked close enough to dip my hands into the shadows under their vines; and where a stream flowed between adjacent ridges, I could see the water shedding itself in pewter-colored fragments on the dry stones that rose above its surface.

I was reminded of a sixteenth-century painting in which every element of a landscape is rendered with careful attention to detail and perspective, where the eye follows a road through wayside flowers, past fields of harvesters and peaks crowned with castles, across a ford where travelers rest in the shade, through all of fifty miles to mountain slopes where armies battle and pennants toss like flocks of enameled birds in the forests. In the compass of a small canvas a whole world is displayed so completely that as it transcends reality it also endows the viewer with abilities he does not ordinarily possess, making of him an omnipotent observer who encompasses in a single glance the whole design of a way of life.

PARADISE   Liz Hymans

SOLOMON ISLANDS

A RARE CHANCE TO EXPLORE the Louisiade Archipelago off the eastern tip of New Guinea, one of the world's richest culture areas, awaits the wind-blown adventurer. We travel from white sands to jungle trails, over the waves and by our whim, and experience the lengendary hospitality of the South Seas at its best. This is the land of Malinowski and Mead, a land where pigs have greater value than cash, where outriggers ply the waters in an ancient "kula-ring" among the islands, where a cult grew up over the cargo of a fallen airship, where an age-old life-style still holds the modern world at bay. Though our main means of transportation are the outriggers so familiar with the islands, we also trek into the interiors of these tropical wonderlands. Here the lush jungles teem with multi-colored parrots, clear streams gush forth from underground sources, idyllic freshwater pools invite the swimmer into cooling soaks, and thatched roof villages thrive beside yards of yams and pens of pigs. This expedition is the first of its kind, not previously offered to the amateur anthropologist or the sailing scholar. Seize the time to see the Solomons, before time catches up with them!

ITINERARY: Day 1: Port Moresby. Day 2: Flight to Louisiade Archipelago; begin sailing. Days 3-12: Sailing and trekking. Day 13: Port Moresby. Day 14: Return.

⛰ 🏕 🚶   Class III   **Medium**
Year-round
Pacific Expeditions   OC42

NEW ZEALAND

NEW ZEALAND MOUNTAINEERING

THERE'S ROOM AT THE TOP even for newcomers to the alpine sports. This complete instruction program will give you the foundation upon which to build the technical skills you'll need for the most rugged of mountaineering exploits. Close instruction by New Zealand's finest mountain guides (with a guide/ student ratio of no more that 1 to 5) will teach the basics and the fine points of glacier travel, roped traverses, belaying, self-arrest, ice and rock climbing, knots, and ice cave building. The course will take place in the vicinity of New Zealand's grandest peaks: mounts Cook, Tasman and Sefton, the 3500-meter summits of the South Island. By the end of the two-week course, you will have graduated from the same elevated classrooms where Edmund Hillary learned the skills that took him to the world's highest peak. Why not you?

ITINERARY: Day 1: Christchurch. Day 2: Mt. Cook. Days 3-13: Climbing course. Day 14: Bus Mt. Cook to Christchurch. Day 15: Return.

⚔ 🏔   Class V   **Medium**
November-February
Australian Himalayan Expeditions   OC46

NEW ZEALAND VIEWS

SEE THE TWIN-ISLAND nation on a unique combination of unparalleled scenic wonders, with the cosmic event of the century: the return of Halley's Comet. Our special itinerary visits the highlights of this Pacific nation, starting with touch-down in Auckland. We travel south through the dairylands typical of New Zealand to the glowworm caves of Waitomo, where we make a special subterranean river trip worth the price of admission alone. Then through the heartland of the native Maori culture to the Coromandel Peninsula for hiking, horseback riding, windsurfing and more, and our first views of the comet overhead. Our second week begins with a flight to Queenstown in the Southern Alps, a backcountry resort second to none for its scenic atmosphere. From here, a short

NEW ZEALAND ALPS   Bart Henderson

three-day trek on historic Milford Track—often cited as the world's best hike—takes us past streaming waterfalls and deep forest to the fjordland of Milford Sound. While Halley's passage makes the 1986 trip unique in this century, the itinerary is worth following in coming years: the attractions of New Zealand are timeless.

ITINERARY: Days 1-2: En route. Day 3: Auckland. Day 4: Waitomo. Days 5-6: Coromandel Peninsula. Day 7: Auckland. Days 8-9: Queensland. Days 10-13: Milford Track. Day 14: Mt. Cook. Day 15: Return to Auckland; flight home. Day 16: Return.

🐍 🎃 🎿   Class II   **Medium**
March-April
Sobek Expeditions   OC56

ALPINE CONTRAST

THE HOARY HEART of New Zealand is our goal on a two-part trek through the Southern Alps. Open tussock flats, shingle-studded rivers, high country tarns, hot springs and beech forests, and dripping rain forests at the foot of snow-covered mountains are just some of the environments through which we pass. Superb views of Mt. Cook, prince of peaks on the South Island, and the other regal summits as well, make our near-solitary tramp on the tracks of New Zealand a lesson in humility as well as a vision of the ultimate. Our first hike, from Lewis Pass to Arthurs Path, was originally a Maori track, and

IT HAS ALWAYS BEEN DIFFICULT for me to leave a place where I have been settled for some time, and it was not easy to walk away from Tofmora knowing that I was unlikely to see it again. I would not have wanted to remain indefinitely, but it was as if in this place I had tested myself and had discovered some personal resources that I had doubted I possessed. I knew now that I was capable of being alone, without others of my own kind, for a considerable length of time; that it was not some personal inadequacy, some failure to make the right response, that prevented me from experiencing the enthusiasms of most of my acquaintances. While I had not found the answers to the questions I asked, I had discovered that there were questions for which answers might be sought and felt myself better equipped to seek them. Some abiding friendships had also been made; they affected me the more deeply because there had seemed to be such little common ground on which to base a personal relationship. Though it was necessary to leave these friends I would never forget them. They were a part of my life from this time onward, and there have been few others to whom I owe so much of my inner development.

"When you go," Maiamuta, the headman of Tofmora, said to me once, "it will be as if you died. I will cut off my finger and cover my head with dirt. Then I will burn your house so I do not have to see it every day." Though he spoke figuratively, I will not believe that he chose his words only for effect. He was ill on the day of my departure, and I said good-by to him in his house, kneeling to look at him where he lay on the ground in the semidarkness. As I walked away, someone told me that he had pulled himself to the door of the hut and called to me. I did not want to look back, and I have not seen him since. ▲

later a route into the area for gold prospectors. We set out on the second trek from Lake Tekapo, one of the island's highest lakes (2280m), and head up from there for thrilling vistas of Mt. Cook, Tasman and Murchison glaciers, and the billowing clouds of the open sky. Just where in this splendor the heart lies is a discovery for each of us.

ITINERARY: Day 1: Arrive Christchurch. Days 2-5: Lewis Pass to Arthurs Path. Day 6: Christchurch. Days 7-10: Lake Tekapo track. Day 11: Christchurch. Day 12: Return.

🚶 🛶   Class III   **Medium**
November-February
Australian Himalayan Expeditions   OC45

AUSTRALIA

RIVERS AND RAIN FORESTS

RAGING THUNDER on Queensland's Johnson River and a bushwalk into Cape Tribulation add up to wilderness action all the way. Things start off quietly enough with the scenic train trip from Cairns to Kuranda in the Atherton Tablelands, and a drive to picturesque Mungalli Falls. But the next morning a helicopter takes us and all our equipment to the banks of the Johnson River, a wild river few have had the pleasure of seeing. From the first tricky rapids to the raging whitewater of the river's lower reaches, we paddle through primitive forests and canyons, and may even sight the occasional crocodile (before it spots us!). Cascading waterfalls, sandy beach camps and a riverside aboriginal sites offer photographic opportunities nonpareil. When we leave the river for Cape Tribulation and the Daintree rain forest, we explore a threatened eco-zone with a local guide and naturalist. A real insight into the nature of rain forests is gained as we camp amidst prehistoric trees which disappeared from the rest of the world millennia ago. Discover for yourself an Australia few know exist.

ITINERARY: Day 1: Cairns to Atherton. Days 2-4: Johnson River. Day 5: Cape Tribulation. Day 6: Daintree Rain Forest. Day 7: Return Cairns.

🚣 🚶 🛶   Class III   **Moderate**
March-November
Australian Himalayan Expeditions   OC62

SNOWY RIVER

AUSTRALIAN FOLKLORE SPRINGS from the Snowy River, and so too do a multitude of rapids, a span of sceneries, and a hoard of wildlife. Eight major adrenalin-pumping rapids and many smaller ones test the mettle of the novice or experienced rafter, while the serene Tullock Ard Gorge soothes the soul. With white sand beaches for camping, abundant wildlife from deer to eagle and good swimming thoughout, we have all the ingredients for an estimable experience of exceptional excitement. Our put-in is at McKillop Bridge, near Buchan, Victoria; from there to our take-out six days later, there is plenty of time for rest, relaxation—and a raft of thrills as we spin and torque through the Great Dividing Range. One of Down Under's best river runs.

ITINERARY: Day 1: Meet near Canberra; begin river trip. Days 2-5: On the Snowy. Day 6: Take-out near Buchan.

🚣   Class III   **Moderate**
October-January
Australian Himalayan Expeditions   OC38

POSTCARD NEW ZEALAND   Bart Henderson

IN THE WHITSUNDAYS   Liz Hymans

WHITSUNDAY DIVE

NEPTUNE'S KINGDOM AWAITS the certified scuba diver. And what better place to earn certification than the Great Barrier Reef of Australia, one of the prime diving areas in the world? This easy week-long course almost guarantees success. Certification is internationally recognized, and with it the whole world becomes a diving platform. The intensive instruction is centered around Whitsunday Island off the Queensland coast, with a teacher-to-student ratio of one-to-four for the best possible underwater education. A week of unparalleled diving for the advanced diver can also be arranged. Rainbow corals, undersea ravines, sunlight refracting through warm tropical waters, untold millions of fish— this is the dream world entered at will by the certified diver.

ITINERARY: Day 1: Proserpine. Days 2-5: Whitsunday Island. Day 6: Great Barrier Reef. Day 7: Return.

🏊 🦢   Class III   **Moderate**
Year-round
Australian Himalayan Expeditions   OC15

SAIL THE TALL SHIPS

FULL AHEAD ON THE *Golden Plover,* sails billowing aloft as they catch the tradewinds. Sailing a square-rigger is a wonderful and romantic experience, and Australia's Whitsunday Islands may be the world's best sailing waters. Or sail the nimble ketch *Cygnus* and learn to navigate the coral waters. A chain of ancient mountainous islands erupt from the aquamarine of the Great Barrier Reef, providing relatively sheltered waters for us to sail from isle to isle. Enjoy the freedom of these seas, exploring quiet coves and white sandy beaches, and diving into a coral reef fantasia, all from the deck of a brigantine built in 1910 (and subsequently the starring ship in *Blue Lagoon*). Our days are filled with sailing, sailboarding, snorkeling or just relaxing; the instructors and equipment for all are aboard on every trip. We spend our nights on secluded beaches, gloriously deserted, and alive with birdlife and the echoes of our aboriginal predecessors. The elegance of a classic brigantine billowing over the rolling seas will seduce your soul, and induce a love affair with the Tall Ships.

ITINERARY: Day 1: Arrive Airlie Beach; begin sail. Days 2-6: Aboard the *Golden Plover* or *Cygnus*. Day 7: Sail into Airlie Harbor.

⚓ 🏄   Class II   **Moderate**
Year-round
Australian Himalayan Expeditions   OC37

DREAMTIME EXPEDITIONS

KAKADU NATIONAL PARK is a protected aboriginal homeland replete with rich potential. Two week-long journeys let you choose the emphasis on its natural and human aspects: Three days of canoeing plus an equal number on trek, or four days of walking in the bush, or a week's drive through the dream landscape from the Annaburroo Buffalo Station. On all trips we explore the dreamtime rock art, deep gorges and swimming holes of Kakadu. The *Canoe Kadadu* trip starts on the Daly River, where we pair up in canoes to navigate the quiet channels through the creeper-entwined jungle banks. Birdlife is prolific: flocks of white cockatoos, kookaburras laughing from the treetops, and the rainbow flashes of many different parrots wheeling overhead. We then shift to four-wheel drive vehicles to camp in the rugged beauty of the Arnhem escarpment. The *Dreamtime Drive* is a first-ever opportunity to live off the land with an aboriginal family. We'll learn the dreamtime lore of Australia's original inhabitants, light fires with sticks, make shelters and throw spears with a *woomera*, and visit places unknown to outsiders. The *Bungle Bungle* safari makes a four-wheel entrance to Bungle Bungle, a land of peaks and domes rising like surreal excrescences above sandstone plateaus. Here we trek for 48 kilometers through gorges, past waterfalls and beneath the science-fiction skyline of the outback.

ITINERARIES: *Canoe Kakadu:* Day 1: Darwin to Daly River. Days 2-6: Canoeing. Day 7: Return. *Dreamtime Drive:* Day 1: Darwin to Kakadu. Days 2-7: Overlanding. Day 8: Return. *Bungle Bungle:* Day 0: Darwin. Day 1: Kununurra to Bungle Bungle. Days 2-6: Hiking. Day 7: Return.

🚶 🛶 🎒   Class III   **Moderate**
May-October
Australian Himalayan Expeditions   OC59

WEEKEND ADVENTURES

GOT AN EXTRA WEEKEND in Australia? Don't waste it. Maybe you can be floating over golden fields in a balloon, or joining newfound cycling friends for a drink at the pub. You may be checking your skis, tightening your sail or running through the take-off sequence for hang gliding. These adventure weekends are designed to give you the best of everything, with the same top equipment, expert instructors, fine cooking, comfortable accommodations and great company you find on longer holidays. Rafting on the Mitchell or Murrumbidgee, a kayaking school, balloon weekends, cross-country skiing, sea kayaking near Melbourne, horseriding, cycling the wineries, rappeling in the canyons, caving, rockclimbing, sailboarding, hang gliding, Ultralight piloting and day hiking are all on the menu. No one can go away hungry from a smorgasbord like this!

ITINERARIES: Most programs begin Friday night or Saturday morning near Sydney, Adelaide or Melbourne, and end Sunday afternoon.

🚴 🎈 📖   Class I-III   **Moderate/Medium**
Year-round
Australian Himalayan Expeditions   OC61

ACROSS THE TOP

AUSTRALIA'S BEST SKI TOUR may well be this snow trek from Harrietville to Falls Creek in the Victorian Alps. You must be fit and able to carry a pack while skiing, but highly technical skills are not as essential as enthusiasm. Our route combines skiing in remote areas with following the old pole trails of wintering gold prospectors of the past. We also climb Mt. Feathertop (1922m) and Mt. Nelse, two of the highest peaks in the Victorias. After seven days in the wild, a hot shower and warm bed await at Mt. Beauty to wind down from a truly wondrous experience. Don't be limited to this premier week in the Australian Alps—if you want more down-under skiing, try weekend hut skiing, telemark workshops, cross-country and ski mountaineering courses. Whatever your level of accomplishment, whatever your time schdule, Australia beckons.

ITINERARY: Day 1: Harrietville. Days 1-6: Ski tour. Day 7: Mt. Beauty. Day 8: Return.

⛷   Class IV   **Moderate**
July-September
Australian Himalayan Expeditions   OC19

HIGH COUNTRY BY HORSE

RIDE THE SNOWY MOUNTAINS of New South Wales or Victoria's Bogong High Plains, and blend into the equine traditions that gave birth to the legends and folklore of Australia's pioneering days, including the verses and tales of the country's greatest bush poet, Banjo Paterson. We gallop, canter and trot through the picturesque mountains of his "Man from Snowy River," stopping at night to light homey campfires and share in the solitude and companionship of a life in the outback. Both regions sparkle with the joys of summer – wildflowers erupt from grass-carpeted fields, fish leap in the streams, swimming holes pool naturally beneath superb views. The terrain is pleasantly varied, yet not difficult for the novice rider. Choose between the trails of New South Wales or Victoria, and relive a part of Australia's heritage by clopping in the tracks of the early stockmen.

SNOWY MOUNTAIN ITINERARY: Day 1: Cooma, NSW; begin ride. Days 2-5: On the trail. Day 6: Return.
BOGONG ITINERARY: Day 1: Mt. Beauty, Victoria; begin ride. Days 2-5: On the trail. Day 6: Return.

🐎 Class III **Moderate**
November-March
Australian Himalayan Expeditions OC36

CAPE YORK ROCK ART

THE WILDERNESS OF CAPE YORK Peninsula in the far north of Australia is home to the rock art galleries of the Gugu-Yelangi Aboriginals. Hundreds of caves secreted in the gorges of Quinkan Reserve contain some of the world's finest specimens of rock art, graphic descriptions of aboriginal culture and the dawn of Australian history. Our trek leaders, who in many cases were actually involved in the rediscovery and recording of these treasures, also take us through a rugged sandstone country of open eucalyptus forest, pristine streams and a wealth of natural history. Wake to a riot of blue-winged kookaburras and flashing honeyeaters; encounter kangaroos, dingoes, freshwater crocs and tortoises, eels and brush turkeys. The chances of seeing anyone else outside of our own party once we leave the trailhead at Jowalbina are minimal; the opportunities for unearthing something new among the natural and cultural wonders of Australia are not.

ITINERARY: Day 1: Meet in Cairns. Days 2-4: Hiking. Day 5: Cairns and return.

🛶 🥾 🐫 Class III **Moderate**
May-October
Australian Himalayan Expeditions OC35

NYMBOIDA RIVER

WHEN THE WATER IS UP, the Nymboida is the most reliable beginner's run in New South Wales. And in the Australian autumn, the water is at its best for a rousing race through bushland and thick rain forest out to the sea. Coffs Harbour, a popular Pacific coast resort accessible by train or plane, is easier to reach than the put-in for the Nymboida. Rough roads through dense brush bring us to Dorrigo, where we begin our five-day aquatic adventure. The first day is filled with practice riffles that warm us up for the rousing best, a raft of hot and fast rapids that powers us through the ever-changing countryside. Playful platypus, wallowing wallabies, and leaping lizards carouse along the water-course, while kingfishers dive and ducks dip. Let the nimble Nymboida turn you on to rafting, Aussie-style.

ITINERARY: Day 1: Coffs Harbour, NSW. Days 2-5: On the river. Day 6: Coffs Harbour and return.

✈	Class III	**Moderate**

December-May
Australian Himalayan Expeditions　　　OC16

ALICE SPRINGS CAMEL TREK

LISTEN: THE GENTLE THUD of camel hoof on spinifex is the only sound. As far as the eye can see there is only sand, a deeper hue of red than any artist can paint. This is the ochre center of Australia, the soul of an ancient continent, where aboriginies have lived for 30,000 years and the winds have crafted their sculptures for far longer. Here is where camels escaped from Afghan traders following the British colonization, the feral forebears of some 50,000 wild Australian camels alive today. We ride the domesticated version of these ships of the desert for five days through either the Finke River or Rainbow Valley near Alice Springs, the aura of desert surrounding us night and day. And don't worry about riding the camels—you'll soon discover that it is easy to stay aloft on these novel creatures, and hard to traverse the outback without them.

ITINERARY: Day 1: Meet at Alice Springs. Days 2-6: Ride to Rainbow Valley or Finke River. Day 7: Alice Springs and return.

🐫	Class II	**Medium**

Year-round
Australian Himalayan Expeditions　　　OC40

WINERIES BY BALLOON

CHAMPAGNE BREAKFASTS and vintage vantages should persuade anyone that ballooning is more than just a lot of hot air. We float in wicker gondolas up and above wineries, over the historic towns of northeastern Victoria, and along the flanks of the snowy Victorian Alps. The Murray River winds like a sluggish blue python through the rolling countryside, while we drift with the wind over new perspectives and old farmlands. Accommodation is at antique pubs in venerable country towns such as Rutherglen, Beechworth, Yackandandah and Mt. Beauty. Within reach are Australia's best ski resorts, so those who long for the vertigo of the slopes to match their aerial balletics can spend some afternoons skiing, after our early morning balloon flights. Three-day champagne balloon weekends are also available for a taste of the fragrant air over wine country; or drift over the dry heart of Australia out of Alice Springs. The truly ambitious can even arrange a balloon charter anywhere in Australia, with nothing to tie you down. An uplifting adventure indeed!

ITINERARY: Day 1: Springhurst, Victoria. Days 2-4: Balloon flights. Day 5: Farewell flight and return.

🎈	Class I	**Medium**

May-August
Australian Himalayan Expeditions　　　OC39

RIVER RELAXATION　　Liz Hymans

TASMANIAN PANORAMA   David Ripley

BUSHWALKING DOWN UNDER

THREE DIFFERENT ROUTES in the hills of Australia offer new discoveries at every switchback. In the Snowy Mountains, alpine heathlands are checkered with flowers, crystal mountain lakes are hidden in forests of gnarled gums, and endless rolling hills grace our passage through Kosciusko National Park. Superb views of Lake Albina, Watson's Crags, neighboring valleys and gorges await us from the top of Kosciusko, at 1800 meters alpine Australia's apogee. Or join a horseback trek through the Flinders Range, with bluffs of amber rock etched against the cobalt sky, and venture deep into the continent's desert heart. We walk at a leisurely pace, pausing when we can by rock pools to swim and sun, then pack deeper into rugged gorges and across the flat desert floor of Wilpena Pound. Or choose to penetrate the cool stillness of the Blue Mountains Wilderness not far from Sydney on a five-day backpack. Warm up with a walk through the Blue Gum Forest to Jenolan caves, then hoist the rucksacks at Kanagra Walls for a fantastic wilderness journey. A 1000-meter deep gorge and mounts Cloudmaker and Stormbreaker are the breathtaking habitat of wildlife including wallabies, dingos, wombats, goannas, echidnas, possums and possibly platypus—a naturalist's delight! Pick your own point-of-view on Australia, or combine them all for an active appreciation of the island content.

FLINDERS ITINERARY: Day 1: Adelaide, SA and begin hike. Days 2-4: In the Flinders. Day 5: Adelaide and return.

BLUE MOUNTAINS ITINERARY: Day 1: Blackheath Station, NSW, and begin hike. Days 2-4: In the Blues. Day 5: End hike and return.

SNOWY MOUNTAINS ITINERARY: Day 1: Tredbo, NSW. Days 2-5: Backpacking. Day 6: Tredbo and return.

   Class III   **Moderate**
Year-round
Australian Himalayan Expeditions   OC58

TASMANIA
FRANKLIN RIVER

AUSTRALIA'S WILDEST WHITEWATER is on the Franklin, a demonic yet tantalizing run on the wooded isle of Tasmania. Our 10 days on the river gives us time to explore the eucalyptus groves lining the stream, lay over in case of rain and make portages when necessary. This is not an easy river trip, but a great one, demanding intense concentration in the tricky rapids, patience and enthusiasm. From its icy headwaters in the Cheyne Range through its narrow gorges, serene pools, boulder-strewn drops and radical S-turns, the Franklin calls upon the complete spectrum of whitewater skills even before it enters the Great Ravine. Here the Churn, Corruscades, Thunderrush and the Cauldron push boatmen to the limit and rafts to the wall for three nail-biting days. Yet the small scale of the river demands the use of Avon Redshank rafts, at less than 12 feet (4 meters) roomy enough for only four. Emerging from the Ravine, we look back in wonder at the limestone cliffs, glacial headwalls, wheeling and screeching cockatoos, rich rain forest and remarkable rapids of the Franklin.

ITINERARY: Day 1: Meet in Hobart, drive to river. Days 2-9: On the river. Day 10: Return to Hobart. Duration from 8-12 days depending on weather.

          Class IV   **Moderate**
December-March
Australian Himalayan Expeditions   OC12

TASMANIAN TRACKS

THE ISLAND OF TASMANIA boasts one of the world's great wilderness areas in its southwest corner. It is a land virtually untouched by man, a kaleidoscope of natural grandeur, precipitous sea cliffs, vast plains of buttongrass, windswept beaches, dense forests, lofty mountains, hidden coves and serene estuaries. Our two-week backpack trip allows plenty of time to rest, layover in case of weather, and explore thoroughly as much of the region as we can reach along its rugged trails. We walk the entire length of the south coast, starting at Scotts Peak and finishing at Catamaran, with two boat crossings and a food drop at Melaluca half way through our journey. A shorter walk on Tasmania, a backpack along the pine-fringed shores of Lake St. Clair to Cradle Mountain, is a celebration of wilderness. Five days in grassy valleys lined with lakes and rocky crags offer a kaleidoscope of natural beauty. Give in to the Tasmanian tempter and celebrate the New Year with a wild walk along the South Coast.

CRADLE MOUNTAIN ITINERARY: Day 1: Launceston, Tasmania. Days 2-6: On the trail. Day 7: Launceston and return.

SOUTH COAST ITINERARY: Day 1: Hobart, Tasmania. Day 2: Scotts Peak. Days 3-13: On the South Coast. Day 14: Hobart and return.

⏃ ⏃ Class IV **Moderate**
December-March
Australian Himalayan Expeditions OC22

TASMANIAN PANORAMA

TASSIE HAS IT ALL. The "Adventure Island" has the wildest rivers in Australia, great tracts of wilderness, lakes and mountains, a rugged coastline and a rich history. This sampler offers the best of Tasmania by bicycle, foot and raft. Two easy day trips on foot in Cradle Mountain/Lake St. Clair National Park, to the Ballroom Forest and the summit of Cradle Mountain, warm us up for more. We hoist backpacks for a three-day wilderness walk across the Central Plateau and the Walls of Jerusalem, a once-glaciated region of five main peaks dissected by open, grassy valleys. After a comfortable hotel night, we mount our cycles to pedal the wildly beautiful east coast as our gear is carried by a support vehicle. Rolling green farms and rugged coastal cliffs keep our eyes wide and our wheels turning. At Coles Bay, relax with a leisurely walk through Freycinet National Park, and feast on freshly-caught scallops and lobsters.

Then south to the banks of the Picton River, with its exciting rapids, to sample all the wondrous fruits of adventure in Tasmania.

ITINERARY: Day 1: Launceston, Tasmania. Day 2: Cradle Mountain. Days 3-5: Wilderness backpack. Day 6: Launceston. Days 7-10: Cycle. Day 11: Coles Bay. Day 12: To the Picton. Days 13-14: Raft and end trip in Hobart.

⏃ ⚲ ⚓ Class II **Moderate**
November-March
Australian Himalayan Expeditions OC60

CYCLE TASMANIA

THE WILD AND RUGGED east coast, steeped in a history brew of conquerors and convicts, stirred with devilishly beautiful scenery, is the riled side of Tasmania. Cycling down its winding roads, cooled by sea breezes, with a meal of freshly-caught scallops and lobsters ahead, we earn a wheeler's feel for Tasmania. From the first day's pedal out of Launceston, the island's capital, to the long haul along the Forestier Peninsula to Port Arthur, this leisurely wheel tour takes your breath away then leaves time to catch it back. Sightseeing, pub stops, lazing about or rolling along in Freycinet National Park are all part of experiencing Tasmania from atop a two-wheeler.

ITINERARY: Day 1: Launceston. Days 2-12: Cycle trek. Day 13: Hobart. Day 14: Return.

⚲ Class III **Moderate**
November-March
Australian Himalayan Expeditions OC14

END OF THE DAY   Michael Nichols

GRAND SUNSET   Bart Henderson

NORTH AMERICA

ALSEK ICE FANTASY   Bart Henderson

THE DRUID AND THE ENGINEER

by John McPhee

"I hate all dams, large and small," David Brower informs an audience.

A voice from the back of the room asks, "Why are you conservationists always against things?"

"If you are against something, you are for something," Brower answers. "If you are against a dam, you are for a river."

When Brower was a small boy in Berkeley, he used to build dams in Strawberry Creek, on the campus of the University of California, piling up stones in arcs convex to the current, backing up reservoir pools. Then he would kick the dams apart and watch the floods that returned Strawberry Creek to its free-flowing natural state. When Brower was born — in 1912 — there was in the Sierra Nevada a valley called Hetch Hetchy that paralleled in shape, size and beauty the Valley of the Yosemite. The two valleys lay side by side. Both were in Yosemite National Park, which had been established in 1890. Yet within three decades — the National Park notwithstanding — the outlet of Hetch Hetchy was filled with a dam and the entire valley was deeply flooded. Brower was a boy when the dam was being built. He remembers spending his sixth birthday in the hills below Hetch Hetchy and hearing stories of the battle that had been fought over it, a battle that centered on the very definition of conservation. Should it mean preservation of wilderness or wise and varied use of land? John Muir, preservationist, founder of the young Sierra Club, had lost this bitter and, as it happened, final struggle of his life.

THE WEST

GRAND CANYON BY MOTOR

THE MAGNIFICENCE THAT IS the Grand Canyon of the Colorado can be appreciated by adventurers with a tight schedule on a motor trip down the Colorado River. And what a trip: the big, stable pontoon rafts navigate the biggest waves and holes on the river while carrying a cornucopia of taste treats and comfortable extras for every indulgence. Yet none of the canyon's beauty and elegance is sacrificed; Vasey's Paradise, Redwall Cavern, Unkar Indian Ruins, Shinumo Creek, Elves' Chasm, Deer Creek Falls, Havasu Creek, Fern Glen Grotto—the evocative names resonate in harmony with the natural splendor of the 280-mile (450kms) float. See the Grand Canyon from the deluxe comfort of big rigs.

ITINERARIES: *Full trip:* Day 1: Lee's Ferry and begin. Days 2-7: On the river. Day 8: Temple Bar and return. *Upper only:* Day 1: Lee's Ferry and begin. Days 2-6: On the river. Day 7: Whitmore and return. *Lower only:* Day 1: Las Vegas, fly to Whitmore and begin river. Day 2: On the river. Day 3: Temple Bar to Las Vegas.

⚓ 🦆　　　Class III　　**Premium**
April-September
Del Webb's Wilderness River Adventures　　NA95

MOUNTAIN SPORTS WEEK

TAKE A REVIVIFYING BREAK from the commonplace and enjoy a potpourri of action in Colorado's Sangre de Cristo Mountains. We sample rock climbing, mountain cycling and whitewater rafting on this seven-day trip based at a 5,000-acre ranch in Bear Basin. On horseback or rugged mountain bicycles, we explore the environs, stopping to investigate an old gold mine or Indian camp or visiting an industrious community of beavers at alpine ponds that teem with trout. The last part of the trip finds us tackling the Arkansas River, where swift water fed by mountain snow spills downstream toward rapids like Zoom Flume, Widowmaker and Slidell's Suckhole. Most evenings are spent enjoying hearty meals around a campfire, but for the final two we indulge ourselves with candlelight and elegant cuisine at the Ponderosa Guest Ranch. From raw wild rock to smoked trout, this is a week of quality.

ITINERARY: Day 1: Colorado Springs, CO, to Bear Creek Ranch; horseback riding. Day 2: Riding. Day 3: Rock climbing. Day 4: Mountain cycling. Day 5: Cycling and move to Ponderosa. Days 6-7: Rafting and return to Colorado Springs.

🚴 ⚓ ✕　　　Class III　　**Moderate**
June-September
Ultimate Escapes　　NA114

FLOYD ELGIN DOMINY raises beef cattle in the Shenandoah Valley. Observed there, hand on a fence, his eyes surveying his pastures, he does not look particularly Virginian. Of middle height, thickset, somewhat bandy-legged, he appears to have been lifted off a horse with block and tackle. He wears bluejeans, a white-and-black striped shirt, and leather boots with heels two inches high. His belt buckle is silver and could not be covered over with a playing card. He wears a string tie that is secured with a piece of petrified dinosaur bone. On his head is a white Stetson . . .

Growing up on a farm that had been homesteaded by his grandfather in the eighteen-seventies, Dominy often enough saw talent and energy going to waste under clear skies. The situation was marginal. In some years, more than twenty inches of rain would fall and harvests would be copious. In others, when the figure went below ten, the family lived with the lament that there was no money to buy clothes, or even sufficient food. These radical uncertainties were eventually removed by groundwater development, or reclamation — the storage of what water there was, for use in irrigation. When Dominy was eighteen years old, a big thing to do on a Sunday was to get into the Ford, which had a rumble seat, and go out and see the new dam. In his photo album he put pictures of reservoirs and irrigation projects. ("It was impressive to a dry-land farmer like me to see all that water going down a ditch toward a farm.") Eventually, he came to feel that there would be, in a sense, no West at all were it not for reclamation.

MUDDY WATERS   Bart Henderson

GRAND CANYON OF THE COLORADO

AMERICA'S GREATEST NATURAL WONDER is at its most dramatic when seen from the churning waters of the Colorado River. Rafting the Grand Canyon is always a premium experience, but even in nature's temple there are little extra services which differentiate the trips one from another. With a low guide-to-passenger ratio, full logistical support before the trip and a more leisurely pace on the river, O.A.R.S. gives the prospective canyoneer a classy option. The 5-meter inflatables carry a maximum load of just four passengers per oarsman, creating an intimate atmosphere and a high degree of personal attention on all facets of the trip. This same attention will be welcome before your trip when an efficient and experienced office staff will handle all the annoying details of planning a vacation: air ticketing, hotel reservations, flights or car shuttles to Flagstaff, and more. Throw in an extra day in the grandeur of the canyon for good measure and you've got a raft trip as special as its setting.

ITINERARY: Day 1: Flagstaff, AZ to put-in. Days 2-4: Marble Canyon section. Day 5: Phantom Ranch. Days 6-12: Lower Canyon. Day 13: Diamond Creek to Flagstaff. *Note:* Marble Canyon only, 5 days; Lower Canyon only, 9 days.

	Class IV	**Premium**
April-October		
O.A.R.S.	NA94	

THE GRAND CANYON

THE NAME SAYS IT ALL: the Grand Canyon, most impressive cut on the skin of the Earth, a living museum of geological forces. And a white-water run to beat all, to boot: with rapids like Hance, Hermit, Crystal and the incomparable Lava Falls — the world's fastest rapid — the Canyon is the standard for big water excitement the world over. Yet there's a quiet side of the river too: the spectral beauty of Elves Chasm, the haunting timelessness of Nankoweap's Anasazi ruins, the multifaceted pleasures of Havasu. We ride oar rafts down 226 miles (363 kms) of the Colorado River over a dozen days of sunshine and excitement, penetrating nearly a mile deep into the earth's crust on a million-year-old waterway, and enjoy eleven campfires and as many starlit nights between the walls of one of the world's wonders. Or take the five-day Upper Trip from Lees Ferry to Phantom Ranch for an inviting glide into the heart of the Canyon, with just a taste of its world-class white-water; or the eight-day Lower Trip from Phantom to Diamond Creek, featuring the mightiest rapids on this, the magnificent Colorado.

ITINERARY: Day 1: Meet in Lees Ferry; put on the river. Days 2-4: Upper Trip. Day 5: Phantom Ranch; end Upper Trip. begin Lower Trip. Days 6-11: Lower Trip. Day 12: Diamond Creek and return.

	Class IV	**Medium**
May-September		
Outdoors Unlimited	NA76	

RIO GRANDE ESCAPE

WILD AND UNTAMED, like the Old West itself, the Rio Grande below Big Bend National Park cuts through desert country as primitive as it was a century ago. Above Big Bend, its historic waters are siphoned off for irrigation; but below the Park, it springs to life again as the Rio Conchos joins it from Mexico's Sierra Madre. And what a life it has — spires, arches, and natural bridges line its route, rugged walls stretch a thousand feet overhead, hawks and falcons, burros and pumas roam, and white-water excitement punctuates the sinuous course. We travel through 120 kilometers of wilderness in one of the most isolated stretches of river in the Lower 48: past the Sioux Peaks and Del Carmine Limestone, down Hot Springs and Burro Bluff rapids, and through the relics of past centuries. From the soaring scenery of the day to the hot springs that soothe us at night, the Rio Grande float is an escape from the mundane into the eternal.

ITINERARY: Day 1: Meet in Odessa, TX; drive to put-in. Days 2-6: On the river. Day 7: Return to Odessa.

Class III	**Moderate**	
March, November-December		
Ultimate Escapes, Ltd.	NA92	

SAN JUAN RIVER

THE CONTORTED CANYONS of the Colorado Plateau have been sculpted and painted by the erosion of rainfall, high country heat, wind and the twisting San Juan. Swift currents and gentle rapids entice family groups to the joys of backcountry river rafting; deep red gorges, towering cliffs, precipitous pinnacles and unusual formations such as Mexican Hat Rock provide an outdoor classroom of unusual grandeur. Evidence of the culture of the lost Anasazi Indians is everywhere: petroglyphs, ruins of cliff dwellings, ancient footpaths cutting across the river's meanders. The river opens the book of the earth, and the geological lessons revealed are a delight to both photographer and rockhound. Choose between relaxing in an oar boat for the full 83 miles (133km) or taking turns paddling inflatable kayaks. Five-day trips depart on Mondays from Bluff, Utah; shorter four-day trips of 63 miles (101km) meet on-going trips in Mexican Hat for the float to Clay Hills Crossing.

ITINERARY: Day 1: Meet in Bluff, Utah; put on river. Day 2: Arrive Mexican Hat, continue down river. Days 3-4: On the San Juan. Day 5: Arrive Clay Hills Crossing.

Class III	**Medium**	
April-September		
O.A.R.S.	NA33	

DURING THE YEARS WHEN Brower was developing as a conservationist, many of his most specific and dramatic personal accomplishments had to do with proposed dams. Down the tiers of the Western states, there are any number of excellent damsites that still contain free-flowing rivers because of David Brower — most notably in the immense, arid watershed of the Colorado. Anyone interested, for whatever reason, in the study of water in the West will in the end concentrate on the Colorado, wildest of rivers, foaming, raging, rushing southward — erratic, headlong, incongruous in the desert. The Snake, the Salmon, the upper Hudson — all the other celebrated torrents — are not in the conversation if the topic is the Colorado. . . . The Colorado lights and slakes Los Angeles. It irrigates Arizona. The odd thing about it is that all its writhings and foamings and spectacular rapids lead to nothing. The river rises in the Rockies, thunders through the canyons, and is so used by mankind that when it reaches the Gulf of California, fourteen hundred miles from its source, it literally trickles into the sea. The flow in the big river and in its major tributaries — the Green, the Yampa, the Escalante, the San Juan, the Little Colorado — is almost lyrically erratic, for the volume can vary as much as six hundred per cent from only year to the next. The way to control that, clearly enough, is storage, and this is accomplished under programs developed and administered by the federal Bureau of Reclamation. The Bureau of Reclamation, all but unknown in the American East, is the patron agency of the American West, dispenser of light, life, and water to thirty million people whose gardens would otherwise be dust. Most of the civil servants in the Bureau are Westerners — from the dry uplands as well as the deserts of the Great Basin. They have lived in the problem they are solving, and they have a deep sense of mission. There are many people in the Bureau of Reclamation — perhaps all nine thousand of them — who hope to see the Colorado River become a series of large pools, one stepped above another, from the Mexican border to the Rocky Mountains, with the headwaters of each succeeding lake lapping against the tailrace of a dam. The river and its tributaries have long since been thoroughly surveyed, and throughout the basin damsites of high quality and potentiality stand ready for river diversion, blast excavation, and concrete.

FISH STORY   Mark Jensen

MIDDLE FORK OF THE SALMON

HOT SPRINGS AND REMOTE CANYONS make this whitewater adventure through the Idaho Primitive Area one of North America's premier river trips. Beginning amidst the jagged peaks of the Sawtooth Mountains as a small clear stream plunging through narrow chutes and channels, the wild and scenic Middle Fork builds to major proportions before joining the Main Salmon, the infamous River of No Return. The dense forest greenery of the mountains gives way to sheer granite cliffs as we sweep downriver. Scenery never looked as good as it does from one of many natural hot pools along the river. Dozens of top-rated rapids, great fishsing, time to explore and relax offer good reasons for modern-day adventurers to follow eagerly in the footsteps of the gold miners, homesteaders and Indians along the Middle Fork of the Salmon.

ITINERARY: Day 1: Meet in Salmon, Idaho; begin river. Days 2-4: On river. Day 5: Return to Salmon.

Class IV   **Medium**
May-September
Steve Currey Expeditions   NA98

MAIN FORK OF THE SALMON

"THE RIVER OF NO RETURN," decided Lewis and Clark when they looked down its churning length and rerouted their expedition. We don't avoid a thing – not the big wilderness or the big canyon, not even the big rapids on the big river itself. For 50 kilometers we follow the Salmon as it cuts across Idaho's vast Primitive Area in the second deepest canyon in North America, a journey of drama and quietude, huge standing waves and lazy calms. As if the river's own variety is not enough, there's human history aplenty – from the Shoshone campsites and petroglyphs to abandoned gold mines coddled among the pines. Golden eagles glide above the river's moody course, and bighorn sheep, brown bear, cougar and a few surprises lurk in the wilderness. A six-day journey through the largest undeveloped land area in the Lower 48, teeming with delights hydraulic, historic and human.

ITINERARY: Day 1: Boise to Salmon, ID. Days 2-5: On the river. Day 6: Return.

Class III   **Medium**
May-September
Steve Currey Expeditions   NA43

THE ROGUE RIVER

THE ROWDY REPUTATION of the Rogue is well-earned, its playfulness giving way to unpredictable fits of passion, thundering whitewater and spirited swirls. Then it turns pretty, and a lovelier river would be hard to imagine: green scented cedar and fir forests, narrow gorges of black basalt, and the crystalline cascades of side creeks. Our leisurely float down the Rogue allows plenty of time to savor its special charms, sight its osprey and deer, swim in its warm waters and doze in its shady groves. Enjoy the respite, for rapids like Blossom Bar, Wildcat, Mule Creek Canyon and the all-but-unrunnable Rainie Falls are inevitable. One of the original Wild and Scenic Rivers, the Rogue is a perfect river for paddle-boating, so everyone can enjoy the thrills and chills of running one of the West's best.

ITINERARY: Day 1: Put-in near Galice. Days 2-4: On the Rogue. Day 5: Return to Galice.

Class III   **Medium**
June-September
O.A.R.S.   NA36

DESOLATION CANYON

DESOLATION CANYON EARNED its name when John Wesley Powell first explored it in 1869, and has re-earned it over the years as settlers, trappers and outlaws strove to eke out a living or lose a posse in its tortured mazes. Rock spires, arch formations and natural monuments rise high above sandy river banks, pinion and juniper slopes and the petroglyphs of the Anasazi. Where legend and landscape are so impressive, river running is a revelation: enjoy the introductory-level whitewater in paddle-boats while a supply raft carries all the necessary camping gear down the river for a fun, family-oriented trip. Or choose a six-day oar option and relax in superb surroundings. Swim, fish, take pictures, and listen to the lore of Butch Cassidy and the Wild Bunch, Indian history and the spectacular geological record of the Green River.

ITINERARY: Day 1: Meet in Green River, UT, fly to Sand Wash for river trip. Days 2-4 or 2-6: River trip; to Green River.

⚓ 🐫 Class III **Moderate**
June-September
Sheri Griffith River Expeditions NA47

RIDING AND RAFTING THE TETONS

COMBINE THE EXCITEMENT of rafting and riding in the unparalleled mountain majesty of Grand Teton National Park. With experts to guide us, we ride through the lush meadows and pine forests of the Snake River canyon, glimpsing herds of elk and bighorn sheep grazing in the rolling alpine countryside of their summer range. Meals around the campfire are hearty, befitting our new-won cowboy status. Then for a change of pace we ease into the still, blue waters of Jackson Lake to explore the trout-laden western shore area. After a couple of relaxing days, we leave the lake and put in on the Snake River, riding the rapids between a shoreline rich in scenery and wildlife—beavers, osprey, otters and moose. To end our adventure, it's only fitting that we all take a bracing dip in the river as a farewell salute to this spectacular land.

ITINERARY: Day 1: Jackson Hole to trailhead. Days 2-3: Trail riding. Days 4-5: Jackson Lake. Days 6-7: Snake River; return to Jackson Hole.

🐫 ⚓ 🦆 Class II **Premium**
July, August
Parklands Expeditions, Inc. NA110

THERE IS NO DAM at the confluence of the Green and the Yampa [in Dinosaur National Monument]. Had it not been for David Brower, a dam would be there. A man in the public-relations office of the Bureau of Reclamation one day summed up the telling of the story by saying, "Dave won, hands down."

Brower feels that he can win nothing. There is no dam at the Green and the Yampa now, but in 2020 there may be. "The Bureau of Reclamation engineers are like beavers," he says. "They can't stand the sight of running water." Below the Utah-Arizona border, in Marble Gorge, a part of the Grand Canyon, there is likewise no dam. The story is much the same. The Bureau of Reclamation had the dam built on paper, ready to go. A battle followed, and Brower won, hands down. In the lower Granite Gorge, another part of the Grand Canyon, there is also no dam, and for the same reason. These Grand Canyon battles were the bitterest battles of all. The Bureau felt that Brower capitalized on literary hyperbole and the mystic name of the canyon. He implied, they said, that the dams were going to fill the Grand Canyon like an enormous bathtub, and that the view from the north rim to the south rim would soon consist of a flat expanse of water. Brower's famous advertising campaigns reached their most notable moment at this time. He placed full-page ads in The New York Times *and the* San Francisco Chronicle, *among other places, under the huge headline "SHOULD WE ALSO FLOOD THE SISTINE CHAPEL SO TOURISTS CAN GET NEARER THE CEILING?" Telegrams flooded Congress, where the battle was decided. . . . There are no dams in the Grand Canyon, and in the Bureau of Reclamation it is conceded that there will not be for at least two generations. The defeat of the high dams if frankly credited, within the Bureau, to David Brower. . . .*

Popular assumptions to the contrary, no federal bureau is completely faceless — and, eyeball to eyeball with David Brower, there was a central and predominant figure on the other side of these fights, marshalling his own forces, battling in the rooms of Congress and in the canyon lands of the West for his profound and lifelong belief in the storage of water. This was the Bureau's leader — Floyd E. Dominy, United States Commissioner of Reclamation. . . .

"Commissioner," I said, "if David Brower gets into a rubber raft going down the Colorado River, will you get in it, too?"

"Hell, yes," he said. "Hell, yes."

COLORADO RIVER ACTION   Mark Jensen

NA PALI COAST   Kebos

CATARACT CANYON

THE COLORADO RIVER CUTS its fair share of canyons, and alongside the Grand its lesser-known cousin, the Cataract, may appear pale from a distance. But not from the bottom of a trough, looking up at a huge standing wave cresting overhead, framed within the red rock sculptures of its canyon walls. This is some of the biggest and most challenging springtime whitewater in the country, with rapids like Mile Long and Teapot, and the affectionately-named Satan's Seat and Satan's Gut. While waves and holes provide the thrills, it's the grandeur of the gorges that lingers in the memory: abstract sandstone spires, mesas, monuments and cliffs that tower above the racing river. The trip begins in Moab, joins the confluence of the Colorado with the Green, and roars down to Lake Powell, with side canyons to explore, sunny beaches to sprawl along, rapids to scout and photographs to frame. A six-day option allows time to absorb the multitudinous attractions of Cataract.

ITINERARY: Day 1: Meet in Moab, UT, put on river. Days 2-3 or 2-6: Down Cataract Canyon, to Lake Powell.

Class IV   **Medium**

May-September
Sheri Griffith River Expeditions   NA48

HAWAII

NANI LOA ADVENTURE

THE EARTHLY PARADISE of Hawaii is a mythical kingdom so kaleidoscopic in color, mood and miracle that you wonder what keeps your feet on its igneous soil. We explore the hidden niches of Kauai, Maui, Hawaii and Lanai for their secrets, snorkeling beneath the azure waves of Hulopoe Bay and climbing to the chilly summit of Haleakala (3055m) for a tropical sunrise. In between, the petroglyphs of Polynesian precursors, the whaling port of Lahaina, and the roiling crater of Kilauea Volcano dowse our sense of histories natural and human with wonderment. Hiking, swimming, sailing, flying and above all sharing the spectacle of Hawaii for 14 days will make a believer out of anyone – if there be heaven on earth, it is in Hawaii.

ITINERARY: Day 0: Arrive Honolulu. Days 1-4: Kauai. Days 5-7: Hawaii. Days 8-11: Maui. Days 12-13: Lanai. Day 14: Honolulu and return.

Class III   **Medium**

Year-round
Pacific Quest   NA49

ALASKA

TATSHENSHINI RIVER

THE WORD IS SPECTACULAR, and it was invented for the Tatshenshini. Slicing south through the Yukon to the Pacific, the river bisects the St. Elias Range and reveals one of the world's most beautiful wildernesses. Bald eagles soar overhead; grizzly bears and moose stalk the banks. Ice-bedecked peaks rise more than 5000 meters above our boats, while their folding green foothills are home to mountain goats. But it is the glaciers that incontestably highlight the trip: the awesome frozen blue rivers dominate the landscape while skyscraper-sized chunks of ice calve off the glaciers and become our floating escorts down the river. We experience the ice floes close-up when we stop for a day to scamper across the moraine onto the living face of a glacier. The river itself grows from a sparkling stream in a constricted canyon to a vast expanse of moving water after its confluence with the Alsek. The scale of the Tatshenshini, its mountains, glaciers and banks, is immense in a way only Alaska can be.

ITINERARY: Day 1: Arrive Haines. Day 2: Bus to put-in. Days 3-11: Tatshenshini. Day 12: Haines. Day 13: Return.

	Class III	Premium
July-August		
Sobek Expeditions	NA1	

MT. McKINLEY TREK

TRAVERSE AN EXQUISITE WILDERNESS at the foot of Denali ("The Great One", as the Indians call McKinley). Isolated and independent, the base of McKinley is a special world of tundra, snow and ice, 37 species of mammals, 130 types of birds, willow, birch, alder, wildflowers, ponds, lakes and rushing rivers. Ever present looms the mute, majestic peak: solitary, splendid, visible for miles, dominating the central Alaskan skyline. A small plane flight to the remote west end of Denali National Park leaves us at a hunting camp over 150 kilometers from the nearest dirt road. We shoulder packs and head into the interior of a private, primeval place along the base of the great massif. Grizzly bear feast on abundant berries, bull moose shed their velvet, and tundra flora display their splendid and colorful designs as we step across the wilds of the park. The roadhead at Wonder Lake signals the hike's end, and we board the scenic Alaska Railroad to return to Anchorage. A rousing ramble through Denali's dazzling landscapes.

ITINERARY: Day 1: Anchorage to McKinley. Days 2-10: Hiking. Day 11: Wonder Lake, Camp Denali. Day 12: Return to Anchorage.

	Class IV	Medium
August		
Sobek Expeditions	NA2	

MILE 130. The water is smooth here, and will be smooth for three hundred yards, and then we are going through another rapid. The temperature is a little over ninety, and the air is so dry that the rapid will feel good. Dominy and Brower are drinking beer. They have settled into a kind of routine: once a day they tear each other in half and the rest of the time they are pals.

Dominy is wearing a blue yachting cap with gold braid, and above its visor in gold letters are the words "LAKE POWELL." His skin is rouge brown. His nose is peeling. He wears moccasins, and a frayed cotton shirt in dark, indeterminate tartan, and long trousers secured by half a pound of silver buckle. He has with him a couple of small bags and a big leather briefcase on which is painted the great seal of the Bureau of Reclamation — snow-capped mountains, a reservoir, a dam, and irrigated fields, all within the framing shape of a big drop of water. Dominy has been discoursing on the multiple advantages of hydroelectric power, its immediacy ("When you want it, you just throw a switch") and its innocence of pollution.

"Come on now, Dave, be honest," he said. "From a conservationist's point of view, what is the best source of electric power?"

"Flashlight batteries," Brower said.

Brower is also wearing an old tartan shirt, basically orange, and faded. He wears shorts and sneakers. The skin of his legs and face is bright red. Working indoors and all but around the clock, he has been too long away from the sun. He protects his head with a handkerchief knotted at the corners and soaked in the river, but his King Lear billowing white hair is probably protection enough. He travels light. A miniature duffelbag, eight inches in diameter and a foot long — standard gear for the river — contains all that he has with him, most notably his Sierra Club cup, without which he would be incomplete.

CLIMBING DENALI   Michael Speaks

DENALI   John Kramer

DENALI CLIMB

AN ASCENT UP THE WEST BUTTRESS of Denali, North America's highest point, is a peak experience indeed. Stand at the summit of the continent, 6194 meters above sea level, while the mighty mass of McKinley spreads out its bulk from horizon to horizon. This is no slick packaged tour, for there is no easy way up. We spend nearly three weeks on the mountain, living and climbing in true expedition style as we set up a base camp at 7,000 feet on the tongue of Kahiltna Glacier, relay loads over the course of a week to the 14,000-foot level, and finally reach our high camp at 17,200 feet. Then we wait: wait for the crystal clear morning when the wind is still, and the horizon-line sharp, and the snowy route to the summit firm. Our final push to the 20,320-foot apex makes the most of the mountaineering skills we have developed over the previous two weeks on Denali. Although previous climbing experience is helpful, it is not essential. Far more useful is the physical and mental health necessary to cope with the long days of glacier travel, moderate snow and ice climbing, and the possibility of poor weather delaying the summit attempt. All expenses on the expedition are covered, from departure from Talkeetna to our return nearly three weeks later.

ITINERARY: Days 1-2: Talkeetna. Day 3: Charter flight to Kahiltna Glacier; begin climb. Days 4-21: On the mountain. Day 22: Talkeetna. Day 23: Return. Date of return to Talkeetna approximate.

✗   Class V   **Medium**
April-June
Genet Expeditions   NA93

IN THE SHADOW OF McKINLEY

ALASKA'S MOST POPULAR attraction would be a stand-out in any land — Mount McKinley, the huge mountain at the heart of the 49th State. Named for the president who led the U.S. into the turn of the century, the parklands around the peak were recently renamed "Denali National Park" in respect of the Native American name for the mountain. Few appellations are better suited: the white-cloaked bulk tower over blue glaciers, green meadowlands and the rainbow of wildflowers surrounding it. The result is breath-snatching, a natural history museum in the most spectacular of settings. We hike to photograph the wildlife and scenery, camp in the shadow of McKinley, and test the whitewaters of the Nenana River. A moonlit hot tub soak rounds off our brief encounter with the Great One.

ITINERARY: Day 1: Anchorage to Denali. Day 2: Hikes. Day 3: Nenana River. Day 4: Anchorage and return.

⌂ ✈ ⚞   Class II   **Moderate**
June-September
Alaska Travel Adventures   NA100

ALASKA SAFARI

FROM THE HEIGHTS OF DENALI to the coastal waters of Prince William Sound, Alaska offers its charms to whomsoever it pleases. This comfortable overview of its natural parks and wildlife refuges features more than enough intimacies with Alaska to satisfy the natural history buff, as we explore the home of the giant Kenai moose, the historic waters of the Copper River, a homestead within Denali National Park, and other spectacular sights and scenes. We visit an Alaskan artist who works in octopus ink, and explore the town of Homer; float down the Kenai River between forested and wildlife-infested banks; ferry across Prince William Sound beneath the mighty face of the Columbia Glacier; stop at mining towns and roadhouses where a turn-of-the-century frontier atmosphere still prevails; dine on sourdough pancakes and toast the sun rising over Denali. A potpourri of places and people that showcases the best of Alaska!

ITINERARY: Day 1: En route to Homer, AK. Day 2: Kachemak Bay. Day 3: Kenai River. Day 4: Valdez. Day 5: Chitina. Day 6: Matanuska Valley. Day 7: Eagle River. Day 8: Denali Park. Day 9: Nenana River. Day 10: Mt. McKinley. Day 11: Fairbanks. Day 12: Return.

⌒ ⊙ ✈   Class III   **Premium**
June-September
Alaska Travel Adventures   NA101

HUBBARD GLACIER

The fastest moving glacier in North America is the Hubbard, a massive wall of ice spilling out of the St. Elias Mountains into the Gulf of Alaska. Calving almost constantly, it creates instant hotel-sized icebergs before our enchanted eyes in a boom and a crash of adventure. There are moments when the Hubbard is silent; then, the cries of hundreds of pelagic birds from nearby rookeries fill the skies in a cloudburst of sound. Our kayak caravan takes us up Russell Fjord, a recently-designated wilderness area, to Osier Island some 500 meters from the face of the Hubbard. Porpoises and seals inhabit the waters of the fjord, and bear, moose and mountain goat patrol its inlets. An intimate encounter with the icy jowls of nature's grandest juggernaut.

ITINERARY: Day 1: Yakutat to Russell Fjord; camp. Days 2-6: Kayaking. Day 7: Float-plane pick-up. Return to Yakutat.

↔↔ ⌒   Class III   **Medium**
June-August
Alaska Discovery   NA15

GRIZZLY   Bart Henderson

CANS OF BEER ARE KNOWN as sandwiches in this red, dry, wilderness world. No one questions this, or asks the reason. They just call out "Sandwich, please!" and a can of Coors comes flying through the air. They catch the beer and drink it, and they put the aluminum tongues inside the cans. I threw a tongue in the river and was booed by everyone. No detritus whatever is left in the canyon. Used cans, bottles — all such things — are put in sacks and go with the raft all the way. The beer hangs in the water in a burlap bag from the rear of the raft, with Cokes and Frescas. The bag is hauled onto the raft before a heavy rapid but rides through the lighter ones. . . .

This is isolation wilderness: two or three trails in two hundred miles, otherwise no way out but down the river with the raft. Having seen the canyon from this perspective, I would not much want to experience it another way. Once in a rare while, we glimpse the rims. They are a mile above us and, in places, twelve miles apart. All the flat shelves of color beneath them return the eye by steps to the earliest beginnings of the world — from the high white limestones and maroon Hermit Shales of Permian time to the red sandstones that formed when the first reptiles lived and the vermillion cliffs that stood contemporary with the earliest trees. . . . The river has worked its way down into the stillness of original time.

Brower braces his legs and grips one of the safety ropes that run along the pontoons. He says, "How good it is to hear a living river! You can almost hear it cutting."

Dominy pulls his Lake Powell hat down firmly around his ears. He has heard this sort of thing before. Brower is suggesting that the Colorado is even now making an ever deeper and grander Grand Canyon, and what sacrilege it would be to dam the river and stop that hallowed process. Dominy says, "I think most people agree, Dave, that it wasn't a river of this magnitude that cut the Grand Canyon."

Brower is too interested in the coming rapid to respond.

TALKEETNA RIVER

FROM HIGH ALPINE TO LUSH FOREST, the Talkeetna River whistles toward its confluence with the Susitna in the eastern shadow of Mount McKinley. Along the way: the best wilderness whitewater in Alaska, gold panning and salmon running, wild moose and grizzly bear – the "whole enchilada" of Northwest attractions. Highlighting the six-day rafting adventure is a two-day whoosh through the Talkeetna's mighty central gorge, where the river drops 60 feet per mile (11 meters per kilometer) for exhilarating Class IV whitewater. One rapid, Sluice Box, is 14 miles (23km) long – the longest commercially run rapid in the world. Local prospectors tell legends and lies, wolves stalk caribou herds, freshly-caught salmon sizzle in our fry pans, and Denali, the Great One, looms over our take-out at the historic town of Talkeetna.

ITINERARY: Day 1: Talkeetna. Days 2-5: River trip. Day 6: Talkeetna and return.

Class IV   **Medium**
June-August
Adventure River Company   NA10

GLACIER BAY   Bart Henderson

GLACIER BAY KAYAKING

GEOLOGICAL HISTORY IN THE MAKING underscores every moment in Glacier Bay, a region which, when first observed by John Muir less than 100 years ago, was covered by ice. Now it's a water inlet, fringed by still-calving glacial walls that thunder and groan, icy fjords that harbor seals and puffins, and a wilderness wonderland for eagles, bears, coyotes and mountain goats. We kayak along the cliffs of the glacier, and beneath bird rookeries which nest murrelets, guillemots and kittiwakes. Sourdough gold mines and the snow-capped Fairweather Range, as well as the rapid advance and retreat of the surrounding glacial system, makes this trip a photographer's, naturalist's, and kayaker's delight. Shorter trips of four days are also available.

ITINERARY: *Seven-day:* Day 1: Gustavus to Ptarmigan Creek. Days 2-6: Paddling. Day 7: Russell Island to Gustavus. *Four-day:* Day 1: Gustavus to Muir Arm. Days 2-3: Paddling. Day 4: Muir Inlet to Gustavus.

Class III   **Medium**
June-August
Alaska Discovery   NA16

TRACY ARM KAYAKING

SHEER CLIFFS RISING HIGH above the icy waters of Southeastern Alaska make kayaking in Tracy Arm a vertiginous adventure for the novice or expert kayaker. We cruise up the Tracy Arm, which winds its way 40 kilometers into Alaska's coastal range, to our base camp site almost 1000 meters below snowy spires of granite and glacier. After kayaking instruction and practice, we load up and paddle into the deep fjord for two nights of remote camping near cascading falls, crystalline icebergs and rain forested shoreline. Bald eagles, black bears and deer are seen ashore or asky, while we match maneuvers with nimble porpoises. Paddling back toward the mouth of Tracy Arm, we pay our respects to the ancient home of the Sumdum tribe of the Tlingit Indians who guided John Muir a century ago on his foray into this region. Put a fjord in your future!

ITINERARY: Day 1: Depart Juneau for Tracy Arm camp. Days 2-3: Kayaking. Day 4: Pick-up and return to Juneau.

Class III   **Medium**
June-August
Alaska Discovery   NA18

YUKON / CHARLEY NATIONAL PRESERVE

GREAT SCENERY AND GRAYLING fishing combine in a tasty feast of outdoor fun, preserved in a wilderness of unrivalled wildlife. Dall sheep and mountain goats graze near the put-in on the Charley River, a hinterland tributary of the historic Yukon River, and the 40 Mile Herd of caribou summers nearby. We float down 100 kilometers of the Charley through the heart of the newly formed Yukon/Charley National Preserve before reaching its confluence with the Yukon, then continue another 96 kilometers to the gold rush town of Circle. The entire region is alive with the legendary treasures of past strikes and dead mines, though its human use extends even farther into history as a major transportation corridor for the Athabascan Indians of the Alaskan interior. We fish for grayling, pike, char and salmon, sharing the wealth of the streams with bears black and grizzly, and eagles bald.

ITINERARY: Day 1: Anchorage to Fairbanks, then to Circle. Day 2: Circle to Charley River. Days 3-8: River trip. Day 9: Arrive Circle, night in Fairbanks. Day 10: Return to Anchorage.

⚞ 🐎 ✈   Class III   **Premium**
August
NOVA   NA7

MOUNTAIN GOAT   Bart Henderson

TRANS-ADMIRALTY ISLAND

NESTLED IN THE INSIDE PASSAGE, Admiralty Island is a unique and uniquely Alaskan phenomenon, an island large enough to support its own lake system, network of trails and native villages, yet one of America's foremost wilderness areas. Our canoe-based overland tour of Admiralty takes in its diversity, from the Alaskan brown bear and American bald eagle to

---

DIRECTLY IN FRONT OF US, a mile ahead and high against the sky, is a broad and beautiful Redwall mesa. The river disappears around a corner to the left of it. Meanwhile, the big, uncompromising mesa seems to suggest a full and absolute stop, as if we were about to crash into it in flight, for spread below it in the immediate foreground is a prairie of white water.

There is a sense of acceleration in the last fifty yards. The water is like glass right up to where the tumult begins. Everything is lashed down. People even take hats and handkerchiefs off their heads and tie them to the raft. Everyone has both hands on safety ropes — everyone but Dominy. He giggles. He gives a rodeo yell. With ten smooth yards remaining, he lights a cigar. . . .

Running the rapids in the Colorado is a series of brief experiences, because the rapids themselves are short. In them, with the raft folding and bending — sudden hills of water filling the immediate skyline — things happen in slow motion. The projector of your own existence slows way down, and you dive as in a dream, and gradually rise, and fall again. The raft shudders across the ridgelines of water cordilleras to crash softly into the valleys beyond. Space and time in there are something other than they are out here. Tents of water form overhead, to break apart in rags. Elapsed stopwatch time has no meaning at all.

Dominy emerged from Deubendorff the hero of the expedition to date. Deubendorff, with two creeks spitting boulders into it, is a long rapid for a Grand Canyon rapid — about three hundred yards. From top to bottom, through it all, Dominy kept his cigar aglow. The feat was something like, say, a bumblebee's flying through a field of waving wheat at shock level and never once being touched. Dominy's shirt was soaked. His trousers were soaked. But all the way down the rapid the red glow of that cigar picked its way through the flying water from pocket to pocket of air. Actually, he was lucky, and he knew it. "Lucky Dominy," he said when we moved into quiet water. "That's why they call me Lucky Dominy." The whole raftload of people gave him an organized cheer. And he veiled his face in fresh smoke.

the lush climax forests of hemlock and Sitka spruce. Recently named a National Monument, Admiralty Island presents a clear case for the preservation of wilderness. More convincing evidence would be hard to find. Shorter, four-day Admiralty Island canoe trips are also available.

ITINERARY: *Four-day:* Day 1: Juneau to Angoon village. Days 2-3: Paddling. Day 4: End paddling; plane to Juneau. *Seven-day:* Day 1: Juneau to Admiralty. Days 2-6: Paddling. Day 7: Angoon to Juneau.

⧫ 🦆   Class III   **Medium**
July-August
Alaska Discovery   NA14

HULAHULA RIVER

UNDER THE MIDNIGHT SUN the feisty flows of the Hulahula take us on a rapid ride through the Arctic Wildlife Refuge. We fly in near its headwaters high in the Brooks Range, taking the first couple of days to hike up towards a glaciated corner of the range. Then we navigate exciting whitewater out of the mountains and onto the arctic tundra, from where the river drains into the Arctic Ocean and the polar icecap. Arctic char fishing, caribou, wolves, bear, foxes, mountain goats, glaciers, rapids, tundra, and the long days of the Alaskan spring all contribute to the tempting smorgasbord of adventure offered by the Hulahula.

ITINERARY: Day 0: Fairbanks. Day 1: Kaktovik. Days 2-11: Hulahula River. Day 12: Fairbanks.

⧫ 🦆   Class III   **Medium**
July
Alaska River Expeditions   NA4

SATISFIED CUSTOMERS   Mark Jensen

KONGAKUT RIVER

THE PORCUPINE CARIBOU HERD is one of only two wild herds which survived the press of modern civilization. When the 100,000-strong herd masses for its annual migration from the barren northern slope of the Brooks Range across to the forests of Canada, its route leads up the Kongakut Valley. There can be no guarantee on the exact timing of this natural spectacle, but we time our Kongakut float to coincide with the normal early July migration. The midnight sun, arctic wildlife, Brooks Range scenery, and a fine river produce a superb experience with or without the caribou. The Kongakut can hold big water rapids or easy navigation depending on the spring melt, but it is always a winner.

ITINERARY: Day 0: Fairbanks. Day 1: Kaktovik. Days 2-11: River. Day 12: Return to Fairbanks.

⧫ 🦆   Class III   **Medium**
July
Alaska River Expeditions   NA3

LUPINE   Mark Jensen

THE SOUTH

EVERGLADES CANOEING

"River of grass" is the meaning of Everglades, and it is this distinctive feature of the region that makes it an ecosystem unique in all the world. Hundreds of square miles of water filter slowly through saw-grass prairies into the sea, creating mangrove swamps that protect the land from violent Atlantic storms, a maze of narrow twisting channels and islands, and rocky tidal pools brimming over with unusual flora and fauna. We paddle down these channels, explore mangrove forests, beachcomb in tidal pools to sample the pacific quality of the Florida Everglades. The scenery changes daily as we canoe between our four campsites, photographing orchids and spectacular sunsets, fishing for dinners of snapper and watching herons and egrets gracefully bend their long necks to feed. A layover day on a remote Gulf Coast island is relaxing and educational. The camping is often primitive, as we must dig our own latrines and carry our drinking water with us, but it is a primitive world we visit. To do the Everglades justice, and do justice to ourselves, we acknowledge rather than combat its timelessness.

ITINERARY: Day 1: Meet in Ft. Myers; travel to Everglades. Days 2-5: Canoeing. Day 6: End canoeing; to Ft. Myers and return.

⧺ 🦆   Class III   **Moderate**
February
Wilderness Southeast   NA84

OKEFENOKEE SWAMP

Southeastern Georgia harbors the vast watery wilderness of the Okefenokee Swamp National Wildlife Refuge, where a multiplicity of birds and mammals, amphibians and orchids live in primitive splendor. Peat prairies are pierced by cypress forests, alive with otter, raccoon, bear and deer; in the low lakes alligators lounge and sandhill cranes stalk the slower glow-worms. It is the kind of environment that takes a lifetime to understand, but our six-day canoe traverse along the celebrated Suwanee River is the next best thing to living there. We follow the elevated prairie boardwalk to a camping area uplifted over the bog on wooden platforms; then canoe amidst the cypress, tupelo

OKEFENOKEE SWAMP   Wilderness Southeast

INSIDE DOMINY'S BIG LEATHER briefcase is a bottle of Jim Beam, and now, at the campsite, in the twilight, with the sun far gone over the rimrocks, we are going to have our quotidian ration — and Dominy is a generous man. After dinner, if the pattern holds, he and Brower will square off for battle, but they are at this moment united in anticipation of the bourbon. Big steaks are ready for broiling over the coals of a driftwood fire. There is calm in the canyon. The Commissioner steps to the river's edge and dips a half cup of water, over which he pours his whiskey. "I'm the nation's waterboy," he says. "I need water with my bourbon."

. . . Jerry Sanderson, the river guide who has organized this expedition, calls out that dinner is ready. He has cooked an entire sirloin steak for each person. We eat from large plastic trays — the property of Sanderson. Brower regularly ignores the stack of trays, and now, when his turn comes, he steps forward to receive his food in his Sierra Club cup. Sanderson, a lean, trim, weathered man, handsome and steady, has seen a lot on this river. And now a man with wild white hair and pink legs is holding out a four-inch cup to receive a three-pound steak. Very well. There is no rapid that can make Sanderson's eyes bat, so why should this? He drapes the steak over the cup. The steak covers the cup like a sun hat. Brower begins to hack at the edges with a knife. Brower in wilderness eats from nothing but his Sierra Club cup.

gum trees and moss-draped cathedral forests along the same aquatic trails the alligators use. More than just a canoe trip, this venture is a school of the outdoors in an environmentally sensitive and significant part of America's natural heritage.

ITINERARY: Day 1: Meet in Savannah at Refuge headquarters. Days 2-5: Canoeing in the Okefenokee. Day 6: To Savannah and return. Shorter 4-day option also available.

⚓ 🚣   Class III   **Moderate**
February-May, October-November
Wilderness Southeast   NA85

THE NEW RIVER

FROM NORTH CAROLINA'S mountains to the green foothills of West Virginia, the ironically-named New—actually the oldest river on the continent—carves its way north. Along this age-old route, it has dug a thousand-foot gorge that whitewater enthusiasts call the Grand Canyon of the East. On our 48-mile rafting and kayaking trip, we thrill to some of the finest whitewater rapids in the East, but also take time to explore old mining claims, hike among the waterfalls and swim in calm, quiet pools. A day's training in kayaking begins the trip, and the first couple days on the New are perfect for learning the skills necessary for negotiating the Lower Gorge, if you so desire.

ITINERARY: Day 1: Meadow Creek, WV; kayak orientation. Days 2-4: New River. Day 5: Take-out at Teays Landing, W.V.

⚓ 🏕   Class IV   **Medium**
April-November
Class VI River Runners   NA112

BAREFOOT CRUISING

SAIL A SCHOONER through the Bahamas and Caribbean with Cap'n Mike Burke, explorer of Caribbean ports-of-call for almost 40 years. Whether your pleasure is a white sand beach like Gun Cay, a duty-free port like Nassau, the night life of Freeport or the pirate caves of Norman Island, these windjamming voyages can fulfill your fantasies. The seven ships of the fleet feature modern accommodations, but the crews sail them using techniques as old as Columbus. You can sit back and relax or, if the pirate's life has its appeal, take an active part in the sailing. Each ship has a different home port—Nassau, Freeport, Grenada, Tortola, St. Martin or Antigua—so the entire outer rim of the Caribbean becomes your playground.

ITINERARY: Day 1: Meet at home port and begin sail. Days 2-5: Windjamming. Day 6: Return to home port. 13-day cruise also available.

⛵ 🚣   Class II   **Moderate**
Year-round
Windjammer Barefoot Cruises   NA113

ADVENTURE ESCAPE

THE ROMANCE OF THE ISLANDS of the Florida Gulf Coast is an anchor-drop away on this week-long adventure in sailing. We sail several types of craft, especially built for stable cruising, through the small islands off Fort Myers for seven dawns and dusks in groups of up to six boats at a time. The boats are designed for four adults, and qualified sailors can captain their own craft for the entire duration of the trip. For others there's plenty of time to learn how, exploring tropical barrier islands inhabited only by gulls, pelicans and man o'war birds. Dolphins lace your bow, red snappers snap at your line, living shellfish color your snorkeling and Gulf breezes fill your foresail.

ITINERARY: Day 1: Ft. Myers Beach, FL. Days 2-5: Sailing. Day 6: Ft. Myers. Day 7: Return. *Shorter 4-day trip also available.*

⛵   Class II   **Medium**
Year-round
Royal Palm   NA64

DIG IN!   Liz Hymans

CANADA

STRAIT OF GEORGIA

THE SHELTERED WATERS of the Strait of Georgia, between Vancouver Island and the British Columbia mainland, are surrounded by excellent anchorages, lushly-forested mountains and steep fjord-like inlets that make sailing here a pleasure and a revelation. Thundering falls drop from high cliffs into the Strait; oyster beds exposed by the tide give up their luscious secrets; eagles, cormorants and herons wing overhead, while clean breezes fill the sails and send us flying over the waters. For willing novices, the crews of our sailing ships are expert teachers; for those who are content to sun, swim and speculate, ample deck space and free time make for a relaxing trip.

ITINERARY: Day 1: Depart Vancouver for sail. Days 2-8: Sailing in the Strait. Day 9: Arrival Vancouver.

Class II **Medium**
June-August
Whitewater Adventures NA60

SAN JUAN ISLANDS

SCATTERED LIKE PRECIOUS JADES within the sheltered waters of Washington's coastal zone, the San Juans are a treasure, with natural abundance and scenic splendor to spare. Bald eagles swoop to scan the emerald waters; orcas dance and dine in the salmon-laced tides; scaups and scoters dive for fry near the forested isles. And sea kayakers meet them all, eye to eye and beam to beak. Even for the novice kayaker, these sea-going craft are easy to handle from the first day onward. With small groups of no more than six sea-lovers under the guidance and tutelage of expert 'yakers, five days in the plentiful wonders of the San Juan, will make a convert of the most devout desert-lover. Come find the plenty of life's fullest horn in these lush northern waters. Charter trips available.

ITINERARY: Day 1: Bellingham, WA, to Gooseberry Point; begin trip. Days 2-4: Sea kayaking in the San Juans. Day 5: To Bellingham; sauna and return.

Class III **Medium**
March-October
Tide-Rip Tours NA102

MILE 144.8. "Here we are," Brower says. He has the map in his hand. Nothing in the Muav Limestone walls around us suggests that we are anywhere in particular, except in the middle of the Grand Canyon. "We are entering the reservoir," Brower announces. "We are now floating on Lake Dominy."

"Jesus," mutters Dominy.

"What reservoir?" someone asks. Brower explains. A dam that Dominy would like to build, ninety-three miles downstream, would back still water to this exact point in the river.

"Is that right, Commissioner?"

"That's right."

The cloud has left the sun, and almost at once we feel warm again. The other passengers are silent, absorbed by what Brower has told them.

"Do you mean the reservoir would cover the Upset Rapid? Havasu Creek? Lava Falls? All the places we are coming to? one man asks Dominy.

Dominy reaches for the visor of his Lake Powell hat and pulls it down more firmly on his head. "Yes," he says. . . .

Our fellow-passengers have become a somewhat bewildered — perhaps a somewhat divided — chorus. Dominy assures them that the lake would be beautiful, like Powell, and, moreover, that the Hualapai Indians, whose reservation is beside the damsite, would have a million-dollar windfall, comparable to the good deal that has come to the Navajos of Glen Canyon. The new dam would be called Hualapai Dam, and the reservoir — Brower's humor notwithstanding — would be called Hualapai Lake.

"I'm prepared to say, here and now, that we should touch nothing more in the lower forty-eight," Brower comments. "Whether it's an island, a river, a mountain wilderness — nothing more. What has been left alone until now should be left alone permanently. It's an extreme statement, but it should be said."

"That, my friend, is debatable."

The others look from Brower to Dominy without apparent decision. For the most part, their reactions do not seem to be automatic, either way. This might seem surprising among people who would be attracted, in the first place, to going down this river on a raft, but nearly all of them live in communities whose power and water come from the Colorado. They are, like everyone, caught in the middle, and so they say they'll have to think about it.

BARKLEY SOUND

THE WILD WEST SIDE of Vancouver Island features a few havens of quiet that the storming seas cannot reach. Barkley Sound is such a place, and such a place is made for kayaking. Tree-shrouded mountain walls surround its quiet waters. Silent green coves are fringed with narrow beaches, piled high with driftwood. Deer come to these strands to watch the mink play in the tides, and fish fly from the waters to dare the eagle's eye. And sea lions, hundreds of them, share the waters with the kayakers who come here in the spring and fall to enjoy the bounty of nature's wonders. On shore, cabins are available for use as luxury base camps. The summer's crowds are either not yet here or just gone, leaving the beaches and harbors to the clever kayaking few. Exploring and paddling these remote shores is an adventure for anyone with an interest in natural history and scenic spectacle. Custom itineraries and charter trips also available.

ITINERARY: Day 1: Ferry from Bellingham, WA or Vancouver, B.C. to Vancouver Island. Day 2: Paddle to Jacques Island. Day 3: Dempster and Gibralter islands. Day 4: Clark Island. Day 5: Wowuer Island. Day 6: Toquart Bay and ferry return.

++ ᨈ   Class III   **Medium**
March-May, September, October
Tide-Rip Tours   NA103

ORCA WATERS

THE KILLER WHALE ENJOYS a new-found reputation as one of nature's most intelligent species, a huge dolphin of incredible beauty. We join this distinctively marked black and white sea mammal in its native waters, the cedar-lined inlets of the Pacific Northwest, kayaking among the Queen Charlotte Islands off the coast of British Columbia. Acoustic hydrophones tune us in to the shrills and shrieks of the orca communication, which some experts feel carries more information than human speech. Our two-person Klepper kayaks allow us to slice through pods of the magnificent creatures, which (incidentally) have never been known to attack humans. We also visit old and new Kwakiutl Indian villages, sea lion rookeries, flocks of rhinoceros auklets and more bald eagles than there are hairs on your head. A voyage of discovery for the biologist, the anthropologist, the birder or the passionately curious.

ITINERARY: Day 1: Meet in Port McNeill, B.C. Days 3-4: Orca watching. Days 5-7: Kayaking along coast. Day 8: Port McNeill and return.

         Class III   **Moderate**
July-August
Ecosummer   NA90

SAN JUANS SUNSET   Bert Sagara

GULF ISLANDS CRUISE

SOFT BREEZES KISS the Canadian Coast in spring and fall creating clear weather, ideal temperatures and the best sailing winds of the Georgia Strait off Vancouver, B.C. These are also the uncrowded seasons, so many isolated anchorages are frequently empty of other craft, but full of charm. The Gulf Islands — just off the sheltered east coast of Vancouver Island — have an abundance of protected bays, good fishing, fine beaches, marine life and interesting exploring both ashore and adrift. Dolphins, seals and otter may be sighted, or murrelets and tufted puffins. At Sidney Spit, hundreds of deer nervously eye our day hike ashore, and our cruise may take us to famous Butchart Gardens and the quaint town of Victoria on the Island. Sailing on comfortable 55-foot (17m) ketches, equipped for snorkeling, fishing, sunning and seafood cookery, makes for an aquatic adventure of variety and repose.

ITINERARY: Day 1: Depart Vancouver, B.C. Days 2-6: Gulf Islands sail. Day 7: Return to Vancouver.

▲ ⛵ ✎   Class II   **Medium**
May-September
Whitewater Adventures   NA61

BANFF BY HORSEBACK

IMAGINE THE PERFECT COMBINATION of mountain scenery, lakeshore serenity, backcountry wildlife and the timeless sense of the wilderness. Now imagine yourself galloping through this scene atop a surging stallion! If it sounds too good to be true, then you haven't been horseback riding in Banff National Park, in the Canadian province of Alberta. Banff has been called "the most beautiful parkland in the world," and when you take the full circle route into the Cascade Valley, where open grassy ridges climb to the glaciated flanks of the Canadian Rockies on every side, you'll think the judgment is justified. Six full days of riding, fire-lit camps in bighorn country, robust Western-style food, and your own ever-increasing knowledge about the art of horsepacking all lead up to a "field day" for photographers, fishermen, and families from tenderfoot youngsters to grizzled seniors.

ITINERARY: Day 1: Banff trailhead; begin ride. Day 2: Stoney Creek camp. Days 3-4: Flint Park Camp. Day 5: Mystic Valley. Day 6: Return to Banff.

🐎 ✎   Class III   **Moderate**
June-September
Warner/MacKenzie   NA111

MILE 171. Beside the minor rapids at Gateway Canyon, we stop, unload the raft, and lay out our gear before settling down to drinks before dinner. . . .

Dominy contemplates the river. Brower goes to the water's edge and dips his Sierra Club cup. He will add whiskey to the water. "Fast-moving water is a very satisfying sound," Dominy says to him. "There is nothing more soothing that the sound of running or falling water."

"The river talks to itself, Floyd. Those little whirls, the sucks and the boils — they say things."

"I love to see white water, Dave. In all my trips through the West over the years, I have found moving streams with steep drops to them the most scenic things of all."

Over the drinks, Brower tells him, "I will come out of this trip a little different from when I came in. I am not in favor of dams, but I am in favor of Dominy. I can see what you have meant to the Bureau, and I am worried about what is going to happen there someday without you."

"No one will ever say that Dominy did not tell anyone and everyone exactly what he thinks, Dave."

"I've never heard anything different, Floyd."

"And, I might say, I've never heard anything different about you."

"I needed this trip more than anyone else."

"You're God-damned right you did, with that white skin."

Dominy takes his next drink out of the Sierra Club cup. The bottle of whiskey is nearly empty. Dominy goes far down into his briefcase and brings out another. It is Jim Beam. Dominy is fantastically loyal to Jim Beam. At his farm in Virginia a few weeks ago, he revived a sick calf by shooting it with a hypodermic syringe full of penicillin, condensed milk, and Jim Beam. Brower says he does not believe in penicillin.

"As a matter of fact, Dave Brower, I'll make a trip with you any time, anywhere."

"Great," Brower mutters faintly.

"Up to this point, Dave, we've won a few and lost a few — each of us. Each of us. Each of us. God damn it, everything Dave Brower does is O.K. — tonight."

CHILKO RIVER   Thompson Guides

JOHNSTONE STRAIT

THE BOLD COLORATION of the orca, black with white markings, makes it the most beautiful creature in its native Northwest waters. Its historical reputation as a "killer whale" is counterbalanced by its acknowledged status as one of the sea's most intelligent creatures. Only by reaching into the very waters where pods of these magnificent ocean mammals feed and fest can the close observation of science and sympathy become possible, and no vessel is more suited to this purpose than the sea kayak. With the experienced guidance and natural history expertise of your kayak tutors, you can paddle into Robson Bight, one of the core areas for the orcas north of Vancouver Island. The region is a hidden treasure chest of wonders botanical and cultural, as the mature virgin forests of the Tsitika watershed shelter an abandoned Northwest Indian village, complete with hand-carved totems. Sea lions and seals, grebes and gulls, bald eagles and black bears add an unnecessary extra dimension to an already kaleidoscopic kayak cruise.

ITINERARY: Day 1: Bellingham, WA to Campbell River, B.C. via ferry and drive. Day 2: Begin kayak cruise at Telegraph Cove. Days 3-4: Robson Bight. Day 5: Paddle to Mamalilacula. Day 6: Explore village. Day 7: Return to Bellingham.

⇥ 🌊 🐋   Class III   **Medium**
June-August
Tide-Rip Tours   NA104

TASEKO RIVER

PICTURE YOURSELF IN A BOAT on the river, with towering peaks and wilderness guides to lead you through the tough and choosy Class IV-V runs of the Taseko River. A distant cousin of the Northwest's mightiest flow, the Fraser, the Taseko was considered unrunnable only a few short years ago. Now it's the scene of infrequent raft runs and frequent wildlife sightings, amid the raw and untouched landscapes of the Coast Range. We put in at the regal wilderness setting of Taseko Lake, where jagged granite peaks scrape the sky, their snow-draped shoulders rimmed by a fringe of fir. Then we take on the river, rafting 135 kilometers over dozens of rapids, including awesome Taseko Falls and four other major drops worthy of a first look, if not a second and third. Our river camps are a model of natural integration with the environment, yet we enjoy first-class meals, friendly company and a lucid skyfull of diamonds. The word to describe it is "taseko" – a stream wandering in the wilderness. Join the stream, and its native Chilcotin spirit, on a stunning four days of all the best a river trip can be.

ITINERARY: Day 1: Meet in Williams Lake, travel to Taseko. Days 2-3: On the river. Day 4: Return.

⇥   Class IV   **Medium**
June-September
Thompson Guiding Ltd.   NA67

RIVER CAMP   Bart Henderson

WHEN DOMINY STEPPED UP on the ledge and into the immediacy of Lava Falls, he shouted above the thunder, "Boy, that's a son of a bitch! Look at those rocks! *See that hole over there? Jesus! Look at that one!"*

Brower said, "Look at the way the water swirls. It's alive!"

The phys.-ed. teacher said, "Boy, that could tear the hell out of your bod."

Brower said, "Few come, but thousands drown."

Dominy said, "If I were Jerry, I'd go to the left and then try to move to the right."

Lava protruded from the banks in jagged masses, particularly on the right, and there was a boulder there that looked like an axe blade. Brower said, "I'd go in on the right and out on the left."

My own view was that the river would make all the decisions. I asked Sanderson how he planned to approach what we saw.

"There's only one way to do it," he said. "We go to the right."

The raft moved into the river slowly, and turned, and moved toward the low white wall. A hundred yards. Seventy-five yards. Fifty yards. It seems odd, but I did not notice until just then that Brower was on the raft. He was, in fact, beside me. His legs were braced, his hands were tight on a safety rope, and his Sierra Club cup was hooked in his belt. The tendons in his neck were taut. His chin was up. His eyes looked straight down the river. From a shirt pocket Dominy withdrew a cigar. He lighted it and took a voluminous drag. We had about fifteen seconds of calm water. He said, "I might bite an inch off the end, but I doubt it." Then we went into Lava Falls.

Water welled up like a cushion against the big boulder on the right, and the raft went straight into it, but the pillow of crashing water was so thick that it acted on the raft like a great rubber fender between a wharf and a ship. We slid off the rock and to the left — into the craterscape. The raft bent like a V, flipped open, and shuddered forward. The little outboard — it represented all the choice we had — cavitated, and screamed in the air. Water rose up in tons through the bottom of the raft. It came in from the left, the right, and above. It felt great. It covered us, pounded us, lifted us, and heaved us scudding to the base of the rapid.

For a moment, we sat quietly in the calm, looking back. Then Brower said, "The foot of Lava Falls would be two hundred and twenty-five feet beneath the surface of Lake Dominy."

Dominy said nothing. He just sat there, drawing on a wet, dead cigar. Ten minutes later, however, in the dry and baking Arizona air, he struck a match and lighted the cigar again. ▲

NORTHWEST DOGSLEDDING

THE CALL OF THE WILD rings out over the frozen wastes of the Northwest Territories, and answering it in the terms it deserves is an adventure like no other. The inhabitants of this rugged land are the hunters, trappers and traders of a far domain, many of whom are Chippewa or Cree Indians. For those willing to share in this timeless way of life, arrangements can be made to allow small groups of visitors to join an Indian guide on his established rounds, whispering over the trails on an oak toboggan behind teams of nine huskies. Two major destinations are suggested: the Tazin Highlands, in the heartland of caribou free range on the tundra, with wolves, red fox and other wintering creatures; or Wood Buffalo National Park, a wilderness of forest and prairie where wild bands of bison and wolf continue their ancient relationship. Visitors may bring snowshoes or cross-country skis, but are encouraged to take an active role in making camp and harnessing dogs. In exchange, they can learn the art of driving a team, camp beneath the Northern Lights and be serenaded by the eerie, lonesome howling of wolves — the call of the wild.

ITINERARY: Trips of 1-5 days by arrangement. Departures from Fort Smith, NWT, and Fort Chipewyan, Alberta.

🐕🛷   Class III   **Premium**
February-April, November-December
SubArctic Wilderness Adventures   NA54

MOOSE   Bart Henderson

THE MIGHTY FRASER

THE LARGEST RIVER in the Northwest is the Fraser, a huge current draining nearly all of British Columbia's abundant watersheds. One of its most thrilling tributaries, the Chilcotin, provides a short, steep passage of Class IV whitewater. We combine both these rivers into a single mighty float trip, riding motorized rafts for 60 kilometers through pastureland, forest and canyon. Gooseneck, Railroad and Caboose rapids decorate the Chilcotin, and abandoned gold mining operations and homesteads line the banks of the Fraser's historic course. Floating at a relaxed pace gives us time to visit Indian rock paintings, gold digs, waterfalls and high meadows with views of the surrounding scenery. And our hearty appetites are satiated by delicious campfire cuisine and dutch oven delights.

ITINERARY: Day 1: Meet in Williams Lake, drive to Hanceville put-in. Days 2-3: Chilcotin. Days 4-5: Fraser. Day 6: Railway to Vancouver.

✈🛶   Class III   **Medium**
August
Whitewater Adventures   NA55

NAHANNI RIVER

"AN EXCEPTIONAL NATURAL SITE forming part of the heritage of mankind" is how the United Nations described the Yukon's Nahanni National Park, in naming it one of the first World Heritage Sites, and we can't say it better. It is so isolated that only a few have seen its waterfalls, its canyonlands, its wildlife or its unique geological formations, but so incredible that more should. Our expedition begins with a float plane flight to Virginia Falls, a 100-meter drop (twice the size of Niagara) that roars and spits with the fierce volume of the Nahanni. Then it's onto the river, careening down the rapids of Five Mile Canyon, Third Canyon, Deadman Valley and more toward the meandering channels of The Splits. Mineral licks frequented by Dall sheep, hot springs, long days and Northern Lights-illuminated nights combine to make the Nahanni a river wilderness experience unlike any other in the united nations of the world.

ITINERARY: Day 1: Watson Lake, Yukon. Day 2: Flight to Virginia Falls. Day 3: Virginia Falls. Days 4-11: Nahanni River. Day 12: Flight to Fort Nelson.

✈🛶   Class IV   **Medium**
June-August
Whitewater Adventures   NA56

CHILKO RIVER

TO IMAGINE A RAPID two miles long, bearing the weighty name of Lava Canyon, is to conjure the Chilko River. Clean, green and meant to be seen, the Chilko is a week's worth of pure air, bright sun, seclusion and wild whitewater. It drops over 100 feet per mile for 15 miles, creating a whitewater experience without peer beneath the rugged scenery of British Columbia's Coast Range. Then the Chilko joins the Taseko to form the Chilcotin, whose turquoise waters flow fast and furious toward the Fraser River through hoodoo canyons and pasturelands, joining B.C.'s prime waterway in the semi-arid grasslands of the Fraser Plateau. More than just a summer vacation, the Chilko River trip is the whitewater experience of a lifetime, a complete and varied world of wildlife and wonder, laced with rapids and an ever-changing summer scenery in the lush Canadian west.

ITINERARY: Day 1: Williams Lake, B.C.; to put-in. Days 2-4: On the river. Day 5: Williams Lake and return.

⌖	Class IV	**Medium**
June-September		
Thompson Guiding Ltd.		NA66

SKI THE MIDNIGHT SUN

THE HUGE ICEFIELDS of the St. Elias Range can be a gigantic playground for the ski tourer. Although much of the year the region is subject to the extreme cold of the highest peaks in Canada, in May and June the budding summer warms the air without melting the season's snows, creating enviable conditions for adventure. From small peaks to broad valley floors, from seracs to glaciers, the terrain is alternately rugged and forgiving, but always a beautiful backdrop for telemarks, snowplows, or hairball downhill runs. After flying to our base camp at the 2500-meter level, we spend our time tripping on nordic skis throughout the long days of late spring, exploring as the clock reads midnight and the sun slowly sinks. Instruction in safe glacier travel and crevasse rescue are offered, but most of our travel is on uncrevassed snowfields for a dream-like week in a skier's paradise.

ITINERARY: Day 1: Whitehorse, Yukon Territories, to base camp. Days 2-9: Ski camping. Day 10: Whitehorse and return.

⚚	Class IV	**Premium**
June		
Ecosummer		NA99

CALIFORNIA

FORKS OF THE KERN

THE MOST DEMANDING STRETCH of whitewater now run in the United States is thought by many to be the Forks of the Kern. The two mile walk into the put-in portends the true wilderness that lies ahead: 18 miles of continuous Class IV and V whitewater, a river so jam-packed with action that some suggest there aren't really 83 rapids, only one long one. Riding a raft down the Forks is akin to being shot out of a cannon: you aim for the right spot and hope for the best. The Kern flows from the heights of Mt. Whitney and Sequoia National Park through polished glacial beds and granite chasms unmarred by dam or diversion. Heart-thumping rapids, scenic grandeur comparable to Yosemite, isolation, challenge, beauty: the Forks of the Kern beckon to every wildwater enthusiast.

ITINERARY: Day 1: Hike to put-in, begin rafting. Day 2 or 2-3: On the Forks.

⌖ 🐫	Class IV	**Premium**
April-September		
The Forks		NA97

IN THE SLOT   Stan Boor

TUOLUMNE RIVER

NOT ONLY THE CHAMPAGNE of Sierra white-water rivers, it is the Dom Perignon. The Tuolumne bubbles with the wildest rapids and most breath-taking scenery in California. It pours forth from Yosemite National Park in an almost continuous cascade of rousing, rip-roaring rapids — Hackamack Hole, Gray's Grindstone, India and the notorious Clavey Falls among them. The intoxicating ride through the bucolic and bacchic wilderness of the tempting Tuolumne is an ideal two or three day immersion in river-running, in high adventure style, with plenty of time for side hikes into enchanting canyons. Visits to gold mining relics along this Mother Lode flow, and the enjoyment of the epicurean delights of on-river cookery, escalate this trip to a stratospheric level.

ITINERARY: Days 1: Meet near Groveland, CA; begin trip. Days 2-3: Complete river trip.

| | Class III | **Medium** |
March-October
Sobek Expeditions   NA27

HOOVER WILDERNESS AREA

CALIFORNIA'S HIGH SIERRA is a rough and ready landscape of lodgepole pine and red fir, arid desert and U-shaped glacial valleys, solitude and spectacle. The Hoover Wilderness is 42,800 acres of primitive countryside in the east-central part of the state, touching on Yosemite National Park at the Sierra Crest — some of the most remote and special acreage in the West. Here we hike for five days among the sagebrush and the thistle, the escarpments and late summer snowfields while South American llamas carry our cargo. Bobcats and coyote live here, as do mule deer, bear and an occasional mountain lion. The streams are choking with trout, while the high peak region — including Matterhorn and Dunderberg (over 3600m) — host technical and amateur climbers. Wildflowers, birdlife, and other features are explained by well-versed guides, so our hike becomes a natural history course, a fishing vacation, a high country adventure and an animal appreciation amusement all in one.

ITINERARY: Days 1-5: Hiking.

| | Class III | **Moderate** |
August
Mama's Llamas   NA38

CALIFORNIA DISCOVERY

SAMPLE THE WEST, from California's wines and seacoast to the glittering neon nightlife of Tahoe casinos. This comfortable camping journey will have us hiking among the majesty of towering Sequoia redwoods and exploring the pristine wilderness of Mt. Lassen National Park, then changing the pace with visits to Hollywood's Universal Studios and the "happiest place on earth," Disneyland. In the Gold Country, it's all aboard a turn-of-the-century steam train which huffs through towns and countryside redolent with the rough-and-ready '49er past. And of course, no trip to the west would be complete without an awe-inspiring view of Yosemite's granite walls rising sheer and bright from the verdant valley floor.

ITINERARY: Day 1: Depart San Francisco for Santa Barbara. Days 2-3: Los Angeles. Day 4: Las Vegas. Days 5-6: Sequoia/Kings Canyon National Park. Day 7: Mendocino Coast and Sonoma wineries. Day 8: Humboldt Redwoods. Day 9: Mt. Lassen. Day 10: Lake Tahoe. Days 11-12: Yosemite. Day 13: San Francisco.

| | Class II | **Moderate** |
June-August
ExplorAmerica   NA32

THE WHITE MOUNTAINS

THE OLDEST LIFE ON EARTH is short, gnarled and unprepossessing, but was budding when pharoahs trolled the Nile. The bristlecone pines of California's White Mountains lay claim to this title; their rugged beauty, sculpted by millennia of winds and fire, ice and heat, is not for postcards or pretty snapshots, but for the adventurer willing to hike among the ancient groves, far from highways and billboards. Using the patient portage-power of llamas, we pack for four days in the 28,000-acre Ancient Bristlecone Pine Botanical Area of easternmost California, exploring old mine sites, deserted shepherds' camps, along streambeds and ridges, and through the oldest rock in the Sierra. Overnight camps are pitched beneath a crystalline sky at 3500 meters which seems to envelop us in a ball of distant torches, lighting the pathway out of the past, into tomorrow.

ITINERARY: Day 1: Westgard Pass to Botanical Area; day hikes. Days 2-4: Llama trekking. Day 5: End hikes; return.

| | Class III | **Moderate** |
July
Mama's Llamas   NA96

GUANACO AT PAINE   Skip Horner

SOUTH AMERICA

CHINCHERO, PERU   Inge Martin

IN THE GALAPAGOS

by Charles Darwin

*T*he natural history of these islands is eminently curious, and well deserves attention. Most of the organic productions are aboriginal creations, found nowhere else; there is even a difference between the inhabitants of the different islands, yet all show a marked relationship with those of America, though separated from that continent by an open space of ocean, between five hundred and six hundred miles in width. The archipelago is a little world within itself, or rather a satellite attached to America, whence it has derived a few stray colonists, and has received the general character of its indigenious productions. Considering the small size of these islands, we feel the more astonished at the number of their aboriginal beings, and at their confined range. Seeing every height crowned with its crater, and the boundaries of most of the lava-streams still distinct, we are led to believe that within a period, geologically recent, the unbroken ocean was here spread out. Hence, both in space and time, we seem to be brought somewhat near to that great fact, that mystery of mysteries — the first appearance of new beings on this earth.

Excerpts from *The Voyage of the Beagle*, by Charles Darwin (1839).

PERU

ANDEAN ODYSSEY

JOURNEY TO AN EMPIRE OF GOLD to the fabulous realm of the Incas. An adventure for those who like nights of comfort, our Peru program ranges from the coastal capital of Lima to the heights of Machu Picchu, the New World's most famous ruins. We fly from Miami to Lima and on to Cuzco, the ancient Incan capital. Native markets and a blend of pre-Columbian and Spanish architecture combine to create a fascinating city at the foot of the Andes. From Cuzco it's not far to the Urubamba River in the Sacred Valley of the Incas. We paddle past ancient ruins and terraced hillsides for two sunny days, overnighting in a comfortable riverside lodge. The final leg of the trip takes us up to Machu Picchu, where we explore for a day and a half this architectural wonder. A colorful train ride past Indian villages and snowy peaks brings us back to Cuzco, in time for post-trip Peruvian extensions, or your return to Lima and Miami.

ITINERARY: Day 1: Miami to Lima. Days 2-3: Cuzco. Days 4-5: Urubamba rafting. Day 6: Machu Picchu. Day 7: Afternoon return to Cuzco. Day 8: Lima. Day 9: Return to Miami or join *SA13, SA39* or *SA45*.

Class I   **Moderate**
Year-round
Sobek Expeditions   SA37

INCA WAYS

AN ACTIVE ADVENTURE by river and trail through the heart of the exotic Inca Empire. We immerse ourselves in the cultures of Peru, past and present, with ruin tours and backstreet walks in Cuzco, then embark on two days of whitewater rafting on the urgent Urubamba. Our river route takes us through the Sacred Valley of the Incas, to villages, markets and the fortresses of Pisac and Ollantaytambo for further grounding in the legends and lore of this vanished kingdom. From there, we trek the remote reaches of the Andes on rigorous footpaths into Vilcabamba, weaving along the transition zone between alpine grassland and cloud forest until we reach Machu Picchu. Never have the ruins of a lost civilization been so honestly earned, and it is with increased Incan insight that we return to Cuzco.

ITINERARY: Day 1: Lima. Day 2: To Cuzco. Days 3-4: Rio Urubamba. Days 5-7: Inca Trail trek. Day 8: Machu Picchu. Day 9: Cuzco. Day 10: Lima. Day 11: Return.

Class III   **Medium**
May-October
Sobek Expeditions   SA5

SEPTEMBER 15, 1835: *This archipelago consists of ten principal islands, of which five exceed the others in size. They are situated under the equator, and between five and six hundred miles westward of the coast of America. They are all formed of volcanic rocks; a few fragments of granite, curiously glazed and altered by the heat, can hardly be considered as an exception. Some of the craters surmounting the larger islands are of immense size, and they rise to a height of between three and four thousand feet. Their flanks are studded by innumerable smaller orifices. I scarcely hesitate to affirm that there must be in the whole archipelago at least two thousand craters . . .*

Considering that these islands are placed directly under the equator, the climate is far from being excessively hot; this seems chiefly caused by the singularly low temperature of the surrounding water, brought here by the great southern polar current. Excepting during one short season, very little rain falls, and even then it is irregular; but the clouds generally hang low. Hence, whilst the lower parts of the islands are very sterile, the upper parts, at a height of a thousand feet and upwards, possess a damp climate and a tolerably luxuriant vegetation.

SOURCE OF THE AMAZON   Zbigniew Bzdak

COLCA CANYON

THE DEEPEST CANYON in the world surrounds one of the best whitewater runs imaginable, the Rio Colca of Peru. First run by the Polish Cano-andes Expedition in 1981, the Colca was long a secret center of pre-Columbian civilization, and strange petroglyphs and ancient irrigation systems mark the route of the river through its canyon. Cut by a restless current through volcanic ash and stone, the two-mile deep canyon is situated between the snowy peaks of Nevado Ampato (6310m) and Coropuna (6425), which provide unexcelled sky-reaching views for the intrepid river runner. For make no mistake: the Colca is an expert's run, and at times even the most skillful rafters and kayakers are put to the test in the dramatic gorge. The runnable portion of the Colca is reached by a two-day trek from the Colca Valley to the botton of the canyon, with vicuñas, alpacas and vizcachas watching our every step. Then six days on the river for exceptional rapids, superlative side-hikes, mind-boggling views and the experience of a lifetime.

ITINERARY: Day 1: Arrive Lima. Day 2: Flight to Arequipa. Day 3: To Colca Valley. Days 4-5: Trek to river. Days 6-11: On the river. Days 12-13: Arequipa. Days 14-15: Lima. Day 16: Return.

⚊ Class V **Medium**

June-August
Canoandes Expedition   SA52

SOURCE OF THE AMAZON

THE ULTIMATE SOURCE OF THE AMAZON is the Rio Apurimac, an elegant snowstream that spills from high peaks through a grand desert canyon to the steamy jungle, thereby initiating the Amazon's 6400-kilometer run to the sea. We reach it by retracing the retreat of the last militant Incas from Machu Picchu, their mountain stronghold, into the wilderness valleys of Vilcabamba. Past glaciers and cloud forest, hamlets and ruins, we pack a horse or llama train into the rugged heartland of the Andes that never capitulated to the conquistadores. Here the Incas maintained their empire for almost half a century after the fall of Cuzco, and here we find the fortresses and temples of this exiled empire. Dropping out of the Vilcabamba range nearly four kilometers to the Apurimac, we inflate our rafts for a week-long navigation of this source river. The Apurimac takes us on its riparian rambles from mountain stream through boat-drenching rapids in desert gorges to its resigned meanders on the jungle floor.

ITINERARY: Day 1: Lima. Days 2-3: Cuzco. Days 4-9: Apurimac. Days 10-14: Trek. Day 15: Machu Picchu. Day 16: Lima and return. River or trek available separately.

⚊ 🚶 🛶 Class IV **Medium**

June, July
Sobek Expeditions   SA8

PERUVIAN PORT   Dave Heckman

PERU OVERVIEW

PERU'S FASCINATING FACES are revealed on this week-long survey of past and present, an adventure which highlights the three major environmental zones of Peru: sea coasts, mountains, and jungle. A dawn flight wings us over the Andes to Iquitos on the banks of the world's greatest river, the Amazon. Here we wake to the call of macaws and are lulled to sleep by the monkeys' chatter and the mysterious whistles and groans of the rain forest. Next stop is the Pacific, via Lima where we board a van for a scenic drive down the Pacific coast to Paracas Bay. Then we cruise out to the nearby Ballestas Islands Marine Reserve, to see frigatebirds dive, albatross soar, and penguins romp on volcanic rocks. Our boat cruises by the mystifying out-line of a huge candelabra on a mainland hillside, presaging our over-flight later that day of the famous "Nazca Lines." These unexplained etchings in the desert from ancient and silent civilizations never fail to excite the imagination. Finally we explore the mountain regions of the Andes, visiting a vicuña reserve, pre-Incan ruins, and the world's highest navigable lake, Titicaca.

ITINERARY: Day 1: Lima. Day 2: Fly to Iquitos. Day 3: Amazon lodge. Day 4: Lima; drive to Paracas. Day 5: Ballestas Islands cruise; Nazca flight; return to Lima. Day 6: Arequipa. Days 7-8: Puno (Lake Titicaca). Day 9: Train to Cuzco; join with *SA37*.

🏺 🦭 ✝   Class I   **Moderate**

Year-round
Sobek Expeditions   SA38

SEPTEMBER 17: *The* Beagle *sailed round Chatham Island, and anchored in several bays. One night I slept on shore on a part of the island, where black truncated cones were extraordinarily numerous; from one small eminence I counted sixty of them, all surmounted by craters more or less perfect. . . . From the regular form of the many craters, they gave to the country an artificial appearance, which vividly reminded me of those parts of Staffordshire, where the great iron-foundries are most numerous. The day was glowing hot, and the scrambling over the rough surface and through the intricate thickets was very fatiguing; but I was well repaid by the strange Cyclopean scene. As I was walking along I met two large tortoises, each of which must have weighed at least two hundred pounds. One was eating a piece of cactus, and as I approached, it stared at me and slowly stalked away; the other gave a deep hiss, and drew in its head. These huge reptiles, surrounded by the black lava, the leafless shrubs, and large cacti, seemed to my fancy like some antediluvian animals. The few dull-colored birds cared no more for me than they did for the great tortoises.*

THE AMAZON

RIO TAMBOPATA WILDLIFE

DOWN FROM THE CLOUDS to the rain forest floor, the Rio Tambopata of the southeastern Andes flows in a sparkling cascade through the Tambopata Reserve – perhaps the richest nest of birds and land animals on the continent. Otters and ocelots, spider and howler monkeys, coati and jaguar, and at least 800 (count 'em) species of birds have brought this sanctuary to the attention of the World Wildlife Foundation and the National Geographic Society. The only access to the length of the reserve is along the river, as we raft this Andean gem from cloud forest to jungle floor, encountering on the way a vast array of wildlife. A rugged road takes us through flamingo-filled marshes and villages of conical huts, over the crest of the Andes to our put-in on the Tambopata. Then ten days down river to the Amazonian outpost of Puerto Maldonado; a healing dose of solitude, beauty and wildlife.

ITINERARY: Day 1: Arrive Lima. Day 2: Lake Titicaca. Day 3: Taquile. Days 4-5: Cross the Andes. Days 6-15: Rio Tambopata. Day 16: Puerto Maldonado to Lima and return. Extension to Cuzco & Machu Picchu available on request.

🛶 ✈ 🏺   Class IV   **Medium**
June, July
Sobek Expeditions   SA17

AMAZON ADVENTURE

THE EARTH'S LARGEST WILDERNESS, and reservoir of a fifth of all the world's fresh water, the Amazon is a place of grand dimensions. But in truth it is even more a world of lush and quiet detail, where a life could be spent documenting the plant and butterfly species of a single square mile. Even the shortest visit is a revelation, and we attain ours by basing our adventure out of a research station-turned-jungle lodge at the spectacular confluence region of the Rios Amazon and Napo. From here we make a three-day rediscovery in the footsteps of Francisco de Orellana, the first Spanish explorer of the upper Amazon basin. We hike and boat to see monkeys, marmosets, macaws and toucans, freshwater porpoises and brilliant butterflies, and plant life beyond description. It's no wonder that early reports of the profusion and variety of life in the Amazon fell on disbelieving ears for centuries, until research expeditions could verify the spectacular claims of the explorers. Seeing is believing—the maxim is as true as ever. So see the Amazon for yourself.

ITINERARY: Day 1: Lima; fly to Iquitos. Day 2: Explorama Lodge. Days 3-5: Jungle exploration. Day 6: Iquitos to Lima and return.

🛶 🏺 ✈✈   Class II   **Medium**
Year-round
Sobek Expeditions   SA46

CONDOR   Liz Hymans

MARIPOSA   George Fuller

JUNGLE RAFTING   Bart Henderson

EMERALD FOREST

THE RAIN FOREST OF Amazonia is one of the world's great treasures, a world with such a multitude of species and relationships that the human mind must acknowledge its insufficiency to understand. Yet for us, it is often easier to destroy than to know; too fast, Amazonia is falling to the saws and bulldozers of "the ant people." To encounter Amazonia on its own terms is to take the first step toward preserving it, and few would argue that a traditional raft trip down the green-fringed currents of the Ucayali River is one of the best ways to visit the land. Two weeks of rafting on "Kon Tiki"-type craft, with side-trips in Indian-style canoes and lay-over days in the native villages of eastern Peru, add up to a memorable immersion in the heritage and adventure of the Amazon. This trip is a complete package, including airfare to Lima and hotels on either side of the Amazon portion.

ITINERARY: Day 1: Miami or Los Angeles to Lima; flight to Tarapoto. Days 2-3: Tarapoto. Day 4: Shapaja. Days 5-14: Rafting. Days 15-16: Lima. Day 17: Return.

🛶 ✈   Class III   **Moderate**
January, May, June-September, November
Amazon Odyssey   SA49

THE JUNGLE EXPEDITION

FEW PEOPLE TASTE THE JUNGLE in-depth and close-up. Ten days in a tiny corner of Amazonia, far from civilization, roads and communications, isolated in the tangled depths of the rain forest, allows us the time to penetrate beneath the surface of jungle life. A motorized canoe takes us far up an insignificant tributary of the Rio Negro, moving without schedule or physical goal at the pace of our surroundings. The journey is dominated by the great trees, the thick underbrush, the tight canopies spreading overhead — the everpresent green. Jungle wildlife and birds, and possible encounters with Indians, enliven this opportunity to absorb the spirit of the world's greatest ecological treasure. Nothing in the world is quite like the Amazon.

ITINERARY: Day 1: To Manaus, Brazil. Day 2: Manaus. Days 3-13: Rios Negro and Cueieras. Day 14: Manaus. Day 15: Return.

🛶 ⇉   Class III   **Premium**
March
Sobek Expeditions   SA18

SEPTEMBER 23: *The* Beagle *proceeded to Charles Island. This archipelago has long been frequented, first by the buccaneers, and latterly by whalers, but it is only within the last six years that a small colony has been established here. The inhabitants are between two and three hundred in number; they are nearly all people of colour, who have been banished for political crimes from the Republic of Equator [sic], of which Quito is the capital. The settlement is placed about four and a half miles inland, and at a height of probably a thousand feet. In the first part of the road we passed through leafless thickets, as in Chatham Island. Higher up, the woods gradually became greener; and as soon as we crossed the ridge of the island, we were cooled by a fine southerly breeze, and our sight refreshed by a green and thriving vegetation. . . . The houses are irregularly scattered over a flat space of ground, which is cultivated with sweet potatoes and bananas. It will not easily be imagined how pleasant the sight of black mud was to us, after having been so long accustomed to the parched soils of Peru and northern Chile. The inhabitants, although complaining of poverty, obtain, without much trouble, the means of subsistence. In the woods there are many wild pigs and goats; but the staple article of animal food is supplied by the tortoises. Their numbers have of course been greatly reduced in this island, but the people yet count on two days' hunting giving them food for the rest of the week. It is said that formerly single vessels have taken away as many as seven hundred, and that the ship's company of a frigate some years since brought down in one day two hundred tortoises to the beach.*

ECUADOR
GALAPAGOS ISLANDS

SCIENCE CAN POINT TO FEW places in the world that have had the impact on human knowledge that the Galapagos Islands have. And what a place to point to — huge land tortoises, marine iguanas, sea lions and seals, birdlife from penguins to albatross, and a host of other species floral and faunal in a wild Pacific archipelago of volcanic stone. The Galapagos have drawn visitors since Tomas de Bertanga first sighted them in 1535; three hundred years later, young Charles Darwin was so intrigued by the many finch species that he developed his theory of natural selection. We spend six full days in the Galapagos, navigating among the isles in small boats and adding up the list of incredible and common species that inhabit these inspirational isles. We'll also visit the interior of Santa Cruz Island before flying back to Guayaquil and home.

ITINERARY: Day 1: Lima to Guayaquil. Day 2: Fly to Baltra, begin cruise. Days 3-6: Yacht cruise. Day 7: Santa Cruz Island, fly to Guyaquil. Day 8: Return.

▲ 🦆   Class II   **Medium**
Year-round
Sobek Expeditions   SA13

ECUADOR'S JUNGLE REALM

FASCINATING. BEAUTIFUL. MYSTERIOUS. These are the words that appear again and again in any description of the Amazon. They are insufficient as we discover when we canoe along its myriad river channels, with the percussive soundtrack of monkeys and macaws ringing in our ears and a tangled canopy of green overhead. We camp at night in jungle huts in true expedition spirit, and by day float in dugout canoes or hike the hidden forest paths to immerse ourselves in the color, the cacaphony, the variety and the majesty of the jungle environment. We also consider the uses and abuses of this threatened environment—ancient native hunting practices, medicinal and recreational recipes for plants, river navigation and pathfinding, and the steady encroachment of the modern world. Only on such an expedition can the fascinating, beautiful, and mysterious Amazon begin to feel familiar.

ITINERARY: Day 1: En route. Day 2: Quito. Days 3-6: Andean highlands. Days 7-14: Jungle canoeing. Days 15-16: Quito. Day 17: Return.

⚡ 🥚 🦆   Class III   **Medium**
February, April, July, October
Wilderness Travel   SA21

IGUANA   John Tichenor

THE ANDES

ACONCAGUA CLIMB

LOOMING OVER ALL OTHER PEAKS in the Western Hemisphere, Aconcagua points to the heavens from the massive fist of the Andes in western Argentina, near the Chilean border. At 22,835 feet (6965m) it would be a sizable peak even in the Himalaya; it turns Denali into a lesser cousin, Whitney into a foothill. Now you can make the climb to the summit—first reached in 1897—in the company of a team of expert guides and those alpinists who like yourself seek to add this jewel to their climber's crown. From Mendoza, the Garden of the Andes and Argentina's wine-growing capital, we drive into the Andes and begin the long and arduous hike to the summit. Mule support lessens the burden up to the 4600-meter (15,000 ft.) base camp; from there three successive camps are established up to the 5900-meter (19,300 ft.) level. It's a slow move up to the summit, as we harbor every breath and watch each footfall sink into the elevated snows. Due to weather, an exact itinerary is impossible; but time permitting, we spend a few days in Mendoza, sampling the local beverages. Lift a glass to toast Aconcagua, pride of the Andes!

ITINERARY: Day 0: Lima to Buenos Aires to Mendoza. Day 1: Mendoza. Day 2: Drive to Punta del Inca; begin hike. Days 3-14: The Ascent. Day 15: Summit day. Days 16-17: The Descent. Days 18-19: Mendoza. Day 20: Return.

⚔   Class V   **Medium**
January
Genet Expeditions   SA41

BODY RIG   Stan Boor

ANDES TO AMAZON

AN EXTRAORDINARY JOURNEY down from the world's highest lake to the Amazon Basin. We begin in La Paz, Bolivia, then venture to the culturally rich Lake Titicaca region for explorations of the birthplace of the Incas. Here the Sun God appointed his son, Manco Capac, to found

---

THE TORTOISE IS VERY FOND of water, drinking large quantities and wallowing in the mud. The larger islands alone possess springs, and these are always situated towards the central parts, and at a considerable height. The tortoises, therefore, which frequent the lower districts, when thirsty, are obliged to travel from a long distance. Hence broad and well-beaten paths branch off in every direction from the wells down to the sea-coast; and the Spaniards by following them up first discovered the watering places. When I landed at Chatham Island, I could not imagine what animal travelled so methodically along well-chosen tracks. Near the springs it was a curious spectacle to behold many of these huge creatures, one set eagerly travelling onwards with outstretched necks, and another set returning, after having drunk their fill. When the tortoise arrives at the spring, quite regardless of any spectator, he buries his head in the water above his eyes, and greedily swallows great mouthfuls, at the rate of about ten in a minute. The inhabitants say each animal stays three or four days in the neighbourhood of the water, and then returns to the lower country; but they differed respecting the frequency of these visits. It is, however, certain that tortoises can subsist even on those islands where there is no other water than what falls during a few rainy days in the year.

PERUVIAN GIRL   Jack Hollingsworth

CORDILLERA BLANCA

TOWERING CLIFFS, ARID BASINS and flowering mountain meadows are a perfect arena for trekking, and few places in the world can boast as perfect a combination of these elements as can the Cordillera Blanca in the Peruvian Andes. Our trek route lies along the spine of the Andes, through a "geological knot"—a concentration of peaks and glaciers over 20,000 feet high (6000 meters) surrounding Huascaran, Peru's highest point. From Huaraz, the trail takes us ever-deeper into an incredible realm of scenery, spectacular sunrises and sunsets, and a skyfull of southern stars. Pack animals carry the loads so we travel free and easy on the trail. Our route arcs through the Cordillera, then leads back to Huaraz on the sixth day just in time for a hot bath and a soft bed.

ITINERARY: Day 1: Lima to Huaraz. Days 2-6: On trek. Day 7: Huaraz. Day 8: Lima and return.

⋔   Class IV   **Moderate**
May-October
Sobek Expeditions   SA39

CORDILLERA HUAYHUASH

CLOUD-SCRAPING ANDEAN PASSES are the portals to the wonders of the high cordillera of Peru. Seven tendon-stretching passes ranging from 15,400 to 16,400 feet guard the hidden valleys and lakes of the Huayhuash, testing the mettle of the fittest of trekkers but offering commensurate rewards. Careful acclimation and a moderate pace make this high altitude assault feasible, and a well-planned series of lay-over days allows both recovery and exploration of lakes Carhuacocha, Quesillacocha and Jahuacocha. The Indian population from whom our regular trek staff is drawn is both friendly and knowledgeable, sharing their traditional perspective on life in the inhospitable heights of the Andes. Far-reaching vistas of peaks, broad glaciers and cascading mountain creeks, and a variety of landscapes—barren and lush, icy, rocky and verdant—entertain the eye at every bend. Rise to the challenge of an Andean high!

ITINERARY: Days 1-2: To Lima. Days 3-5: Huaraz. Day 6: Chiquian. Days 7-19: On trek. Day 20: Chiquian. Days 21-22: Lima. Day 23: Home.

⋔   Class V   **Moderate**
July
Exodus   SA50

an empire, in South America's pre-historic past; here, today, snowy peaks loom over the broad waters of Titicaca and ancient religious sites on the islands of the Sun and of the Moon. Then we make a memorable trek through the Valley of Dreams, over the glaciated crest of the Andes to the rich eastern foothills, in the drainage of the mighty Amazon. By the time we return to La Paz, we have a fund of memories for future dreams: marketplaces colorful as a Crayola pack, ruins shimmering in the moonlight, vicuñas dancing on the cliffside and condors swaying in the thermals.

ITINERARY: Day 1: Depart U.S. Days 2-3: La Paz. Days 4-7: Lake Titicaca. Day 8: La Paz. Day 9: To Illimini; begin trek. Days 10-16: On trek. Day 17: La Paz. Day 18: Return.

⋔ 🚙 🛶   Class III   **Moderate**
July
Wilderness Travel   SA10

CHILE

PATAGONIAN EXPRESS

IMAGINE A WEEK OF ROMANCE, lost in the time-warp of an earlier world. Ride the sleeper trains and luxury steamboats of a bygone era on this week-long introduction to the people and places of southern Chile, the land at the end of a continent. From Santiago we board the Patagonian Express, and rock south to Puerto Montt past vineyards and villages, supping in a full-service diner car and drowsing to the clackety-clack of the track beneath our sleepers. Then we explore the Andean Lake District, steamboating across the continental divide and overnighting in a classic lodge near the crest. As we enter Argentina, a new series of national traditions begins: chocolate shops and knitting houses crowd the streets, a more cosmopolitan cuisine is favored, and our accommodations in Bariloche on the shores of Lake Nahuel Huapi expose us to some of nature's most favored scenery. The final passage speeds us across the vast pampas that make Argentina a major source of the world's wheat and beef, and we spill into Buenos Aires to enjoy the "Paris of the Americas." A comfortable, classy crossing from one century into another.

ITINERARY: Day 1: Santiago and board train. Day 2: Arrive Puerto Montt. Days 3-4: Andean Lake District. Day 5: Bariloche. Day 6: Evening train. Day 7: Buenos Aires. Day 8: Return.

🦆 🚙 🛥️   Class I   **Medium**
Year-round
Sobek Expeditions   SA45

CHILEAN MARKET   Peter Fox
TORRES DEL PAINE   Tom Moody

THE TORTOISES, WHEN PURPOSELY MOVING towards any point, travel by night and day, and arrive at their journey's end much sooner than would be expected. The inhabitants, from observing marked individuals, consider that they travel a distance of about eight miles in two or three days. One large tortoise, which I watched, walked at the rate of sixty yards in ten minutes, that is, three hundred and sixty yards in the hour, or four miles a day — allowing a little time for it to eat on the road. During the breeding season, when the male and female are together, the male utters a hoarse roar or bellowing, which, it is said, can be heard at the distance of more than a hundred yards. The female never uses her voice, and the male only at these times; so that when the people hear this noise, they know that the two are together. They were at this time [October] laying their eggs. The female, where the soil is sandy, deposits them together, and covers them up with sand; but where the ground is rocky she drops them indiscriminately in any hole. . . . The egg is white and spherical; one which I measured was seven inches and three-eights in circumference, and therefore larger than a hen's egg. The young tortoises, as soon as they are hatched, fall a prey in great numbers to the carrion-feeding buzzard. The old ones seem generally to die from accidents, as from falling down precipices; at least, several of the inhabitants told me that they had never found one dead without some evident cause.

BIO-BIO   Bart Henderson

RIO BIO-BIO

RAPIDS REIGN SUPREME on the Bio-Bio, the world's wildest river run commercially, pioneered by Sobek in 1978. If the excitement and challenge of heavy whitewater in an exotic setting quickens your pulse, this is your river. Clear, crisp water, cascading almost continuously on its course through the Andes; hot springs, a smoking 3000-meter volcano, spectacular tributary waterfalls; Chilean cowboys, the Southern Cross, and above all, *rapids* put the Bio-Bio at the apex of river adventure. An overnight train ride Orient Express-style trundles us up the river, and the eight-day river odyssey begins. We cap this trip of supreme whitewater, Yosemite-like day hikes and great food with a visit to the bustling market of Chillan, and a no-holds-barred farewell celebration there. If you like your adventure wet and wild, look south to the Bio-Bio.

ITINERARY: Day 1: Santiago, Chile. Day 2: Manzanar. Day 3: En route. Days 4-11: On the river. Day 12: Santa Barbara. Day 13: Chillan. Day 14: Santiago and return.

⚓   Class IV   **Premium**
December-March
Sobek Expeditions   SA1

TORRES DEL PAINE

AT THE UTTERMOST ENDS of the earth, in the southern extremes of Chile on the Straits of Magellan, lies the former whaling station of Punta Arenas. It is our gateway to Torres del Paine National Park, a captivating assemblage of reeling mountains and spilling glaciers, of rampaging rivers and quiet fjords. The famous Towers of Paine, skyline-scratching extrusions of granite, dominate the parklands. Options from gentle strolls mixed with fishing and guanaco viewing to challenging treks into the wilds behind the Paine massif are all possible to impress these picturesque pinnacles indelibly into imaginations.

ITINERARY: Day 1: Puerto Montt. Day 2: Punta Arenas. Days 3-6: Torres del Paine. Day 7: Punta Arenas. Days 8-9: To Santiago and return.

🚶 🛶 🦅   Class III   **Medium**
January
Sobek Expeditions   SA3

COSTA RICA

PARKS OF COSTA RICA

A TROPICAL GARDEN of flora, fauna and cultural wealth, the "rich coast" of Costa Rica is only the outer edge of a land of variety and beauty. This week-long visit to Central America's natural paradise highlights the national parks and resorts which have made the country respected by the world's environmentalists and naturalists. We begin with a night in San Jose, one of the New World's oldest cities, then rise early the next morning to visit Poas Volcano on our way into the cloud forests at Monteverde. Here we may have the opportunity to see the rare and elusive quetzal, most beautiful of America's birds with its colorful streaming tail and red breast. The quetzal is only one of 300 bird species here, in a wonderland of orchids and ferns. Then we head for the Reventazon, a sprightly river that chugs along beside the railroad toward the Caribbean coast. Next up is two days in Manuel Antonio Beach Park, where the rain forest meets the sea in a parkland of squirrel monkeys, two-toed sloths, butterflies and birdlife beyond count. By the time we return to San Jose, we will have discovered that there's more to Costa Rica than a week's exploration can reveal.

ITINERARY: Day 1: San Jose. Days 2-3: Monteverde. Day 4: San Jose. Day 5: Rio Reventazon. Days 6-7: Manuel Antonio. Day 8: San Jose and return.

🛶 ✈ 🚙　　Class I　　**Medium**
Year-round.
Sobek Expeditions　　SA48

RAIN FOREST FLORA　　Bett Lonergan

CUSTOM NATURAL HISTORY

DESIGN YOUR OWN TOUR through the natural history paradise of Costa Rica, the crowning glory of Central America. What's your interest—exploring the sandy covers where tortugas lay their eggs by night? Hooting at the howler monkeys whose cries fill the virgin forests? Or trekking into the cloud-socked highlands in pursuit of the elusive resplendant quetzal? Costa Rica is blessed with a wide range of habitats, parklands and species, and for the natural history enthusiast there are few destinations as rewarding. These complete tour packages include all accommodations, flights and expert guides, and the "modules"—three- to six-day packages—can be linked together. Featured destinations include Manuel Antonio Beach National Park

---

THE INHABITANTS BELIEVE that these animals are absolutely deaf; certainly they do not overhear a person walking close behind them. I was always amused when overtaking one of these great monsters, as it was quietly pacing along, to see how suddenly, the instant I passed, it would draw in its head and legs, and uttering a deep hiss fall to the ground with a heavy sound, as if struck dead. I frequently got on their backs, and then giving a few raps on the hinder part of their shells, they would rise up and walk away; but I found it very difficult to keep my balance. The flesh of this animal is largely employed, both fresh and salted; and a beautifully clear oil is prepared from the fat . . .

There can be little doubt that this tortoise is an aboriginal inhabitant of the Galapagos; for it is found on all, or nearly all, of the islands, even on some of the smaller ones where there is no water. Had it been an imported species, this would hardly have been the case in a group which has been so little frequented. Moreover, the old buccaneers found this tortoise in greater numbers even than at present; Wood and Rogers also, in 1708, say that it is the opinion of the Spaniards that it is found nowhere else in this quarter of the world. It is now widely distributed; but it may be questioned whether it is in any other place an aboriginal.

with its coastal birds and plant life; Finca La Pacifica, a progressive farm along Rio Corobici with howlers, trogons and herons; Monteverde Cloud Forest Preserve, where the quetzal is but one of over 300 bird species amid a spectacular forest of 2,000 plant species and over 100 mammals; and trout fishing at the highland retreat of Rio Savegre.

SAMPLE ITINERARY: *Finca La Pacifica and Monteverde:* Day 1: Bus from San Jose to La Pacifica; hotel. Day 2: All day at the La Pacifica. Day 3: Morning at finca; afternoon bus to Monteverde; lodge. Days 4-5: Explore Monteverde. Day 6: Return to San Jose.

Class II   **Moderate**
Year-round
Costa Rica Expeditions   SA40

RIOS CHIRRIPO AND PACUARE

TUMBLING FROM ITS SOURCE on Mt. Chirripo, the Rio Chirripo's juicy jungle whitewater is but half our Central American river odyssey. Its companion, the Rio Pacuare, is a tantalizing tropical river, one of the choice rafting rivers of the world. These two courses careen out of highland Costa Rica through an evergreen environment rich with birdlife, fern-festooned gorges, clear pools and leaping waterfalls, while jaguar and ocelot lurk in the shadows. The rivers themselves feature countless Class III and IV rapids (and perhaps a portage or two), powerful hydraulics, and a gradient of up to 100 feet per mile! The trip includes one of these rivers, plus the Reventazon one-day, as well as time in San Jose. Complete 9-day packages include airfare from Miami in trip cost.

ITINERARY: Day 1: Miami to San Jose. Days 2-5: Chirripo or Pacuare. Day 6: Reventazon. Day 7: Island sail. Day 8: San Jose. Day 9: Return.

Class III   **Medium**
Year-round
Costa Rica Expeditions   SA27

JUNGLE RAFTING   Dave Shore

JAMAICA

JAMAICA EAST

YOUR BLOOD WILL LEAP to the native beat of reggae, your heart will warm to the people, and you'll be feelin' alright when you surrender to the temptations of Jamaica. As a complement to the Jamaica West trip, Sobek offers another side of the isle of magic during a second week of adventure overlanding, scheduled to allow two full weeks of fun in the Caribbean. Once again winning elements of sun and scenery blend together with the cultural facets of this historic pleasure center to create a week of discovery. We indulge ourselves in the notorious ports of St. Ann's Bay and Port Antonio, the reef diving at Port Maria, the botanical gardens of Castleton, the quiet flow of the Rio Grande and sensuous pleasures of Blue Lagoon. From the coffee plantations on the slopes of Blue Mountain to the Folly Ruins that haunt the outskirts of Port Antonio, from isolated Maroon towns in the hills to the crowded marketplaces overflowing with tropical fruit and local color, you can't help but enjoy Jamaica.

ITINERARY: Day 1: Arrive Montego Bay. Days 2-8: Overlanding. Day 9: Return.

🚙 🛖 🛶   Class III   **Moderate**
Year-round
Sense Adventures   SA30

JAMAICA WEST

THE ISLE OF MANY RIVERS is an ideal location for a unique combination of sun, fun and jungle whitewater. Jamaica still has many secrets, despite its enduring status as a tourist mecca, and we uncover some of these hidden treasures — coves, waterfalls and sparkling creeks slipping through the overgrowth. Every day brings something new: from sunning and snorkeling at Negril, waterfalls and wildlife sanctuaries on the outskirts of Cockpit Country, miles of deserted shore at Treasure Beach, mineral baths and pirate lore. To these we add our own unique discovery: running the rivers of Jamaica by inflatable canoe, a first ever offering on such feisty flows as Great River and Black River, which we share with the egrets and herons, hummers and the "john crow" bird. And of course, we delve into the distinctive aspects of Jamaica that make it what it is — feasts of ackee and rice, the easy tempo of the tropics, the throbbing pulse of reggae coursing through daily life like the heartbeat of a people. Travel is by minibus, accommodations in relaxed guest houses and historical hotels. Rock with us to the rhythms of Jamaica!

ITINERARY: Day 1: Arrive Montego Bay. Days 2-8: Island overlanding. Day 9: Return.

🚙 🛖 🛶   Class III   **Moderate**
Year-round
Sense Adventures   SA29

I WILL CONCLUDE MY DESCRIPTION of the natural history of these islands by giving an account of the extreme tameness of the birds.

This disposition is common to all the terrestrial species; namely, to the mocking-thrushes, the finches, wrens, tyrant-flycatchers, the dove, and the carrion-buzzard. All of them often approached sufficiently near to be killed with a switch, and sometimes, as I myself tried, with cap or a hat. A gun is here almost superfluous, for with the muzzle I pushed a hawk off the branch of a tree. . . . Formerly the birds appear to have been even tamer than at present. Cowley (in the year 1684) says that the "turtle-doves were so tame, that they would often alight upon our hats and arms, so as that we could take them alive: they not fearing man, until such time as some of our company did fire at them, whereby they were rendered more shy" . . . At present, although certainly very tame, they do not alight on people's arms, nor do they suffer themselves to be killed in such large numbers. It is surprising that they have not become wilder; for these islands during the last hundred and fifty years have been frequently visited by buccaneers and whalers; and the sailors, wandering through the woods in search of tortoises, always take cruel delight in knocking down the little birds. . . .

From these several facts we may, I think, conclude, first, that the wildness of birds with regard to man is a particular instinct directed against him, *and not dependent on any general degree of caution arising from other sources of danger; secondly, that it is not acquired by individual birds in a short time, even when much persecuted, but that in the course of successive generations it becomes hereditary. . . . We may infer from these facts what havoc the introduction of any new beast of prey must cause in a country, before the instincts of the indigenous inhabitants have become adapted to the stranger's craft or power.*

▲

JUNGLES OF JAMAICA   John Kramer

BLUE MOUNTAIN TREK

THE MOST CELEBRATED COFFEE in the world is grown on the slopes of Blue Mountain in Jamaica. A rich, deeply aromatic brew, it breathes the spirit of the Caribbean island-nation's tropical fecundity and flavor. This magnificent coffee is grown only along the lushly-foliated central spine of Jamaica's Blue Mountains, where a developing trail system winds through tropical montane forest, plantation land and mist-shrouded mountain vale. It is an area perfect for a backpacking discovery of Jamaica's heartland, and we rise and fall with the sun through this magical mountain terrain, accompanied by hundreds of fern species, orchids, butterflies and birds galore, for a rapturous and rewarding four days. Our trip reaches culmination with a pre-dawn conquest of the 7,402-foot peak for a view of the sun rising over the sea 2256 meters below. Then share a steaming cup of the world's best brew with the colorful Rastafarians who live in the hills, spend a night in Kingston, birthplace and capital of reggae, and find your own reasons to remember Jamaica.

ITINERARY: Day 1: Arrive Kingston. Day 2: Port Royal. Days 3-7: Hiking. Day 8: Return.

Class III   **Medium**
Year-round
Sense Adventures   SA31

JAMAICA BY CANOE

THE LIFEBLOOD OF JAMAICA is its rivers, the many crystal flows that lace across the Caribbean island like the veins of a living organism. As such, they provide the best possible avenues into the heart and soul of Jamaica. This week-long tour penetrates into the dense forests of the island's western half, and the limestone reaches of Cockpit Country, where erosion has created countless caves and subterranean waterways—all by riding the "cool running" currents of several different rivers. After a few days orientation near the casual tourist mecca of Negril, we venture onto no fewer than four of the streams of the island: the Roaring River, past herb farms and caves; the Y.S. River with its falls, and the verdant scenery of the nearby Broad River; and the Great River, a whitewater surprise outside of Montego Bay. Comfortable villas, cottages and guest houses, plus colorful locals, add to our visit the kind of cultural dimension available only on Jamaica.

ITINERARY: Day 1: Arrive Montego Bay; to Negril. Days 2-3: Negril. Day 4: Roaring River. Day 5: Treasure Beach. Day 6: Y.S. Falls; Broad River. Day 7: Great River; Montego Bay. Day 8: Return.

Class III   **Moderate**
Year-round
Sense Adventures   SA51

MEXICO

VOLCANOES OF MEXICO

THE LEGEND OF POPOCATEPETL and Ixtaci-huatl is a familiar one to every Mexican school-child, and it is at least peripherally familiar to every habitue of Mexican restaurants in the States. These are two of Mexico's largest volcanoes, which together with Orizaba provide a wondrous experience in the high country south of the border. Our program begins with a visit to one of the New World's most impressive museums, the Museo Nacional de Antropologia in Mexico City, where a literal mile of exhibits details the many different and distinctive native cultures of Mexico, ancient and modern. We travel on to the small town of Amecameca in the highlands, at the foot of Volcanoes National Park, where we set out to climb "Popo" (17,887 feet, 5455m), the fifth highest peak in North America; and "Ixta", the "Sleeping Woman" (17,342 feet, 5289m), the seventh highest. After these adjustments to the altitude of central Mexico, we head east to Mt. Orizaba, or Citlaltepetl, at 18,710 feet (5704m) the third highest of the continent's mountains. A remarkable tour for the culturally curious climber.

ITINERARY: Day 0: Fly to Mexico City. Days 1-2: Mexico City. Day 3: Amecameca. Day 4: Popocatepetl. Days 5-6: Ixtacihuatl. Day 7: Puebla. Days 8-9: Orizaba. Day 10: En route to Mexico City. Day 11: Return. (Two extra days should be allowed for variable weather.)

⚔ ⛄   Class IV   **Medium**
December
Genet Expeditions   SA43

BARRANCA DEL COBRE

THE COPPER CANYON of Mexico's state of Chihuahua is one of the Western Hemisphere's unknown wonders: a vertical world of rock and mystery almost as deep and much more inaccessible than the Grand Canyon of the Colorado. From our rendezvouz in the west Texas town of El Paso, we travel to the colonial-style town of Chihuahua, Mexico. From there, the fabled Ferrocarril Barranca del Cobre takes us deep into the Sierra Madre Occidental, along the rim of this fabulous and fabled gorge cut by the Rio Urique. Then it's down, down and down some more, into a world of tropical canyons charmed by hot springs, centuries-old cliff dwellings and the farms of our hosts, the Tarahumara. These are the world's most remarkable runners, at home racing over distances that would make a marathon seem a stroll — 50, 100 or even 300 kilometers without a stop. Our own hikes are more modest 10-20 kilometers a day, with 1200 meters of altitude gain on our last day as we leave the canyon. In the reeling world of the Barranca del Cobre, every step takes us closer to the extraordinary.

ITINERARY: Day 1: El Paso, TX, to Chihuahua. Day 2: Train to Barranca. Day 3: Tarahumara village. Days 4-7: Hiking. Day 8: Barranca. Day 9: Train. Day 10: Chihuahua. Day 11: Return. *Optional itinerary:* Day 9: Train to San Blas at coast. Day 10: Train to Mazatlan. Day 11: Return.

🚶 🐫 🦎   Class IV   **Moderate**
February-April, October
Ultimate Escapes   SA36

BAJA CAVE PAINTINGS

ONE OF THE HIDDEN SECRETS of American archaeology is the series of cave paintings scrawled on rock in Baja California's forbidding interior. The Sierra San Francisco is a Grand Canyon-like terrain where a secluded ranching community still lives in the style of the 17th century — herding goats, making their own saddles and shoes, surviving on the fringes of time. We use their skills, their horses and mules, and their ancient trails into the central maze of canyons, to reach the largest cave painting site in the Western Hemisphere. Bighorn sheep, deer, dolphins and whales, birds and men: all represented life size, wrapped in dynamic interdependence, an affirmation of life that has survived into the centuries since its prehistoric etching. Our journey into the depths of Arroyo el Parral is arduous, our scrambles into the caves often difficult. But the rewards of discovery and inspiration make every bead of sweat a jewel earned in a very special rite of passage.

ITINERARY: Day 1: Los Angeles to Santa Inez. Day 2: Sierra San Francisco. Days 3-8: On trek. Day 9: Sierra San Francisco. Day 9: Santa Inez. Day 10: Return.

Class IV   **Medium**
April, December
Pacific Adventures   SA34

BAJA SAIL CAMPING

A DESERT WILDERNESS ADVENTURE along a seldom-traveled Baja coastline is a rugged week for the true adventurer. Sailing from cove to port in 6-meter Drascombe Lugger open cruising boats, we see Baja close-up and without the frills. Uninhabited islands and remote coastline offer campsites and bases for hiking and snorkeling. The watery wilderness also shelters dolphins, seals, whales, a wealth of marine bird-life and, on land, coyote. Itineraries will vary with the season to take advantage of the best wildlife, weather and water. A light camping style fits the arid, survival-oriented nature of the region, so we eat simply and must ration water, and adjust our daily destinations to the winds and whims of the climate. Baja is a unforgettable environment for anyone ready to accept her non-too-tender mercies.

ITINERARY: Day 1: To Loreto. Days 2-6: Sailing. Day 7: Loreto and return. *Note:* 14-day itinerary also available.

Class IV   **Medium**
March-May, December
Small Boat Cruising Center   SA44

SEA OF CORTEZ

BENEATH THE AZURE SKIN of the Sea of Cortez, braced between the beaches of Baja and the Mexican coast, are schools of angelfish, neon gobies, sea bass and yellow-tail — whole universities of game fish and colorful hangers-on, circulating around reef campuses off the white sandy shores, no motorcycles feeding dust to the footborne. Just the sea 'yaks and Hobie cats of our encampment on the unihabited islands of Danzante and Carmen, base camps for nine days of diving, sailing, sunning and lazing. We drive from Los Angeles down the coast, sail away to islands in the sun, and live and learn the curriculum of the casual. Watch the pelicans hit the waters as they dive off-shore. Hear the wind moving in the bushes, lap at the shore, carry our campfire music over the sea. Sip the beer, sample the ceviche, and feel the rugged placidity of Baja.

ITINERARY: Day 1: Drive Los Angeles to Santa Inez. Day 2: Cave paintings; continue to Mulege. Days 3-6: Island hopping. Day 7: Loreto. Day 8: Flight to L. A.; return.

Class II   **Medium**
April, October
Pacific Adventures   SA35

PELICAN   Bart Henderson

ICEFISHING LAKE HAZEN   Skip Horner

ANTARCTICA   Al Erickson

THE BALLAD OF THE NORTHERN LIGHTS

by Robert W. Service

We watched the groaning ice wrench free, crash on with a hollow din;
Men of the wilderness were we, freed from the taint of sin.
The mighty river snatched us up and it bore us swift along,
The days were bright, and the morning light was sweet with jewelled song.
We poled and lined up nameless streams, portaged o'er hill and plain;
We burnt our boat to save the nails, and built our boat again;
We guessed and groped, North, ever North, with many a twist and turn;
We saw ablaze in the deathless days the splendid sunsets burn.
O'er soundless lakes where the grayling makes a rush at the clumsy fly;
By bluffs so steep that the hard-hit sheep falls sheer from out the sky;
By lilied pools where the bull moose cools and wallows in huge content;
By rocky lairs where the pig-eyed bears jeered at our tiny tent.
Through the black canyon's angry foam we hurled to dreamy bars,
And round in a ring the dog-nosed peaks bayed to the mocking stars.
Spring and summer and autumn went; the sky had a tallow gleam,
Yet North and ever North we pressed to the land of our Golden Dream.

From *Best Tales of the Yukon* by Robert W. Service. Copyright © 1983 by Running Press.

ARCTIC

ARCTIC KAYAK

SLICE THROUGH THE WAVES of the legendary Northwest Passage, the water route across the continent, amidst the dolphins, the whales, and the seabirds of Devon Island. The south coast of Devon is the breeding grounds for fully half of the Arctic's sea bird population, and summer home of 85% of North America's narwhal population. The expedition begins with a flight from Resolute Bay to Ellesmere Island, and then takes us on a two-day hike in search of a small, isolated herd of musk ox. Then we slip into the comfortable, sturdy sea kayaks for up-close studies of narwhal, seal, walrus, white whales and possibly polar bear as we glide along the wild, isolated coastline by day, camp ashore by night. Since this is such a treasured and delicate region, every trip here is of scientific value, and our sightings and recordings will help researchers for years to come.

ITINERARY: Day 1: Resolute Bay. Day 2: Fly to Ellesmere Island. Days 3-4: Day hikes. Days 5-12: Sea kayaking. Day 13: Beechjey Island. Day 14: Fly or kayak (depending on weather) to Resolute. Day 15: Return.

⧓ 🎿 ☺   Class IV   **Premium**
July-August
Ecosummer   PO7

DISCOVER THE HIGH ARCTIC

EXPERIENCE THE OTHER-WORLDY arctic, where the sun circles endlessly without setting, the peaks soar, the glaciers groan, and delicate flowers and lichen live in a treeless home. We meet in Yellowknife, capital of Canada's Northwest Territories, for appetizing foretastes of the feast to come: visits to the surprising Prince of Wales culture museum and spectacular Cameron Falls. Then it's into the mystic, with a flight across the Barrenlands of northernmost Canada to Pond Inlet, where immense glaciers pour into the sea and birdlife from Patagonia returns each summer for sanctuary. We shop for soapstone carvings, search for seals and watch stunning birdlife at the prime Baylot Island Reserve. Another flight over sculpted snowfields brings us to Ellesmere Island, where Lake Hazen holds court as the most northerly lake in the world. Here, the char weigh up to 6 kilograms, a wily lot that make fishing a sport worthy of the captivating scenery. We include three days at Grise Fiord, a small settlement of 82 at the base of a steep cliff — the northernmost non-military settlement in North America. An arctic adventure of majesty, magnetism and mystery.

ITINERARY: Day 1: Yellowknife, NWT. Days 2-3: Resolute Bay. Days 4-5: Pond Inlet. Days 6-8: Lake Hazen. Days 9-11: Grise Fjord. Day 12: Resolute Bay. Day 13: Return.

🐟 ⤷   Class III   **Premium**
August
Special Odysseys   PO3

GREENLAND ODYSSEY

A KAYAK ADVENTURE in the far reaches of North America, slicing through the icy waters of Baffin Bay above the Arctic Circle. From our arrival in Godthab, Greenland's capital and a major fishing port, we fly north to the village of Jakobshavn, perched on the edge of Disco Bay. This is our gateway to a stunning complex of fjords, surrounded by clippers and galleons of towering ice walls and rocky rookeries for arctic birdlife. We paddle amidst this ultimate wonderland of scenery and isolation, our hearts bursting with the beauty of the far north. But there is human company here, and we find it in small settlements of Inuit natives who thrive on the abundance of fresh fish and other game. A hearty and unforgettable adventure, an inundation of sensation, a Greenland odyssey.

ITINERARY: Day 1: Arrive Godthab. Day 2: Godthab. Day 3: To Jakobshavn. Days 4-11: Sea kayaking. Day 12: Godthab. Day 13: Return.

⧓ 🐟 ☺   Class IV   **Medium**
July
Ecosummer   PO9

NORTH POLE   Michael Dunn

KING GEORGE ISLAND   Tom Moody

THE NORTH POLE

THIS IS IT — the apex, the zenith, the apogee, Ultima Thule: the North Pole. A swift but serious expedition to the top, where few have been since Robert Peary's 1909 classic journey. Our eight day highest adventure begins in Resolute Bay, in Canada's Northwest Territories, from where we fly to Lake Hazen near the tip of Ellesmere Island. We fish for arctic char, walk the tundra, savor the penetrating silence and wait for the perfect weather to make our Polar flight. It's 557 miles (700 kilometers) from camp to Pole, a long and incredibly scenic sky-cruise to the top of the world, the axis of daily rotation. We spend an hour where the sun stands still, sipping iced champagne, savoring caviar and snapping photos. We unwind with a visit to Grise Fiord, a friendly Inuit village where we snowmobile, track seals and sleep on caribou hides. Then we fly to where the compass skids to a stop — Magnetic North, a short but exciting trip over the wildlife-rich Parry Islands of northernmost Canada. After an adventure like this, it's all downhill.

ITINERARY: Day 1: Resolute Bay. Days 2-4: Lake Hazen/North Pole. Days 5-6: Grise Fiord. Day 7: Magnetic North. Day 8: Resolute Bay.

✝ 🦭   Class III   **Premium**
April
Special Odysseys   PO2

ANTARCTIC

ANTARCTIC ADVENTURE

EXPLORATION IS AN ONGOING PROCESS for scientists and researchers in Antarctica. As knowledge about the icy wasteland accumulates, access to the bottom of the world becomes a reality. Those who have dreamed of trekking and boating the frozen frontier can now realize this ambition by joining another Sobek first, the Antarctic Adventure. We fly into King George Island when the weather is at its best, and tour the island and the area from a secure camp at Eduardo Frei, the Chilean air base. On foot we visit an elephant seal colony and a penguin rookery, taking care to avoid disrupting the animals. In motorized rubber rafts we then cruise the coast of the island and visit some of the research bases maintained by various governments. By helicopter we strike out for either wondrous Deception Island, a volcanic cone that cradles an inland sea with sandy beaches, hot springs, calm water and an abandoned whaling station; or to the equally charged Paradise Bay on the mainland. No fixed daily itinerary is possible; much depends on the weather. Group limited to twelve.

ITINERARY: Day 1: Santiago, Chile. Day 2: Punta Arenas. Days 3-12: In Antarctia (conditions permitting). Day 13: Punta Arenas. Day 14: Return.

🦭 ✝   Class III   **Premium**
March, November
Sobek Expeditions   PO1

ACTIVITY INDEX

GENERAL INFORMATION

THE TRIPS

Every trip listed in *Sobek's Adventure Vacations* is available to the general public interested in the excitement and discovery of adventure travel. For more information on any of these programs—including current dates and prices, equipment lists, health and travel advice, day-by-day itineraries, suggested reading and more—simply send the name and number code of the trip (e.g., *AS78, Gateway to Nepal*) with your name and address to: SOBEK EXPEDITIONS, Angels Camp, CA 95222. All information and a trip reservations form will be immediately sent to you.

Participation: If you are in good health, enjoy sleeping under the stars and want to explore remote areas, you qualify for most of our trips. Whitewater experience is not required on any of our river trips. On mountain and trekking expeditions, a medical certificate from your doctor certifying a clean bill of health is required. All potential participants should be aware of the stresses of climate and remoteness. We place no age limitations on our trips, but ask that those interested prudently judge qualifications, physical and mental health, desire and experience for each departure.

Leadership: All of our guides share a deep love and respect for wilderness and its special, ethereal qualities. They are highly skilled rafters, trekkers and mountaineers whose knowledge of the flora, fauna, language and lore of a region qualify them to lead our expeditions. Special interest trips (e.g. birding) are led by persons trained in the particular field or region. Personalities, ages, backgrounds and styles are diverse but every leader shares the ability and the commitment to make your trip safe, enjoyable and educational. Details on trip leaders and assistants are available.

Food: Our menus would tempt the palate of the most discriminating outdoor gourmet. Food is an important part of a wilderness trip, and we take pride in supplying the best. If you have special dietary requirements, let us know well in advance and we will try to accommodate you. Special diets are not always available and cannot be guaranteed.

Equipment: SIES and participating outfitters provide all group camping or rafting equipment including cooking gear, medical supplies, safety items and in some cases tents. Participants are expected to bring their own sleeping gear, clothing, liquor and other items of a personal nature. A detailed equipment list is sent out on receipt of deposit. Details on airline or other restrictions on baggage size and weight will also be forwarded.

See your travel agent for assistance in all booking arrangements.

RESERVATIONS

To reserve space on any trip, return the completed application form with your $300 deposit to Sobek's International Explorers Society. (For trips with a land cost of $600 or less, deposit is $150.) We will notify you of acceptance on the trip or of the alternate possibilities should the trip requested be unavailable. Reservations are accepted in some cases up to the date of trip departure, though many trips fill up early. Please make your reservations well in advance.

Final Payment: In all cases final payment is due two months before trip departure. In case of late bookings payment is required at the time of the reservation. If payment has not been received and no special arrangements have been made, we reserve the right to assume cancellation and fill the space from our waiting list.

Waiting List: If you wish to be wait-listed for a full trip, the normal deposit is required. If an opening occurs on the trip, you will be automatically informed and transferred to the trip roster if you wish to join the trip, subject to normal cancellation policy should you accept the slot. Otherwise your deposit will be refunded in full.

Supplemental Information: On receipt of deposit you will receive a confirmation packet including visa and medical information forms, equipment list, reading list, special travel considerations in the area of the trip, number of participants signed up, etc. Also included are air travel information, invoice for land cost and optional insurance policy forms. Any updates to this information or to our printed trip supplement will be sent to you as changes occur.

Individual Travel: Outfitters listed herein will custom tailor your travel arrangements in all the areas of the world in which we operate. If you have a special trip you or your group would like to try, or if your schedules don't fit ours, just give us a call.

ITEMS OF INTEREST

SOBEK's International Explorers Society: For yourself or as a gift, an SIES membership is perfect. If your soul yearns to adventure, take advantage of the special opportunities available to SIES members. Membership is $30; a special $25 membership is available to the purchaser of this book. Instead of a copy of *Sobek's Adventure Vacations (The Adventure Book)*, a Sobek visor will be sent to special members. Other membership benefits include discounts on trips listed in *The Adventure Book*, a bimonthly newsletter and special rates on equipment. A new edition of *The Adventure Book* will be published every year, with added trips and up-to-date departures and costs. Copies of this compendium of the world's finest adventures are available from SIES, c/o SOBEK, Angels Camp, CA 95222.